I am Not a Brain

T0087849

For Marisa Lux
Become who you are!

I am Not a Brain

Philosophy of Mind for the Twenty-First Century

———————————

Markus Gabriel

Translated by Christopher Turner

polity

First published in German as *Ich ist nicht Gehirn. Philosophie des Geistes für das 21. Jahrhundert* © by Ullstein Buchverlage GmbH, Berlin. Published in 2015 by Ullstein Verlag.

English edition © Polity Press, 2017

This paperback edition © Polity Press, 2019

Reprinted 2020, 2021, 2022 (twice)

Polity Press
65 Bridge Street
Cambridge CB2 1UR, UK

Polity Press
101 Station Landing
Suite 300
Medford, MA 02155, USA

ISBN-13: 978-1-5095-1475-5
ISBN-13: 978-1-5095-3872-0 (pb)

A catalogue record for this book is available from the British Library.

Library of Congress Cataloging-in-Publication Data

Names: Gabriel, Markus, 1980- author.
Title: I am not a brain : philosophy of mind for the 21st century / Markus Gabriel.
Description: Malden, MA : Polity, 2017. | Includes bibliographical references and index.
Identifiers: LCCN 2017010106 (print) | LCCN 2017030527 (ebook) | ISBN 9781509514779 (Mobi) | ISBN 9781509514786 (Epub) | ISBN 9781509514755 (hardback)
Subjects: LCSH: Philosophy of mind. | Consciousness.
Classification: LCC BD418.3 (ebook) | LCC BD418.3 .G33 2017 (print) | DDC 128/.2--dc23
LC record available at https://lccn.loc.gov/2017010106

Typeset in 10.5 on 12pt Sabon by
Servis Filmsetting Limited, Stockport, Cheshire
Printed and bound in United Kingdom by TJ Books Limited

For further information on Polity, visit our website:
politybooks.com

I am Not a Brain

Philosophy of Mind for the Twenty-First Century

———————

Markus Gabriel

Translated by Christopher Turner

polity

First published in German as *Ich ist nicht Gehrin. Philosophie des Geistes für das 21. Jahrhundert* © by Ullstein Buchverlage GmbH, Berlin. Published in 2015 by Ullstein Verlag.

English edition © Polity Press, 2017

This paperback edition © Polity Press, 2019

Reprinted 2020, 2021, 2022 (twice)

Polity Press
65 Bridge Street
Cambridge CB2 1UR, UK

Polity Press
101 Station Landing
Suite 300
Medford, MA 02155, USA

ISBN-13: 978-1-5095-1475-5
ISBN-13: 978-1-5095-3872-0 (pb)

A catalogue record for this book is available from the British Library.

Library of Congress Cataloging-in-Publication Data

Names: Gabriel, Markus, 1980- author.
Title: I am not a brain : philosophy of mind for the 21st century / Markus
  Gabriel.
Description: Malden, MA : Polity, 2017. | Includes bibliographical references
  and index.
Identifiers: LCCN 2017010106 (print) | LCCN 2017030527 (ebook) | ISBN
  9781509514779 (Mobi) | ISBN 9781509514786 (Epub) | ISBN 9781509514755
  (hardback)
Subjects: LCSH: Philosophy of mind. | Consciousness.
Classification: LCC BD418.3 (ebook) | LCC BD418.3 .G33 2017 (print) | DDC
  128/.2--dc23
LC record available at https://lccn.loc.gov/2017010106

Typeset in 10.5 on 12pt Sabon by
Servis Filmsetting Limited, Stockport, Cheshire
Printed and bound in United Kingdom by TJ Books Limited

For further information on Polity, visit our website:
politybooks.com

Contents

. . . as we remind ourselves that no age has been more skillful than our own in producing myths of the understanding, an age that produces myths and at the same time wants to eradicate all myths.

Søren Kierkegaard, *The Concept of Anxiety*

Introduction

We are awake and thus conscious; we have thoughts, feelings, worries and hopes. We speak with each other, found states, choose parties, conduct research, produce artworks, fall in love, deceive ourselves and are able to know the truth. In short: we humans are minded animals. Thanks to neuroscience we know, to some extent, which areas of the brain are active when someone shows us a picture, for instance, or prompts us to think of something in particular. We also know something about the neurochemistry of emotional states and disorders. But does the neurochemistry of our brain ultimately guide our entire conscious mental life and relations? Is our conscious self only our brain's user interface, so to speak, which in reality does not contribute at all to our behavior but only accompanies what actually happens, as if it were an unimportant spectator? Is our conscious life thus only a stage upon which a show is performed, in which we cannot really – that is, freely and consciously – intervene?

Nothing is more obvious than the fact that we are minded animals who lead a conscious life. And yet, this most evident fact about ourselves gives rise to countless puzzles. Philosophy has occupied itself with these puzzles for millennia. The branch of philosophy that is concerned with human beings as minded animals, these days, is called *philosophy of mind*. It is more relevant today than ever before, as consciousness and the mind in general are at the center of a whole variety of questions for which we currently have nothing that even comes close to a full explanation in terms of our best natural sciences.

Many consider the nature of consciousness to be one of the last great unsolved puzzles. Why, anyway, should the light turn on, so to speak, in some product of nature? And how is the electrical storming of neurons in our skull connected to our consciousness? Questions such as these are treated in subfields of the

1

philosophy of mind, such as the *philosophy of consciousness*, and in *neurophilosophy*.

Thus it is here a question of our very selves. I first present a few of the main thoughts of the philosophy of mind with reference to central concepts such as consciousness, self-consciousness and self. In the wider public and in various disciplines outside of philosophy, there is much talk about these concepts, mostly without awareness of the philosophical background, which leads to confusion. Hence, to start out with, I discuss this background with as few philosophical assumptions as possible.

My sketch of the philosophical background of many of the conceptual building blocks of our self-understanding as minded animals forms the foundation of the second main goal of this book: the defense of our freedom (our free will) against the common idea that someone or something deprives us of our freedom unbeknown to us – whether it be God, the universe, nature, the brain or society. We are free through and through, precisely because we are minded animals of a particular kind. The particularity of our mind consists in the fact that we constantly work out a historically shifting and culturally varying account of what exactly it takes to be the kind of minded animal we are. Whereas some believe that we have an immortal soul which accounts for the various mental processes we constantly experience, at the other extreme end of possibilities, many are happy to accept that all their mental processes are ultimately identical to brain states.

In this book, I argue that the truth indeed lies between these untenable extremes (and their more sophisticated versions spelled out by contemporary philosophers and mind scientists of various stripes). Here, the main idea is that what we call "the mind" is really the capacity to produce an open-ended list of self-descriptions which have consequences for how humans act. Humans act in light of their self-understanding, in light of what they believe to be constitutive of a human being. For instance, if you believe that your capacity to act morally presupposes that your soul has an immortal nature, you will live differently from someone who (like me) is convinced that they will live only once and this is the source for our ethical claims. Given that nothing would matter to us at all if we weren't conscious, sentient creatures with beliefs about what that very fact means, anything which matters to us, anything of any importance hinges on our self-conception as minded. However, there is a vast plurality of such self-conceptions spread out through human history as we know it from the writings and cultural artifacts of our ancestors as well as from the cultural variation across humanity as we find it on our planet right now.

It will turn out that we are neither pure genetic copying machines, in which a brain is implanted giving rise to the illusion of consciousness, nor angels who have strayed into a body but, in fact, the free-minded animals whom we have considered ourselves to be for millennia, animals who also stand up for their political freedoms. Yet, this fact about ourselves is obscured if we ignore the variation built into the capacity to conceive of oneself as minded.

Mind and Geist

Let me give you an example of the variation we need to explore. Remarkably, there is no real equivalent of the English word "mind" in German. Likewise, the German word *Geist*, which plays a similar role as mind in English, cannot be translated in a literal way – that is, without further explanation. Here are more elements in a list of terms that have a whole variety of meanings even within English and which cannot easily be translated into every language: consciousness, the self, awareness, intuition, belief, cognition, thinking, opinion. Let us call the vocabulary in which our self-conception as minded animals is couched our *mentalistic vocabulary*. This vocabulary has different rules in different languages, and even within a given natural language, such as English or German, there is really a variety of usages tied to specific local ways of understanding ourselves as minded. Depending on the kind of vocabulary to which you explicitly and implicitly subscribe as privileged over alternatives, you will, for example, think of your mind as extended into your computer, as locked in your brain, as spread out over the entire cosmos, or as connected to a divine spiritual realm in principle inaccessible to any modern scientific investigation. However, in order to make sense of this very variation, we have to assume that there is a core concept defining human self-understanding as minded. For simplicity's sake, my choice for the central term here is "mind."

I am aware that this might be more misleading than in the German context in which I started to work out my views about the topic at hand. For, in the German philosophical tradition, we rather speak of *Geist* as the relevant invariant. However, the notion behind the somewhat mysterious term *Geist* can be summarized in roughly the following way: what it is to be a minded (*geistig*) animal is to conceive of oneself in such a variety of ways.

Human beings essentially respond to the question of what it means for them to be at the center of their own lives in different ways. What does not vary is the capacity, nay, the necessity, to respond differently to this question. Our response to the question of what it means to be a human minded animal in part shapes what it is to be such an animal. We turn ourselves into the creatures we are in each case by developing a mentalistic vocabulary.

Let me give you another example. We all believe that there are pressing moral issues having to do with, say, abortion, economic equality, warfare, love, education, etc. At the same time, we all have beliefs about why we are even open to these issues. Again, here are two possible extremes. A social Darwinist will believe that morality is nothing but a question of altruistic cooperation, a behavioral pattern whose existence can be explained in terms of evolutionary biology/psychology. By contrast, a Christian fundamentalist maintains that morality is a divine challenge to humans, whose nature is corrupted by sin. This has consequences for their actions and for their answers to pressing moral questions, as we all know. In both cases, the divergence of opinion results from the way in which the social Darwinist and the Christian fundamentalist think about their mental lives. I suggest that the social Darwinist will turn herself into the kind of altruistically inclined animal she takes herself to be, whereas the Christian fundamentalist will literally have a different mindset, one in which her mind will be shaped in light of her conception of the divine. The Christian fundamentalist might be much more obsessed with the idea that God is watching and judging her every deed (and even her intimate thoughts), which will give rise to thought processes utterly absent in the social Darwinist, and vice versa.

In my view, there is no neutral ground to settle the issue, no pure standpoint from which we can start to answer the question of what human mindedness really is. For human mindedness actually exists only in the plurality of self-conceptions. If we strip it from its differentiation into a plurality of self-conceptions, we wind up with an almost empty, formal core: the capacity to create self-conceptions.

However, this formal core matters a lot, as I will also argue in what follows that this formal core necessarily gives rise to an irreducible variety of self-conceptions, and that this fact about us as minded animals is also at the center of morality in general.

Elementary particles and conscious organisms

A major challenge of our times is the attempt to come up with a scientific image of the human being. We would like to obtain objective knowledge finally of who or what the human being really is. However, the human mind still stands in the way of achieving a purely scientific story, since the knowledge obtainable only from a subjective point of view has eluded scientific research to this point. To address this problem, future neuroscience is decreed as the final science of the human mind.

How plausible is the assumption that neuroscience can finally give us a fully objective, scientific understanding of the human mind? Until recently, one would hardly have thought that a neurologist or a neurobiologist, for example, should be the specialist for the human mind. Can we really trust neuroscience in general, or brain science in particular, to provide us with the relevant information about ourselves? Do they hold the key to the secret which has haunted philosophy and humanity ever since the Delphic oracle told us to know ourselves?

To what extent should we align our image of the human being with technological progress? In order to address central questions such as this in a sensible manner, we should scrutinize *concepts of our self-portrait* such as consciousness, mind, self, thinking or freedom more carefully than we are accustomed to do in an everyday sense. Only then can we figure out where we are being led up the garden path, if someone were to claim, for instance, that there is really no such thing as free will or that the human mind (consciousness) is a kind of surface tension of the brain, as Francis Crick and Christof Koch at some point supposed: synchronized neural firing in the 40-Hertz range – a conjecture which they have since qualified.[1]

In contrast to the mainstream of contemporary philosophy of mind, the proposal introduced in this book is an antinaturalistic one. **Naturalism**[2] proceeds on the basis that everything which really exists can ultimately be investigated in a purely natural-scientific manner, be it by physics alone or by the ensemble of the natural sciences. In addition, naturalism at the same time typically assumes that **materialism** is correct – i.e., the thesis that it is only material objects that really exist, only things which belong to a reality that is exhaustively composed of matter/energy. But what then is the status of consciousness, which until now has not been explained scientifically – and in the case of which it cannot even be foreseen how this is supposed to be at all possible?

Remarkably, the German word for the humanities is *Geisteswissenschaften* – that is, the sciences which deal with the mind in the sense of the invariant structure which is constituted via historically and culturally shifting self-conceptions. The point of dividing academic labor into the natural sciences and the mind sciences corresponds to the fact that it is hard to see how the Federal Republic of Germany, the worlds of Houellebecq's novels, dreams about the deceased, thoughts and feelings in general, as well as the number π could really turn out to be material objects. Do they not exist, perhaps, or are they not real? Naturalists attempt to establish precisely the latter claim by clearing up the impression that there are immaterial realities, which according to them is deceptive. I will have more to say about this in what is to come.

As previously mentioned, I adopt the stance of **antinaturalism**, according to which not everything which exists can be investigated by the natural sciences. I thus contend that there are immaterial realities which I consider essential for any accessible insight of sound human understanding. When I consider someone a friend, and consequently have corresponding feelings for him and adjust my behavior accordingly, I do not suppose that the friendship between him and me is a material thing. I also do not consider myself to be only a material thing, although I would obviously not be who I am if I had no proper body, which in turn I could not have if the laws of nature of our universe had been very different or if biological evolution had taken another course. Antinaturalism does, therefore, not deny the obvious fact that there are necessary material conditions for the existence of many immaterial realities. The immaterial does not belong to another world. Rather, both the material and the immaterial can be parts of objects and processes such as the Brexit, Mahler's symphonies, or my wish to finish this sentence while I am writing it.

The question of whether naturalism or antinaturalism is ultimately right is not merely important for the academic discipline of philosophy or simply for the academic division of labor between the natural sciences and the humanities, say. It concerns all of us, insofar as we are humans – that is, insofar as who we are in part depends on our self-conception. The philosophical question of naturalism vs. antinaturalism also plays an important historical role in our era of religious revival, since religion is quite rightly considered to be the bastion of the immaterial. If one overhastily ignores immaterial realities, one ends up not even being able to understand the rational core of the phenomenon of religion, since one views it from the start as a kind of superstition or cognitively empty ghost story. There are shortcomings in the idea that we could understand human subjectivity by way of scientific, technological and economic advances and bring them under our control by means of such an understanding. If we simply ignore this and pretend that naturalism in the form of futuristic science will solve all existential issues by showing that the mind is identical to the brain and that therefore nothing immaterial really exists, we will achieve the opposite of the process of enlightenment. For religion will simply retreat to the stance of irrational faith assigned to it by a misguided foundation of modernity. Modernity is ill-advised to define itself in terms of an all-encompassing science yet to come. In other words, as the case of scientology proves: we should not base our overall conception of who we are and how absolutely everything hangs together on science fiction. Science fiction is not science, even though it often enables actual science to make progress. But so does religion.

Already in the last century thinkers from different orientations pointed out the limitations of a misguided Enlightenment project based on the notion that we can extend scientific rationality to all spheres of human existence. For instance, the first generation of critical theorists, most notably Theodor W. Adorno (1903–1969) and Max Horkheimer (1895–1973) in their influential book *Dialectic of Enlightenment*, went so far as to claim that modernity was ultimately a misfortune that had to end in totalitarianism. I disagree. But I do believe that modernity will remain deficient for as long as it props up the fundamental materialist conviction that there are ultimately only particles dispersed in an enormous world-container structured according to natural laws, in which only after billions of years organisms emerged for the first time, of which by now quite a few are conscious – which then poses the riddle as to how to fit the obviously immaterial reality of the mind into the assumption that it should not exist according to the materialist's lights. We will never understand the human mind in this way! Arguably, this very insight led the ancient Greeks to the invention of philosophy, which at least holds for Plato and Aristotle, who both resisted naturalism with arguments still valid today.

To reclaim the standpoint of an antinaturalist philosophy of mind, we must give up the idea that we have to choose between a scientific and a religious image of the world, since both are fundamentally mistaken. There are today a group of critics of religion, poorly informed both historically and theologically, who are gathered together under the name of a "New Atheism," among whom are counted prominent thinkers such as Sam Harris (b. 1967),

Richard Dawkins (b. 1941), Michel Onfray (b. 1959) and Daniel
Dennett (b. 1942). These thinkers believe that it is necessary to
choose between religion – that is, superstition – and science – that
is, clinical, unvarnished truth. I have already rebutted at length the
idea that our modern democratic societies have to stage a constitutive conflict of world images in *Why the World Does Not Exist*.
My thesis there was that, in any case, there are no coherent world
pictures, and that religion is no more identical to superstition than
science is to enlightenment.[3] Both science and religion fail insofar
as they are supposed to provide us with complete world pictures,
ways of making sense of absolutely everything that exists, or reality as a whole if you like. There simply is no such thing as reality
as a whole.

Yet, even if I am right about this (as I still believe after several
waves of criticism and polemics against my no-world-view), it
still leaves open the question to be dealt with here of how to conceive of the relation between the mind and its non-mental natural
environment. It is now a matter of developing an antinaturalist
perspective vis-à-vis ourselves as conscious living beings, a perspective happy to join in the great traditions of self-knowledge that
were developed in the history of ideas – and not just in the West.
These traditions will not disappear because a small technological
and economic elite profit from the progress of natural science and
now believe that they must drive out ostensible and real religious
superstitions and, along with them, expel mind from the human
sciences. Truth is not limited to natural science; one also finds it
in the social and human sciences, in art, in religion, and under the
most mundane circumstances, such as when one notices that someone is sad without theorizing about her mental state in any more
complicated, scientific manner.

The decade of the brain

The recent history of the idea that neuroscience is the leading discipline for our research into the self is noteworthy and telling. Usually,
this political background story is not mentioned in the set-up of the
metaphysical riddle of finding a place for mind in nature. In 1989,
the United States Congress decided to begin a decade of research
into the brain. On July 17, 1990, the then president, George H. W.
Bush (that is, Bush senior), officially proclaimed the "Decade of
the Brain."[4] Bush's proclamation ends solemnly and grandiosely
– as is customary in this genre: "Now, therefore, I, George Bush,

President of the United States of America, do hereby proclaim the decade beginning January 1, 1990, as the Decade of the Brain. I call upon all public officials and the people of the United States to observe that decade with appropriate programs, ceremonies, and activities." A decade later, a similar initiative in Germany, with the title "Dekade des menschlichen Gehirns" ["The Decade of the Human Brain"] was launched at the University of Bonn under the auspices of the governor of North Rhine-Westphalia, Wolfgang Clement.

It is irritating that the press release for this very initiative began with a statement that is not acceptable as it stands: "As recently as ten years ago the idea that it could ever be possible to see the brain as it thinks was pure speculation."[5] This statement implies that it is *now* supposed to be possible "to see the brain as it thinks,"[6] which, however, looked at more closely, is quite an astounding assertion, since it is ultimately a preposterous idea that one could *see* an act of thinking. Acts of thinking are not visible. One can at best see areas of the brain (or images thereof) which one might consider to be necessary prerequisites for acts of thinking. Is the expression "to see the brain as it thinks" supposed to mean that one can literally *see* how the brain processes thoughts? Does that mean that now one no longer merely *has* or *understands* thoughts but can also *see* them in a single glance? Or is it just associated with the modest claim of seeing the brain at work, without already implying as a consequence that one can somehow literally see or even read thoughts?

As far as I know, George Bush senior is not a brain scientist (let alone a philosopher), which means that his declaration of a decade of the brain can at best be a political gesture performed in order to funnel more government resources into brain research. But what would need to happen for one to be able to "see" the brain as it thinks?

Neuroimaging techniques such as functional magnetic resonance imaging, to which the German declaration alludes with its claim, constitute progress in medicine. Unlike earlier attempts to understand the living brain, they are not invasive. Thus, we can visualize the living brain with computer-generated models (but not directly!) without serious medical interventions in the actual organ. However, in this case, medical progress is associated with a further promise, the promise to *make thinking visible*. And this promise cannot be honored. In the strict sense, it is quite absurd. That is to say, if one understands by "thinking" the conscious having of thoughts, much more is involved than brain processes that one could make visible by means of neuroimaging techniques. To be sure, one can make brain processes visible in a certain sense, but not thinking.

The two decades of the brain, which officially came to an end on December 31, 2010, were not intended to be restricted to medical progress but offered hope for progress in self-knowledge. In this context, neuroscience has for a while been charged with the task of serving as the lead discipline for the human being's research into itself, since it is believed that human thinking, consciousness, the self, indeed our mind as such can be located in and identified with a spatio-temporally observable thing: the brain or central nervous system. This idea, which I criticize in this book and would like to refute, I call for brevity's sake *neurocentrism*. With the rise of other superpowers, **Eurocentrism** – that is, the old colonialist view of Europe's cultural superiority over the rest of the world – is no longer taken seriously. One must now fight against a new ideological monster, neurocentrism, which is no less a misguided fantasy of omnipotence (and, incidentally, not very scientific either). While Eurocentrism mistakenly thought that human thinking at its peak was bound to a continent (Europe) or a cardinal point (the West), neurocentrism now locates human thinking in the brain. This spurs the hope that, in this way, thinking can be better examined, by mapping it, as Barack Obama's more recent initiative of a "Brain Activity Map" suggests. As if the brain was the continent of thinking such that we could literally draw a map with the structure of neuroimaging models on which we could locate, for instance, the (false) thought that naturalism is true.

The basic idea of **neurocentrism** is that to be a minded animal consists in nothing more than the presence of a suitable brain. In a nutshell, neurocentrism thus preaches: *the self is a brain.* To understand the meaning of "self," "consciousness," "will," "freedom" or "mind," neurocentrism advises us against turning to philosophy, religion or common sense and instead recommends investigating the brain with neuroscientific methods – preferably paired with evolutionary biology. I deny this and thus arrive at the critical main thesis of this book: *the self is not a brain.*

In what follows, I will take a look at some core concepts of our self-understanding as minded, such as consciousness, self-consciousness and the self. I will do so from an antinaturalistic perspective. In this context, I will sketch some of the absurd consequences and extreme views that came out of naturalism, such as **epiphenomenalism** – that is, the view that the mind does not causally interfere with anything which really happens. Along with taking stock of some conceptual bits and pieces of our mentalistic vocabulary, I will scrutinize the troublesome issue of free will. Are we free at all, or are there good reasons to doubt this and to conceive ourselves to be biological machines that are driven by the hunger for life and that really strive for nothing other than passing on our genes? I believe that we are in fact free and that this is connected to the fact that we are minded animals of the sort which necessarily work out conceptions of what this means in light of which people become who they are. We are creative thinkers, thinkers of thoughts which in turn change the thinkers. It really matters how you think of yourself, a fact well known to psychologists and to human subjects in general, as we constantly during our conscious life engage with the realm of thoughts about ourselves and others.

Mainstream philosophy of mind for quite a while has sought to provide a theoretical basis for neurocentrism. This seemed necessary given that neurocentrism cannot yet claim to be based on empirical results, as neuroscience is infinitely far away from having solved even "minor" problems, such as finding a physical/neural correlate for consciousness, not to mention finding a location in the brain which correlates with insight into some complicated quantum-mechanical truth or the concept of justice. It has participated, sometimes even enthusiastically, in the decade of the brain. Yet, in the course of the unfolding of mainstream philosophy of mind it has become apparent to many that it is anything but obvious that the self is a brain.

Many reflections and key results of the last two centuries of the philosophy of mind already speak against the basic idea of neurocentrism. I will thus also refer to long-dead thinkers, since in philosophy one should almost never assume that someone was wrong simply because they lived in the past. Plato's philosophy of mind loses nothing through the circumstance that it emerged in ancient Athens – and thus, incidentally, in the context of an advanced culture to which we owe some of the most profound insights concerning ourselves. Of course, Plato was wrong if he believed that we had an immortal soul somehow invisibly governing the actions of the human body. However, if you actually carefully read Plato, let alone Aristotle, it is far from clear that he believed in what the British philosopher Gilbert Ryle famously derided as "the ghost in the machine."

Homer, Sophocles, Shakespeare, Tom Stoppard or Elfriede Jelinek can teach us more about ourselves than neuroscience.

Neuroscience attends to our brain or central nervous system and its mode of functioning. Without the brain there can be no mind. The brain is a necessary precondition for human mindedness. Without it we would not lead a conscious life but simply be dead and gone. But it is not identical with our conscious life. A necessary condition for human mindedness is nowhere near a sufficient condition. Having legs is a necessary condition for riding my bicycle. But it is not a sufficient one, since I have to master the art of riding a bicycle and must be present in the same place as my bicycle, and so forth. To believe that we completely understand our mind as soon as the brain is understood would be as though we believed that we would completely understand bicycle riding as soon as our knees are understood.

Let us call the idea that we are our brains the **crude identity thesis**. A major weakness of the crude identity thesis is that it immediately threatens to encapsulate us within our skull as minded, thinking, perceiving creatures. It becomes all too tempting to associate the thesis with the view that our entire mental life could be or even is a kind of illusion or hallucination. I have already criticized this thesis in *Why the World Does Not Exist*, under the heading of **constructivism**.[7] This view, coupled with neurocentrism, supposes that our mental faculties can be entirely identified with regions of the brain whose function consists in constructing mental images of reality. We cannot disengage ourselves from these images in order to compare them with reality itself. Rainer Maria Rilke gets to the heart of this idea in his famous poem "The Panther": "To him, there seem to be a thousand bars / and back behind those thousand bars no world."[8]

A recent German radio series called *Philosophie im Hirnscan* [Philosophy in the Brain Scan] asked the question whether it is "not the human mind but rather the brain" that "governs decisions." "Free will is demonstrably an illusion."[9] What is worse, it claimed that neuroscience finally provides support for a thesis allegedly held by Immanuel Kant, namely that we cannot know the world as it is in itself.[10] The German philosopher of consciousness Thomas Metzinger (b. 1958), a prime representative of neurocentrism, is reported to claim that

> Philosophy and neuroscience agree: perception does not reveal the world, but a model of the world. A tiny snippet, highly processed, adjusted to the needs of the organism. Even space and time, as well as cause and effect, are created by the brain. Nevertheless, there is a reality, of course. It cannot be directly experienced, but it can be isolated by considering it from various vantage points.[11]

Fortunately, many philosophers who work in epistemology and the theory of perception would not accept this statement today. The theory that we do not directly experience reality but can only isolate it by considering it from various vantage points proves on closer inspection to be incoherent. For one thing, it presupposes that one can directly experience a model of the world, as the quotation indicates. If one had to isolate this model itself indirectly by considering reality from various vantage points on one's own, one would not even know that, on the one hand, there exists a model and, on the other, a world of which we construct internal models. To know that one constructs or even has to construct a model of reality implies knowing something about reality outright, such as that we can only know anything about it indirectly for some reason or other. Thus one does not always need models and is not trapped within them, so to speak. And why then, pray tell, does the model not belong to reality? Why should, for instance, my thought that it is raining in London, which indeed I do not first need to isolate by considering reality from various vantage points in order to have it, not belong to reality? If my thought that it is raining in London right now does not belong to reality (as I can know it without first having to construct a model of mental reality), then where exactly does it take place? With this in mind, new realism in philosophy claims that our thoughts are no less real than what we are thinking about, and thus that we can know reality directly and need not make do with mere models.[12]

My own view, **New Realism**, is a version of the idea that we can actually grasp reality as it is in itself by way of our mental faculties. We are not stuck in our brains and affected by an external world only via our nerve endings such that our mental life is basically a useful illusion, an interface or computational platform with a basic evolutionary survival value.

After the failures of the loudmouthed exaggerated promises of the decades of the brain, the *Süddeutsche Zeitung*, one of the biggest German newspapers, pithily reported: "The human being remains indecipherable."[13] It is thus time for a reconsideration of who or what the human mind really is. Against this background, in this book I sketch the outlines of a philosophy of mind for the twenty-first century.

Many people are interested in philosophical questions, in particular those pertaining to their own minds. Human beings care about what it means for them to be minded, suffering, enjoying, thinking and dreaming animals. Readers who are interested in philosophy but do not spend the whole day going through philosophical literature often have the reasonable impression that one can only understand a philosophical work if one has read countless other books first. In contrast, the present work should be accessible without such assumptions, insofar as it also provides information about the relevant basic ideas lurking in the background. Unfortunately, many generally accessible books about the human mind in our time either simply assume a naturalistic framework or are driven by the equally misguided idea that we have immortal souls on top of our bodies. My own stance is thoroughly antinaturalistic in that I do not believe that nature or the universe (or any other domain of inquiry or objects) is the sole domain there is. We do not have to fit everything into a single frame. This is an age-old metaphysical illusion. However, there is a further question concerning the structure of human mindedness, as the human mind certainly has neurobiological preconditions (no mind without a suitable brain) but also goes beyond these conditions by having a genuinely immaterial side which we will explore.

Can the mind be free in a brain scan?

My overall goal is the defense of a concept of *the mind's freedom*. This includes the fact that we can deceive ourselves and be irrational. But it also includes the fact that we are able to discover many truths. Like any other science or discipline, philosophy formulates theories, gives reasons for them, appeals to facts that are supposed to be acceptable without further ado, and so forth. A theory consists of propositions – claims that can be true or false. No one is infallible, certainly not in the area of self-knowledge. Sophocles portrayed this harshly in *Oedipus the King*, but hopefully things will not unfold so tragically here.

My main targets in this book, neurocentrism and its pioneering precursors – the scientific image of the world, structuralism and poststructuralism – are all *philosophical* theories. Sometimes it seems as if the empirical findings of brain research entail that the self and the brain are identical. Advocates of what I critically call "neurocentrism" act as though they could appeal to scientific discoveries that should not be doubted by reasonable modern citizens and thus to alleged facts recognized by experts. Yet, with its sweeping assumptions, neurocentrism formulates genuinely philosophical claims, which here means claims that one cannot delegate to some other branch of learning. Science itself does not solve philosophy's problems unaided by philosophy's interpretation of its results. Neurocentrism is ultimately just bad philosophy trying to immunize itself against philosophical critique by claiming to be justified not by philosophy, but by actual neuroscientific discoveries. Notice, though, that no neuroscientific discovery, no fact about our neurobiological equipment without further interpretation, entails anything about human mindedness.

In particular, for its interpretation of neuroscientific knowledge, neurocentrism brings to bear *philosophical* concepts such as consciousness, cognition, representation, thinking, self, mind, free will, and so forth. Our understanding of those concepts by means of which we describe ourselves as minded animals is stamped by a millennia-long intellectual, cultural and linguistic history. There is no possibility for us simply to sidestep this fact and take, as it were, a neutral or fresh look at the human mind, as if from nowhere or from a God's-eye point of view. Our ways of thinking about ourselves as thinkers are mediated by the language we speak and by the manifold cultural assumptions which govern our self-conception, as well as by a huge range of affective predispositions. Our self-conception as minded always also reflects our value system and our personal experience with mindedness. It has developed in complex ways, in the tension between our understanding of nature, literature, legal systems, values of justice, our arts, religions, socio-historical and personal experience. There just is no way to describe these developments in the language of neuroscience that would be superior or even equal to the vocabulary already at hand. Disciplines such as neurotheology or neuroaesthetics are "terrifying theory-golems," as Thomas E. Schmidt sharply puts it in an article on new realism for *Die Zeit*.[14] If a discipline only gains legitimacy by being able to observe the brain while the brain engages with a given topic or object, we would ultimately need a neuro-neuroscience. Whether we then would also still have to come up with a neuro-neuro-neuroscience, time will tell . . .

There is also a suspicious political motivation associated with neurocentrism. Is it really an accident that the decade of the brain was proclaimed by George H. W. Bush shortly after the fall of the Berlin Wall in 1989 and thus with the end of the Cold War looming? Is this just a matter of political support for medical research? Does the idea of being able to watch the brain – and thereby the citizen – while thinking not also imply a new possibility for controlling social surveillance (and the military-industrial complex)? It has long been well known that possibilities for controlling consumers are expected from a better understanding of the brain: think of neuro-economics, another theory-golem out there.

As the German neuroscientist Felix Hasler (b. 1965) plausibly argued in his book *Neuromythology*, the decade of the brain also goes along with various lobbying efforts. By now, more students at American research universities take psychotropic drugs than smoke cigarettes.[15] The higher resolution and more detailed knowledge of our images of the brain promise to contribute to social transformation in the context of what the German sociologist Christoph Kucklick aptly summarizes as a "control-revolution." He observes that we live in a "granular society," where we are no longer merely exploited but are also put in a position to interpret ourselves as objects of medical knowledge.[16] The crude identity thesis corresponds to the fantasy that our self, our entire human mind, turns out to be a physical object among others, no longer hidden from view.

The question, of who or what the ominous self really is, is thus revealed to be significant not merely for the discipline of philosophy but rather in political terms as well, and it concerns each one of us on an everyday level. Just think about the popular idea that love can be defined as a specific "neurococktail" or our bonding behavior be reduced to patterns trained in prehistoric times in which our evolutionary ancestors acquired now hard-wired circuits of chemical flows. In my opinion, these attempts are really relief fantasies, as they defer responsibility to an in itself irresponsible and non-psychological machinery which runs the show of our lives behind our backs. It is quite burdensome to be free and to thus figure that others are free, too. It would be nice if we were relieved of decisions and if our life played out like a serenely beautiful film in our mind's eye. As the American philosopher Stanley Cavell puts it: "Nothing is more human than the wish to deny one's humanity."[17]

I reject this wish, and in this book I argue for the idea that the concept of mind be brought into connection with a concept of freedom, as it is used in the political context. Freedom is not merely a very abstract word that we defend without knowing what we actually mean by it. It is not merely the freedom guaranteed by a market-based economy, the freedom of choice of consumers confronted with different products. On closer inspection, it turns out that human freedom is grounded in the fact that we are minded animals who cannot be completely understood in terms of any natural-scientific model or any combination of them, be it present or futuristic. Natural science will never figure us out, not just because the brain is too complex (which might be a sufficient ground to be skeptical about the big claims of neurocentrism), but also because the human mind is an open-ended process of creation of self-conceptions of itself. The core of the human mind, the capacity to create said images, is itself empty. Without the variation in self-images, no one is at home in our minds, as it were. We really exist in thought about ourselves, which does not mean that we are infallible or illusions.

And thus we come to the heart of the matter. We exist precisely in the process of reflecting on ourselves. This is the lot of our form of life. We are not merely conscious of many things in our environment, and we do not merely have conscious sensations and experiences (including feelings); rather, we even have consciousness of consciousness. In philosophy we call this *self-consciousness*, which has little to do with the everyday sense of a self-conscious person. Self-consciousness is consciousness of consciousness; it is the kind of state you are in right now as I instruct you to think about your own thought processes, to relate mentally to your own minds.

The concept of mental freedom that I develop in this book is connected to the so-called existentialism of Jean-Paul Sartre (1905–1980). In his philosophical and literary works, Sartre sketched an image of freedom whose origins lie in antiquity and whose traces are to be found in the French Enlightenment, in Immanuel Kant, in German Idealism (Johann Gottlieb Fichte, Friedrich Wilhelm Joseph Schelling, Georg Wilhelm Friedrich Hegel), Karl Marx, Søren Kierkegaard, Friedrich Nietzsche, Sigmund Freud and beyond. In contemporary philosophy this tradition is carried on in the United States primarily on behalf of Kant and Hegel, although Kierkegaard and Nietzsche are also assigned a role. So far, Albert Camus and Sartre have played a minor role in the revival of the existentialist tradition in the philosophy of mind.

I mention these names only in order to remind us of an important strand of human thought about ourselves. The philosophical tenet I take over from that tradition I call **neo-existentialism**, which claims that human beings are free insofar as we must form an image of ourselves in order to be individuals. To have a human mind is to be in a position in which one constantly creates self-conceptions in light of which we exist. We project self-portraits of ourselves, who we are and who we want to be, as well as who we should be, and via our self-portraits we relate to norms, values, laws, institutions, and rules of various kinds. We have to interpret ourselves in order to have any idea of what to do. We thus inevitably develop values as reference points for our behavior.

Another decisive factor at this point is that we often project false and distorted self-images onto social reality and even make them politically effective. The human being is that being which forms an idea of how it is included in realities that go far beyond it. Hence, we project visions of society, images of the world, and even metaphysical belief-systems that are supposed to make everything which exists part of a gigantic panorama. As far as we know, we are the only animals who do this. In my view, however, it does not diminish other animals or elevate us morally in any sense over the rest of the animal kingdom which would justify the current destruction of the flora and fauna of our planet, the only home to creatures who are able to orient their actions in light of a conception of a reality that goes beyond them. It is not that we human beings should be triumphantly intoxicated on our freedom and should now, as masters of the planet, propose a toast to a successful **Anthropocene**, as the epoch of human terrestrial dominance is called today.

Many of the main findings arrived at by the philosophy of mind in the twentieth and twenty-first century to this point are still relatively little known to a wider public. One reason for this certainly lies in the fact that both the methods and the arguments that are employed in contemporary philosophy typically rest on complicated assumptions and are carried out in a quite refined specialized language. In this respect, philosophy is of course also a specialized discipline like psychology, botany, astrophysics, French studies or statistical social research. That is a good thing. Philosophy often works out detailed thought patterns about particular matters in a technical language out of sheer intellectual curiosity. This is an important training and discipline.

However, philosophy has the additional and almost equally important task of what Kant called "enlightenment," which means that philosophy also plays a role in the public sphere. Given that all human beings in full possession of their mental powers constantly construct self-images which play out in social and political contexts, philosophy can teach everybody something about the very structure of that activity. Precisely because we are nowhere close to infallible with respect to our mindedness, we often create misguided self-conceptions and even support them financially, such as the erroneous but widespread conception that we are identical with our brains or that consciousness and free will are illusions.

Kant explicitly distinguishes between a "scholastic concept" [*Schulbegriff*] and a "cosmopolitan concept" [*Weltbegriff*][18] of philosophy. By this he meant that philosophers do not only exchange rigorous, logically proficient arguments and on this basis develop a specialized language. That is the "scholastic concept" of academic philosophy. Beyond this, in Kant's view, we are obligated to provide the public with as extensive an insight as possible into the consequences of our reflections for our image of the human being. That is the "cosmopolitan concept" of philosophy. The two concepts go hand in hand, such that they can reciprocally critique each other. This corresponds to the fundamental idea of Kantian enlightenment – a role that philosophy already played in ancient Greece. The word "politics" itself, together with the set of concepts which still structure our overall relation to the public sphere, the polity, derives from ancient Greek philosophy. The idea made prominent by Plato's Socrates is that philosophy, among other things, serves the function of critically investigating our self-conception as minded, rational animals. For many central concepts, including justice, morality, freedom, friendship, and so forth, have been forged in light of our capacity to create an image of ourselves as a guide to human action. Again, we can only act as human beings in light of an implicit or explicit account of what it is to be the kind of minded creature we happen to be. Given that I believe that neurocentrism is a distorted self-conception of the human mind, full of mistakes and based on bad philosophy, it is time to attack in the name of enlightenment.

The self as a USB stick

The *Human Brain Project*, which was endowed with more than a billion euros by the European Commission, has come under heavy criticism. Originally, its aim was to consolidate current knowledge of the human brain by producing computer-based models and simulations of it. The harmless idea was to accumulate all the knowledge there is about the brain, to store it and to make it readily available for future research.

Corresponding to the idea of medical progress based on knowledge acquisition are wildly exaggerated ideas of the capability of artificial intelligence which permeate the *zeitgeist*. In films such as Spike Jonze's *Her*, Luc Besson's *Lucy*, Wally Pfister's *Transcendence*, Neill Blomkamp's *Chappie* or Alex Garland's *Ex Machina*, mind, brain and computer are confused so as to give rise to the illusion that we could somehow (and soon) upload our mental profiles on non-biological hardware in order to overcome the limitations of biologically realized mental life. In order to convince us that there is no harm in such fantasies, in *Her* we are shown a protagonist who falls in love with his apparently highly intelligent software, "who" happens to develop a personality with existential problems so that the program decides to break up with its human lover. In *Transcendence*, the protagonist becomes immortal and omnipotent by uploading his self onto a computer platform in order to disseminate himself on the internet. In *Lucy*, the female protagonist, after she is able consciously to control 100 percent of her brain activity under the influence of a new drug from Asia, succeeds in transferring herself onto a USB stick. She becomes immortal by transforming herself into a pure mass of data on a data carrier. This is a rampantly materialist form of pseudo-Buddhist fantasy represented by the idea that such a mind/brain-changing drug has to come from Asia, of course . . .

Along with the imaginary relief that we get in wishing to identify our self with the grey matter in our skull, our wish for immortality and invulnerability also plays a decisive role in the current world picture. The internet is presented as a platform of imperishability, onto which one can someday upload one's mind purified of the body in order to surf through infinite binary space forever as an information ghost.

Somewhat more soberly, the scientists of the *Human Brain Project* anticipate medical progress through a better understanding of the brain. At the same time, this project also proclaimed on its homepage, under the tab "Vision," that an artificial neuroscience based on computer models, which no longer has to work with actual brains (which among other things resolves ethical problems), "has the potential to reveal the detailed mechanisms leading from genes to cells and circuits, and ultimately to cognition and behaviour – the biology that makes us human."[19]

Scientific and technological progress are welcome, without question. It would be irrational to condemn actual progress merely on the ground that science over the last couple of hundred years has led to problems such as nuclear bombs, global warming, and ever more pervasive surveillance of citizens through data collection. We can only counter the problems caused by modern humanity with further progress directed by enhanced value systems based on the idea of an ethically acceptable sustainability of human life on earth. Whether we resolve them or whether humanity will obliterate itself sometime in the foreseeable future cannot be predicted. This depends on whether we will even recognize the problems and identify them adequately. It is in our hands to implement our insights into the threatened survival conditions of human animals. We underestimate many difficulties, such as, for instance, the overproduction of plastic or the devastating air pollution in China, which already afflicts hundreds of millions. Other problems are hardly understood at all at this point, such as, for example, the complex socioeconomic situation in the Middle East. These problems cannot be dealt with by outsourcing human self-conceptions to objective representations, maps and models of the brain. It is not only that we do not have enough time left to wait for neuroscience to translate everything we know about the human mind into a neurochemically respectable vocabulary. Rather, there is no need to do this, as we are already equipped to deal with the problems, but underfinanced and understaffed in the relevant fields of inquiry.

We certainly do not want to return to the Stone Age, indeed not even to technological conditions in the nineteenth century. A lamenting critique of modernity does not lead anywhere except for those who long for the end of civilization, which more likely than not reflects their own fears of civilization, their "discontent with civilization" (Freud).[20] It is already almost unthinkable for us *digital natives* to write someone a letter via snail mail. If there were no email, how would we organize our workplace? As always, technological progress is accompanied by technophobia and the potential for ideological exploitation, which govern the debates over the digital revolution and the misuse, as well as the monitoring, of data on the internet.

General technological progress is evidently not that bad. On the contrary: I am glad that I can write emails and be electronically connected with my friends around the globe. Furthermore, I am glad that I no longer have to go to a video store in order to rent films. I am glad that I can order pizza, book my vacation online, and find information ahead of time concerning hotels, beaches or art exhibitions. Our technologically sophisticated and scientifically respectable progressive civilization is not in itself a "context of delusion," as pessimistic cultural critics following the philosopher Adorno suppose.

Yet, as always, there are delusions today. The major delusion is that scientific and technological process unaided by cultural, philosophical, ethical, religious and artistic reflection could by itself lead to an enhanced understanding of the human mind in light of which we could improve on our decision-making or courses of action.

Admittedly, our present-day techno-scientific progress has its dark sides, problems of our own making on an undreamt-of scale: cyberwars, ecological degradation, overpopulation, drones, cybermobbing, terrorist attacks prepared in social networks, nuclear weapons, attention deficit disorders, and so forth. Nevertheless, remarkable regressions in the domain of self-knowledge are to be noted, which are this book's concern. When it comes to such regressions, we are dealing with ideology, thus with a certain kind of illusion that proliferates for as long as no one revolts against it. *Ideology critique* is one of the main functions of philosophy in society, a responsibility that one should not avoid.

Neuromania and Darwinitis – the example of Fargo

The British medical physician and clinical neuroscientist Raymond Tallis (b. 1946) coined the terms "neuromania" and "Darwinitis," by which he understands humanity's current misrepresentation of itself.[21] **Neuromania** consists in the belief that one can know oneself by learning ever more about one's central nervous system, especially concerning the workings of the brain. **Darwinitis** complements this view with the dimension of our deep biological past in an attempt to make us believe that typical present-day human behavior is to be better understood, or perhaps only explainable at all, if we reconstruct its adaptive advantage in the struggle for survival amid the tumult of species on our planet. Neurocentrism is the combination of neuromania and Darwinitis, and thus the idea that we can understand ourselves as minded animals only if we investigate the brain while considering its evolutionary prehistory.

A wonderfully ironic example of Darwinitis can be found in an episode of the brilliant television series *Fargo*. The psychopathic killer Lorne Malvo, skillfully played by Billy Bob Thornton, is temporarily arrested by a policeman who recognized him. However, Malvo had already previously come up with the ingenious idea of presenting himself as a priest on a church website, so that he is quickly released, since the police all too credulously take a supposed church's website on the internet for the real thing. When Malvo heads out of the police station, the above-mentioned policeman, who knows his true identity, asks him how he can reconcile his behavior – being a killer who uses a fake identity as a priest – with his human conscience. Malvo replies by asking him why human beings can visually distinguish so many shades of the color green. The policeman is at a loss but later asks his fiancée about it. She answers him as follows. Our refined color palette for green stems from the fact that, back in the time when we were hunter-gatherers, we had to recognize our natural enemies as well as our prey in bushes and dense forests. Natural selection thus brought about our specific color vision, which generally speaking is hard to deny. Without natural selection and the color spectrum consciously available to us due to our biological equipment, our species would probably not exist.

Yet, Malvo does not merely evoke a biological fact. With his response, he actually wants to communicate that he is a hunter and to justify it. He would like to *justify* his behavior by pointing out that we are descended from hunters and killers and hence that his killing represents a kind of natural necessity. He thus advocates a crass form of social Darwinism and consequently a philosophical position. **Social Darwinism** advocates the thesis that every kind of interpersonal behavior between human beings can be understood, explained and justified according to parameters implemented in the survival of biological species that can be investigated by evolutionary biology. What we do is driven by behavioral patterns ultimately rooted in hard-wired facts about our biological make-up and not in ethical reflection which floats free from our biology.

Although *Darwinism*, of course, first emerged in the second half of the nineteenth century, certain basic ideas of *social Darwinism* are much older. The ancient Greeks already discussed it – for instance, Plato in one of his main works, in the first book of *The Republic*. The ancient philosopher Thrasymachus appears there and defines justice as "nothing else than the advantage of the stronger."[22] In the first half of the nineteenth century, Arthur Schopenhauer began describing specifically human behavior in a proto-social-Darwinistic manner. For example, he explained romantic love as well as many other social facts and processes in general on the basis of human sexuality as courtship behavior in the biological sense of the term, which in his case was accompanied by a marked general misanthropy and misogyny in particular. Schopenhauer – to put it lightly – had problems dealing with the opposite sex.

One finds explanations like this everywhere in popular culture and science today. In particular, biological categories are employed to explain the basic structures of human behavior in relationships that we are all involved in on an everyday level. We indeed wish that it might finally be revealed that the human being is "only" an animal, too, and in any case we do not want to be so naïve as to believe that we have completely dropped out of the animal realm. Perhaps, from a bad conscience toward the other animals (whom we gawk at in zoos and happily grill on warm, summer evenings with a bottle of beer in one hand), we wish to pretend that the human being is no exception in the animal realm but rather, simply by coincidence, also a living being with a very peculiar kind of mind – and, by the way, most likely the only animal worried about its position in the animal realm in light of the very idea of such a realm. This is one of the reasons why, as far as I know, we are the only animals that rip other animals to shreds with machines, pack their meat into their intestines, turn this mess into a sausage, and then enter into a dialogue over the most skillful preparations for roasting them. In its sophistication, this goes way beyond any kind of cruelty we find in the animal kingdom, and it serves the function of creating a culture of meat consumption which makes it look as if meat was not really meat, given that sausages are highly artificial products obscuring their origins.

Mind – brain – ideology

One of the main theses of this book is that the issues that have been touched on up to this point, of delegating our self-knowledge to new scientific disciplines, are ideological and thus misguided fantasies. What I criticize here under the heading of **ideology** is a system of ideas and knowledge claims in the realm of self-knowledge, which misconstrues the products of the mind's freedom as natural, biological processes. Seen in this light, it is no wonder that the contemporary ideology of neurocentrism has particularly tried to dismiss the concept of human freedom. It is supposedly for the best that there are no products of human freedom at all.

The goal would be achieved if one were able to trace Heinrich von Kleist's *Amphitryon*, Gioachino Rossini's *Petite messe solennelle*, the hip-hop of the 1990s or the architecture of the Empire State Building as somewhat complex variants of the ludic drive prevalent in the animal kingdom. It is widely acknowledged that our sciences are still infinitely far from achieving this goal. Thus we find, toward the end of the much discussed German "Manifesto: Eleven Leading Neuroscientists on the Present and Future of Brain Research," which appeared in the popular science journal *Gehirn und Geist* [Brain and Mind]:

> Even if we should someday eventually bring to light all of the neural processes that underlie human sympathy, being in love, or moral responsibility, the uniqueness of this "inner perspective" is still preserved. Even one of Bach's fugues is no less fascinating when one has precisely understood how it was composed. Brain research will have to clearly distinguish what it can say and what lies beyond its domain, as musicology – to stick to this example – has a few things to say about Bach's fugue but must remain silent when it is a matter of explaining its singular beauty.[23]

As a representative example of neurocentrism – that is, the thesis that self = brain – one can point to the book by the Dutch brain scientist Dick Swaab (b. 1944) entitled *We Are Our Brains: A Neurobiography of the Brain, from the Womb to Alzheimer's*.[24] Right at the beginning of the introduction we read that:

> Everything we think, do, and refrain from doing is determined by the brain. The construction of this fantastic machine determines our potential, our limitations, and our characters; *we are our brains*. Brain research is no longer confined to looking for the cause of brain disorders; it also seeks to establish why we are as we are. It is a quest to find ourselves.[25]

This quote nicely illustrates how, according to neurocentrists, brain research is no longer supposed to be research only into the mode of functioning of an organ. It now wishes, or at least Dick Swaab wishes, to embark on the "quest to find ourselves." Without a healthy brain, admittedly, we would not exist. We could not think, be aware or live consciously. However, without many more arguments, it does not follow that we are identical to our brain.

An initial distinction which helps to clarify why we should resist the scientifically premature and philosophically deluded claim that we are identical to our brain even if we cannot exist without it is the distinction between *necessary* and *sufficient conditions*. For example, it is necessary that I have a bagel and jelly in order to be able to spread jelly on a bagel. But it is by no means sufficient. If the jelly is in the fridge and the bagel is in China, I do not easily achieve the state of having bagel with jelly smeared on top of it. For that to happen, I must properly blend jelly and bagel, for instance with butter, and all of us – me, jelly, bagel and butter – have to be in the same place. The necessary material conditions for there being an event of bagel consumption do not suffice for this event to happen.

We are in a similar situation when it comes to the brain. One reason why we are not identical to our brain consists simply in the fact that we do not first of all have a body that is composed only of neurons but have many additional organs that consist of other kinds of cells. Furthermore, we would not even be close to being what we are if we did not exist in social interaction with other human beings. We would have no language and would indeed not even be capable of surviving, since human beings are anything but born solipsists, as we cannot have a normal kind of consciousness without communicating with others.

Many cultural facts simply cannot be explained by observing a brain. At the very least, one must take into consideration a variety of brains that are found in mature, healthy human organisms. This makes the subject matter of neuroscientific observation forever too complex, since, because of its individual character and plasticity, even a single brain cannot be anywhere near to being completely described. Good luck to the attempt to investigate, for instance, the sociocultural structure of a current Chinese metropolis or even a small town in the Black Forest with the methods of neurobiology! Not only is such a project completely utopian, but it is also superfluous, since we are in possession of far better means. Our methods of describing and explaining cultural facts stem from the long history of the acquisition of self-knowledge, which besides philosophy includes, of course, literature, music, art, sociology, psychology, the colorful bouquet of the human sciences, religions, and so forth.

For more than a hundred years, the philosophy of mind has been centrally concerned with the relation between mind and brain, a question that became acute in early modern philosophy, especially with René Descartes (1596–1650). Descartes famously formulated a (pretty crude) way of looking at the problem: for he asked how an immaterial (meaning: not material) thing, such as a thought or a series of thoughts, could ever interact with the material world. If it could, it could not really be immaterial, as only matter causally interferes with matter. If it could not, our actions seemed to be utterly mysterious, as we often act by forming a plan in the realm of thoughts about the near future and then carry it out in the world of bodies by moving our limbs accordingly.

However, the mind–brain problem harks back to antiquity, to the question already formulated in ancient Greece, namely, how our body relates in general to our mind or our soul. This has created the general **mind–body problem**, of which our more recent *mind–brain* problem is a variant. The most general formulation of the problem runs as follows. How can conscious subjective mental experience take place at all in an unconscious, cold, purely objective universe that unfolds according to natural laws? How could our subjective conscious states possibly fit into a larger scheme of things in the universe, which is not governed at all by the kinds of psychological or logical laws constitutive of our self-encounter as thinking beings? Suns, moons, fermions and galaxy clusters, dark matter and CO_2 do not have or support an inner life. How come that the brain does? The prominent Australian philosopher of consciousness David Chalmers (b. 1966) has called this the **hard problem of consciousness**. In other words, how does our apparently provincial perspective on the universe fit into the natural order of the universe which exceeds our attempt to conceive it?

At this point, it is very tempting in our current cultural climate to come up with a simplistic solution, one which basically just shrugs its shoulders and flatfootedly denies that there is a problem. For instance, one could suppose that the conscious self is generated by the brain. One could perhaps understand this production as a side-effect of an adaptive advantage in the struggle for survival of species and individuals. Consciousness would then simply exist because certain kinds of brains prevailed in evolutionary terms, namely those generating consciousness. This certainly looks like some kind of explanation. But if our conscious self is *generated* by the brain, it cannot simply and self-evidently be *identical* to what generated it. If A is generated by B, then A and B are in any event not strictly identical. Hence, either the self is *generated* by the brain (perhaps as an illusion that is useful for survival or as our organism's user interface) or it is *identical* with the brain. This is where theorizing begins, as one cannot obtain clarity and coherence in this matter by confusing production and identity, which Sam Harris (b. 1966) absolutely fails to do in his book *Free Will*.[26] Harris there actually claims that the self is generated by the brain and hence is not free, while he also denies the existence of an independent mental level. However, how is it possible that the brain creates something with which it is identical? Traditionally, this model, the model of a *causa sui*, a cause of itself, was reserved to God, and it did not help theology's coherence either ... The problem is that, if there is really only a brain and not in addition to it a mental level (let alone a soul), then, if the brain produces consciousness, it has to produce a brain. Of course, this invites the immediate response that consciousness is identical only to a part of the brain, but again this does not help, as it is not the case that the non-conscious parts of the brain literally produce the conscious parts of the brain – at least there is no known mechanism that instantiates this part–whole relation.

To deny human freedom on the basis of the claim that we are identical to our brain will never work, even if our brain unconsciously makes decisions for us. For one thing, on this model we are precisely still free, since the brain for its part is not supposed to depend on the unconscious decisions of another system. If my brain controls me, but I am my brain, then my brain controls itself, or I control myself. Thus freedom is not imperiled but rather elucidated. If the brain is a self-determining system where the non-conscious parts bring about explicit and conscious decision-making, this does not undermine our freedom but is, rather, an account of it. One of the many sources of confusion in Sam Harris's

wishful thinking that he can eliminate his own free will by theorizing about it in an incoherent manner is that he really provides us
with a (bad) model of free will and not with a way of undermining
it. Also, why would free will require that I consciously create a
conscious decision to do something? This view immediately runs
into a vicious infinite regress, as I would have to pile up infinitely
many conscious decisions in order to act in a conscious manner! I
would have consciously to produce my consciousness of my consciousness, . . . , to act. This will not work. But it has nothing to do
with the brain.

The cartography of self-interpretation

The critique of neurocentrism is nevertheless only one objective
of this book. At the same time, I would like to map the intellectual landscape of our self-knowledge by presenting some central
basic concepts of the philosophy of mind. How are concepts such
as consciousness, self-consciousness, self, perception and thinking connected and how, anyway, do they become part of our
vocabulary?

In what follows, I will hence also be concerned with positive self-
knowledge, and thus with the question of who we really are. The
main positive thesis of the neo-existentialism sketched out here is
the claim that the human mind engenders an open multiplicity of
capacities all of which involve the mind, because the mind creates
an image of itself by way of these self-interpretations. *The human
mind makes an image of itself and thereby engenders a multiplicity
of mental realities.* This process has a structure that is historically
open, and which cannot be conceived only in the language of
neurobiology. Neurobiology will only ever be able to account for
some necessary conditions of human mindedness, even if it informs
us that there are restrictions on human action of which we might
not have been aware before. The fact that no complete form of
self-knowledge of the human mind can ever be achieved via neurobiology alone is grounded in the fact that the human mind is not
purely a biological phenomenon.

Our capacity for developing false world pictures and misguided
self-conceptions is intertwined with the phenomenon of ideology.
What is crucial is that even false self-conceptions express something, as they present those who hold them as taking certain things
to be true and accurately stated even though they are not. We are
in constant dialogue with others about our self-image and general

self-conception precisely because we are constantly negotiating and testing new modules of self-understanding. Some turn out to be delusional. Yet, those suffering from self-delusional models are afflicted by the associated beliefs. It is constitutive of the human mind that it can change according to its beliefs about itself, which includes the false ones. If I mistakenly believe that I am a great dancer and lead my life in light of this illusion regardless of my experience (which should teach me a lesson here), this changes my status as an agent.

The spectrum of the production of mental realities extends from a profound understanding of ourselves in art, religion and science (which includes the human, social, technological and natural sciences) all the way to the quite various forms of illusion: ideology, self-deception, hallucination, mental illnesses, and so forth. We have at our disposal, among other things, consciousness, self-consciousness, thinking, a self, a body, an unconscious, etc. The human mind is irreducibly multifarious and ever-changing. What remains is the core invariant of self-production.

The human mind does not have a reality that is independent from its self-images, such that one could simply compare this independent reality of the mind with its self-images. It exists only in such a way that it makes self-images. It thus always becomes what it makes of itself. It has a history for precisely this reason, the history of mind or *Geistesgeschichte*, as we say in my neck of the woods.

A simple way to illustrate this thought is by the following contrast. As a matter of fact, I hardly know anything about trees. However, I know that elms are trees. But I could certainly not tell an Anhui elm from a Nikko elm without doing some kind of research (at least Google). Now imagine I see a tree somewhere and say to myself or to others that this is a Nikko elm. It might not even be an elm or an Anhui elm. Be that as it may, the tree is what it is regardless of my beliefs about it. It does not turn into an Anhui elm if I believe it to be one. And it does not change its status at all relative to my beliefs, which simply do not matter for the tree's being what it is. By contrast, if I am self-deluded and believe that I am a great tango dancer, I might start behaving in light of these false beliefs which sustain my self-delusion. Maybe I start traveling to Buenos Aires, where no one wants to dance with me, which I explain as a lack of recognition of my true tango genius, etc. In this case, my belief about myself, my capacities, my style, and so forth, changes me from someone with an accurate self-image into a deluded person. My beliefs about myself (including my beliefs about my beliefs) affect me profoundly and constantly. A mind is just not an elm, as you can tell from this little philosophical exercise.

Our epoch of the history of mind, modernity, has produced neurocentrism, which seems to be in harmony with a great basic motif of this epoch: to achieve enlightenment (the realization of a particular value system) through science. However, what we have increasingly forgotten in the recent history of this valuable epoch is the fact that it can founder and run aground. We need more modernity, not less. We currently lack a sufficiently widespread insight into the constitutive historicity of our self-images, which has been a central theme of philosophy for the last two hundred years and which ought not to be erased from our current concept of mind, which threatens to lose touch with its historical reality in the context of its wish to deny its own mindedness by replacing it with a silicon, plastic or neural counterpart.

1

What is at Stake in the
Philosophy of Mind?

At first glance, nothing seems more obvious than that mind is at
stake in the philosophy of mind. But I have already argued that the
mind is not a thing, a natural kind out there in the universe, whose
nature we need to study in some natural scientific way. In the last
century, in particular, a new approach emerged to the fact that
we are creatures who are aware of their surroundings by perceiving them, who have feelings, thoughts and dreams, etc. This new
approach is called "philosophy of mind"[1] and was presented in paradigmatic form in Bertrand Russell's influential book *The Analysis
of Mind*.[2] What is called *Philosophie des Geistes* in German, even
today by many authors in the German-speaking world, stems from
the discipline of the "philosophy of mind" in the English-speaking
world. However, in German, *Bewusstseinsphilosophie* [philosophy
of consciousness] would be a more accurate translation of "philosophy of mind," which I would like to use in order to be able to
distinguish this new orientation from previous currents of thought.
Philosophers from Hegel to Habermas suggested a distinction
between philosophy of consciousness and philosophy which deals
with mind in the sense of *Geist*. This distinction is obscured by the
decision to come up with a unified category, the mind, and think
of it along the lines of consciousness. Consciousness is, roughly
speaking, a subjective process that, for all we know, is somehow
connected with the fact that we have a suitable brain. In order to
be able to sketch the outlines for my contribution to the revival
of self-conceptions in terms of *Geist*, I will distinguish philosophy
of consciousness and philosophy of mind. *Philosophy of consciousness*, then, corresponds to the mainstream discipline called
"philosophy of mind" in the English-speaking world, and *philosophy of mind*, as in the title of this book, refers to an investigation
into human mindedness, into the invariant capacity to produce
self-conceptions and its differentiation into conceptual modules,

31

such as consciousness, self-consciousness, thought, representation, will, etc.

What is problematically new in philosophy of consciousness is not so much to be found in its content but, rather, consists in the fact that the philosophy of consciousness typically assigns the philosophy of mind in general the task of seeking the answer to a specific question: What marks something out as a mental state or a mental event? For, if we ever want to make progress on the mind–brain problem, it seems a good move to carve out the concept of a mark of the mental so that we know what to relate to what. Notice that the concept of a brain is also more complicated than is presented by standard discussions. Usually, we speak of a "normal" healthy adult brain, for which we have a map on which we find the neural correlates of specific mental functions, such as the visual cortex with its subregions. However, this brain is really a model of a brain and not the kind of thing everybody has within their skulls. Brain science can only ever work out a model of the brain on the basis of very limited samples, and it tells us that brains have plasticity – that is, they can be highly individual and even change the function of some areas in order to replace other areas, etc. Yet, for the rest of this book I will simply play along and assume that we know how to individuate a brain. Hence, I will not try to attack neuroscience on that front and simply grant the concept of the brain.

This leaves us with the task of finding a "mark of the mental," as the saying goes, something which helps us to distinguish mind and brain first on a conceptual level in order to find out how they hang together in the natural world (if they do!). The mark accepted by many turns out to be consciousness, which is why the philosophy of mind has been concentrated one-sidedly on a single capacity of the human mind: consciousness.

The question referred to, concerning the mark of the mental, arises against the backdrop of the modern presumption that much of what we once may have considered in terms of mind turned out to be purely natural. Here once more the modern struggle against superstition comes to the fore. While it may once have been believed that the heavenly bodies move in regular paths and constellations in order to transmit the messages of the gods, in modernity we have finally realized that the universe contains no such messages for us. It is meaningless in that it does not contain messages and is not driven by any mind. The regular movements of the heavenly bodies can be explained mechanistically, and neither intention nor mind of any other kind is behind such an explanation. I have no intention to deny this.

Yet, according to this view, the mind was progressively banished from the universe or nature until it was resurrected in the shape of philosophy of consciousness. Mind has turned into consciousness, which, in turn, is supposed to rest on essentially subpersonal, non-conscious processes encapsulated in our brain. Some associate this progressive banishment with **secularization**, and thus with the disappearance of religion in favor of that which is not religious, above all scientific explanations, something supposedly characteristic of modernity. However, the question here is whether we even have criteria for something that can be considered as mental, and under what conditions a religious and a scientific explanation are really incompatible.

Mind in the universe?

The first contrast that is prominent in the modern line of reasoning is that of nature and mind. In this vein, Russell ventures the claim that we should not make use of precisely this contrast, since otherwise the dualism feared and despised by nearly everyone will force itself upon us. This **dualism** is the thesis that the universe consists of two different kinds of objects or events: mental and natural. Most philosophers of consciousness today consider it untenable, because one must then assume that mental events would somehow have to impinge on the mechanism of the conservation and transformation of energy that belongs to purely natural processes. According to many contemporary scientists (but not according to Isaac Newton himself!), the laws of nature that teach us how the conservation and transformation of energy function tell us nothing about there being a mind that impinges causally on what happens. On the contrary, everything which takes place in nature or the universe apparently can be explained without recourse to a mind, since the laws of nature teach us that nothing can impinge causally on something without a transformation of energy/matter. Sure, this assumes that mind itself is not something material. If it were, by this logic it could easily impinge on what happens causally. Mind-matter has not yet been discovered, or so it seems. Thus one prefers to seek mind in the brain, because without the latter we would in fact have no conscious inner life, and therefore no consciousness, which the philosophy of consciousness ultimately considers to be the mark of the mental.

It is easy to imagine a perspective from which the mind-matter problem appears quite striking. Imagine Yonca would like to drink coffee. Accordingly, she goes to the kitchen and turns on the coffee machine. From the perspective of physics, we have no reason to assume that somewhere in Yonca's body a vital force, a soul or a mind is diffused and guides her body into the kitchen. Were something like this the case, its interaction with the body would have been proven long ago, since such a mind can impinge on the material-energetic reality studied by physics only if it leaves material-energetic traces according to the laws of nature. This means that energy would have been put to use, which can be measured. From this perspective, it seems most natural that we have to look for Yonca's apparent wish to drink coffee somewhere in the energetic meshwork of nature. Since, however, no soul is to be found there, but at most a brain, the question of how brain and mind are related to one another starts to look to make sense. We know from the description of the scenario that Yonca wants to drink coffee, and we know from the point of view of physics that this cannot mean that an immaterial soul interacts with her body without leaving any material-energetic trace. In this context, one usually invokes **the principle of the causal closure of nature**, which involves the claim that purely natural processes can never be interfered with by purely mental processes. Nothing which does not leave any material-energetic footprints can interfere causally with processes which require a material-energetic grounding in order to take place. This causes a problem if one wishes to distinguish mind from nature by the fact that the former is understood to be a non-material substance, a purely mental bearer of thoughts, and the latter is understood as the closed realm of the causal world, the universe or nature.

Within this framework, the American philosopher of consciousness Jaegwon Kim (b. 1934) asked somewhat derisively whether an almost immaterial mind, so to speak, could not still be somehow causally connected to our body. But then the question arises as to how the mind manages to accompany the body at great velocity. For example, how does the mind accelerate when an astronaut is sent into outer space? Can one measure it physically, or how does one conceive it? Could our body outrun our mind if only it were quick enough? Or is the mind fastened to the body somewhere, perhaps in the pineal gland in the brain, as Descartes, the great-grandfather of the philosophy of consciousness, supposed?

The very idea of a causal closure of reality relies on the notion that there is a purely natural reality, an objective realm occupied by processes and objects such that everything in that domain can be apprehended, described and explained with scientific precision and objectivity. Let us call the realm of physical reality thus conceived **the universe**.

So far, so good. But what about psychology? Does it not examine something like the human mind with the aid of experiments, and thus also with scientific precision and objectivity? Yet, if this is the case, then the mind must belong to the universe. The contrast between nature and the mind that leads to a mind-matter problem quickly collapses. Notice that dualism looms large as soon as one supposes that there is a problem at all with the embedding of mind in nature. Hence, to be a dualist, one does not need to believe that there is a secret, non-material source of energy (the mind, the soul) which prowls around within our skull.

It is indeed correct that we do not find mind in the universe. But it does not follow from this that the mind does not exist! This only follows if we have an image of the universe as the only realm of what exists, as the one and only true reality. Yet such an image of the world is not scientifically or physically verifiable but has to remain a pure article of faith. At best, one can argue for it philosophically.

One prominent strategy at this point is to try to explain mind away altogether, which is called **theory reductionism**, in order simply to eliminate the problem we have outlined. This thesis has the name it does because we are supposed to reduce every theory that avails itself of mental processes into a theory in which the word "mind" no longer occurs. For instance, **behaviorism** attempted to translate all statements about mental processes into statements about observable, ultimately physical, measurable behavior, and flourished in the early days of reductive views. To be in pain meant only to exhibit pain behavior. The assumption that there are mental processes at all came to seem like a remnant of premodern superstition – a side-effect of the misguided attempt to find mind in the universe while considering the latter to be the one and only true reality.

In the spirit of Hegel

The search for a mark of the mental is largely occupied with the question of how mental states and events can have a place in a purely natural universe. But, in framing the question this way, it is assumed that we should accept a standard or paradigmatic concept of reality: physical reality. In presupposing this, we already oppose mental reality to physical reality by definition. The question then becomes how such a rift can be overcome or resolved.

Let us give this whole way of posing the question a name: **naturalistic metaphysics. Metaphysics** is the theory of reality as a whole, also called "the world," "the universe," "reality (full stop)" or "the cosmos." Metaphysics deals with absolutely everything which exists, with the most encompassing totality of them all. If the world is identified with nature, this means that everything which really exists must be natural. The sense of "naturalism" in "naturalistic metaphysics" is that **naturalism** claims that absolutely everything which exists is natural in the sense of being an object of the best (natural-)scientific theory. We should note that this metaphysics is neither a finding confirmed by research in some particular scientific discipline – or even by all the sciences together – nor a presupposition of research in physics, chemistry, biology or any other branch of natural science. Rather, it is a philosophical theory about how the world as a whole is constituted.

In *Why the World Does Not Exist*, I argued against all metaphysical world pictures which hold that there is a single reality, regardless of whether this is equated with the universe or with a giant hallucination in some god's mind. The assumptions driving a good deal of discussions in mainstream philosophy of mind are thus at least not without an alternative. If it turns out that we simply do not have to fit absolutely everything which exists into a single frame, there is room for a total reconfiguration of the very problems of the philosophy of mind, a reconfiguration I highly recommend given the manifold problems of naturalistic metaphysics.

The first problem is that naturalistic metaphysics relies on a concept of nature that has completely run its course and is even obsolete. That there is a universe, which at best can be completely explained by a unified physics in the sense of a "theory of everything," appears at present to be extremely utopian from the standpoint of science itself. Naturalistic metaphysics emerged in times when it seemed as though first Newton and then Newton + Einstein would suffice to provide a fundamentally complete account of the universe in the language of mathematics. Since the advent of quantum physics, that no longer sounds very plausible. The candidate that, these days, stands for a unified physics, namely string theory with its many varieties, does not appear to be experimentally verifiable at all. Currently, the very notion of absolutely everything which is physical cannot be pinned down by attaching it to physics. Physics is not unified, and it does not have an account of absolutely everything which is physical. At its borders, there are all sorts of speculations and open questions, from the nature of dark matter and dark energy to the hypotheses of a plurality of universes which might in turn be part of a multiverse landscape we will never be able to explore scientifically. In short, we are no longer even close to being able to specify how one could actually investigate the universe as a whole by means of experimentally grounded science.

The second problem of mainstream naturalistic metaphysics is that it does not ever concern itself with the human mind, but at most with consciousness. Thus it excludes the greatest part of the philosophical tradition that does not deem mind to be a subjective phenomenon of the kind that belongs to conscious experience. For example, in German one speaks of the "spirit of the age" [*Zeitgeist*]. Hegel introduces the term "objective spirit" [*objektiver Geist*], by which he means, for example, that a traffic sign is spiritual in the sense that it is the expression of an intention publicly to determine recognized rules for human behavior. Our social reality is defined by a huge array of artifacts which embody meaning so that our everyday experience is one where we constantly encounter objective manifestations of mind. In the philosophical tradition, human mindedness and language are intimately connected. But is language, for instance, purely subjective? Even texts that are handed down from the past can convey to us an impression of a *zeitgeist* that no longer exists but which nevertheless was once a reality. The German philosopher Wolfram Hogrebe (b. 1945) expresses this concisely in an aphorism: "Spirit is outside, but breaks through inside."[3] Our subjective mind is formatted in an encounter not with brute physical objects but with embodied meaning and social interaction. We never merely face an objective physical reality which we take in perceptually. The idea that the human mind in its infant stages, as it were, looks at the physical world and tries to make sense of it, is completely mythical, a modern myth based on the denial of the fact that our first encounter with reality is an encounter with people who interact with an environment consisting both of physical objects and artifacts.

In the nineteenth century in Germany, the concept of mind [*Geist*] led to the adoption of the expression *Geisteswissenschaften* as a designation for the humanities. This led to a bad opposition between the disciplines dealing with the human mind and the disciplines dealing with nature, the natural sciences. In the twentieth century, so-called hermeneutics (from the ancient Greek *hermēneia* = understanding) postulated that the humanities investigate only that which one can understand, while the natural sciences do not *understand* but rather wish to *explain*. Along these lines, the great

Heidelberg philosopher Hans-Georg Gadamer (1900–2002) wrote that language qua "being that can be understood"[4] is the object of the humanities.

The division of sciences into two broad categories over the decades happened to create the notion that ultimately only the natural sciences study the world, as they deal with things that are the way they are regardless of how we take them be, whereas the humanities deal with "softer" topics. But this climate assumes that there is only one true reality, the tough and blind world of physical forces into which we poor creatures are thrown so that our conscious life consists in coming up with illusions which help us to cover up the real.

At the same time, we have also witnessed a revival of serious philosophical interest in the tradition sometimes called German Idealism – i.e., the great philosophical systems that began with Kant and were further developed in the first half of the nineteenth century. This goes hand in hand with a revaluation of the humanities, including philosophy. Hegel's philosophy, which is fundamentally an attempt to give an account of what he calls *Geist*, surprisingly occupies center stage once more. As a matter of fact, he provides us with nowhere near exhausted insights into the relation of "nature" and "spirit." In particular, he proposed a quite plausible version of the idea that the human mind consists in the formation of its own image and of its place in a reality which goes far beyond it.

Hegel puts this as follows: "Spirit is only what it makes of itself; it is the activity of producing itself, grasping itself."[5] He thus takes up a few of the fundamental ideas of Kant and Fichte, both of whom are also relevant for contemporary ethics and practical philosophy, as you will see.

The philosophy of mind should include the tradition of philosophy from Plato to Sartre and beyond. Philosophy of consciousness should be a part of the larger enterprise to understand human mindedness and its relation to non-human reality, which includes the minds of other animals as well as purely physical reality. In any event, we have to reject the starting point of mainstream philosophy of consciousness – that is, first and foremost that we have to grope for a response to the misleading question of how the subjective phenomenon of our interior mental life fits into an anonymous, blind, unconscious nature without purpose, whose regularities can be described scientifically in the language of the natural sciences. When it comes to developing a philosophy of mind for the twenty-first century, it is first necessary to break through this dogma which makes us blind as to who we really are.

The historical animal on the social stage

Hegel's basic idea, that spirit first forms itself by way of self-images, also implies that spirit cannot be a thing among things. One does not come upon it as one comes upon mountain ridges, lakes or algae. The philosophy that immediately followed German Idealism drew upon this fundamental Kantian–Hegelian insight. In this context, Karl Marx believed precisely that the human being to this point had constructed false ideological self-images which must be overcome – admittedly, on the level of political economy and not merely by way of a correction of the images in philosophy, or natural science for that matter. Marx identifies false self-images in the ideological superstructure of art, religion, philosophy and science, a method which presupposes a specific form of the basic existentialist idea that the human being is a historical animal. It should be noted that even Marx did not suppose that the mind belonged to nature in the sense of the universe. This is why in a famous dictum he speaks of a "naturalism of the human being," which at the same time is supposed to be a "humanism of nature."[6] Marx's idea behind this is that the human mind is a piece of nature insofar as we produce artifacts in which human being and nature are united on the basis of social practices and particularly on the basis of labor. Labor, on Marx's account, is blind with respect to its material conditions, which is why it generates mistaken representations of these, which in turn have consequences for the formation of social reality. This feedback loop is the motor of history. In contrast to Hegel, Marx thus believes that the mind is essentially engendered through materially enacted labor, thus through the transformation of the natural environment with which it is sensuously engaged and not primarily in the form of art, religion and philosophy. But even Marx does not consider the human mind to be a subjective phenomenon that is played out within our skull and which could be investigated by psychological experiments, for instance, or even with a brain scanner – had he known of such a thing. Yet, he relegates adequate self-knowledge of the human mind to the discipline of political economy, for which he was trying to provide a philosophically sound foundation.

One of the central thoughts of the mid-nineteenth-century philosophy of mind up to the so-called existentialism of the twentieth century was that the human being is free in that it takes up its own role on the social stage. This thought attained particular prominence in Sartre's novels and plays, but also of course in the literary works of Camus. **Existentialism** is the view that the human being initially discovers itself as simply existing and must continually respond to this situation, and it is precisely this that distinguishes it from all other living beings. "Existence precedes essence."[7] This means that we are surprised by our own existence, by the fact that we find ourselves in this world. This fact as such does not give us the merest clue as to the meaning of it all, which is why Sartre takes the human mind to be a response to this predicament.

The basic idea behind this thought was indeed already the guiding theme of Kant's ethics. Its existentialist undertones also play a crucial role in contemporary philosophy – for instance, in the influential work of Christine Korsgaard (b. 1952), Stanley Cavell (b. 1926), Robert B. Pippin (b. 1948), Judith Butler (b. 1956), Jonathan Lear (b. 1948) and Sebastian Rödl (b. 1967), to mention but a few contemporary philosophers working in that tradition.

The fundamental thought of this neo-existentialism has the advantage of actually being easily understandable. In order to examine it more closely, let us imagine an everyday scenario: we are browsing through the supermarket looking for cucumbers, in the course of which we see someone who moves toward the shelves of bread, picks out a number of packages of bread and is examining them. We now first ask ourselves what appears to be the simplest question of all: What is he doing there? The obvious answer is that he is looking at a bunch of different packages of bread and examining them.

So far, so good. Yet is this actually a suitable description? How many human beings do you know who go to the supermarket in order to take hold of packages of bread and examine them? That would actually be a strange thing to do. It seems more likely to be the kind of thing one would do if one was perhaps drugged or otherwise suffering from an abnormality. But, then, what is going on? What is the man doing?

Now, here is another explanation: he went to the supermarket to buy bread and, because he bought moldy bread in the recent past, he is now examining the bread more closely. The fact that he is examining packages of bread is thus situated in a larger context which bestows meaning on his action in such a way that he does not fall into any specifically abnormal category.

In general, in order to understand what anyone is doing, we refer to a specific structure: someone is doing something *in order* to achieve something. In sociology and philosophy, this is called an *action*. An action is thus always an activity that is oriented toward goals and is accompanied by motives. Actions have a meaning that one must understand in order to know which, if any, takes place before we can set out further to describe, understand or explain it.

Neo-existentialism takes up Sartre's idea – which, as I said, has an influential precursor in Kant – that a person's action is really understandable only when we understand their project, as Sartre puts it. This project consists in the person's not only carrying out individual, idiosyncratic actions but also choosing between different courses of action within the context of a general idea of how they are meaningfully shaping their life.

Why not everything, but at least something, is teleological

This apparently completely trivial observation has quite far-reaching consequences. We are talking here about *teleological action explanation*. **Teleology** (from the Greek *to telos* = goal, purpose) is the doctrine of goal-directed processes. A **teleological action explanation** postulates that someone does something because she is pursuing a goal. It would be completely absurd to claim seriously that teleological action explanations are always objectively false and inadequate. Yet neurocentrism virtually forces just this presumption on us, which is why the very existence of successful teleological action explanation limits the pernicious influence of neurocentric thinking.

Let us for once assume that we are our brain. It follows that the man in the supermarket also is his brain. Thus we would always have to attribute his actions to his brain. His brain looks at bread and so forth (indeed it is certainly not his fingernails that do so, and his eyes are connected with his brain). Yet in what language does one best objectively describe brain processes?

It is a widespread assumption that modern science is so successful in making predictions and understanding nature in general because it gets by without teleology. On such a view, no sort of intention lies behind natural processes, and even the laws of nature are normally conceived of not as purposeful frameworks but as brute facts. There is no further reason why certain brute facts are as they are and, hence, no intention can lie behind them. According to this understanding of the sciences, one should not assume that anything happens in nature *in order for* something else to happen. Rather, purely natural processes are interpreted according to laws of nature by means of which we explain in general terms which event brings about which subsequent event.

The wish not to buy moldy bread, on this view, is not a scientific matter. For it to be a scientific matter, one would first have to translate it into an appropriate language, a language that dispenses with the teleological structure of action explanation. Then it would be a matter of the chemical composition of what we call mold and of the biological fitness of the organism, which is increased to a certain extent by avoiding mold. It would be a matter of photons hitting sensory receptors. It would be a matter of the complex processing of stimuli on the retina, and so forth. But it would not be a matter of the man doing something because he is pursuing a goal. Brains do not pursue any goals in this sense; they fulfill certain functions of processing information in a complex organism, which is situated in a natural environment to which it can react when necessary. Brains have no goals, only people do, who are much more than their brain and much more even than their present, past and future bodies.

One of the repeatedly emphasized breakthroughs of modern science consists in the fact that it formulates laws of nature without teleology. We can see what this means when we recall the glaring contrast between Isaac Newton and Aristotle in this regard, as it is usually represented. Aristotle postulates, among other things, that there are five elements: earth, water, fire, air and the ether, a substance which he introduces in order to account for the movement of the heavenly bodies. Our expression "quintessence" stems from this Aristotelian element, which literally means "the fifth element," ether, which for Aristotle borders on the divine. According to Aristotle, all of the elements have a natural place toward which they strive: fire and air move upward, earth downward, and so forth. In addition, Aristotle assumes in general that everything which occurs in nature has an ideal or perfect form after which it strives. This was the basic thought of his teleology. Nature is ordered and understandable for us, because we know in advance that there is a perfect form of the given natural species to discover. The perfect form makes any natural phenomenon intelligible.

In contrast to this, the modern idea has it that we can discover laws of nature that can be expressed mathematically without invoking anything which has the shape of an intention or a goal-directed activity. Accordingly, nature is understandable for us not because it fulfills our expectations of perfection, but because we are able to recognize relations and formulate them precisely by means of experiments and mathematical equations. Newton discovered gravity in this way, and in this context the Aristotelian doctrine of the five elements can be considered to be refuted once and for all.

Over the course of centuries, science has undermined our tendency to conceive of natural events in terms of the kinds of activities we understand on the model of human agency. Let it be noted in passing that this is not actually true of Newton's understanding of physics, as the context in which he works out laws of nature is highly theological. Be that as it may, modern physics teaches us that nature does not in fact generally function in the way one might think if one investigates it with the naked eye. What we see and perceive with our other senses more or less directly are objects on a specific level of physical reality. If we take only these objects into consideration, as Aristotle does, we do not get very far in explaining nature. Nature is fundamentally different from what meets the eye. Teleological action explanations hold true only on a limited everyday spectrum, in which, for example, people bump into us. In light of these considerations it seems perfectly legitimate to wonder how the reality of human action looks from the standpoint of natural science, a standpoint not accessible to the naked eye and one which dispenses with teleological explanations on all levels. This thought first spurred the attempt to seek a science of human behavior based on a scientific psychology.

The realization that nature, in a scientifically precise manner, is scaled entirely differently than it appears to us at first sight has resulted in massive disillusionment. Without this disillusionment we would never have been able actually to figure out (and not merely conjecture in a speculative way) the fact that we are situated in a possibly infinite universe and perhaps even in only one universe among infinitely many. We would have no telephones, no internet, no trains, indeed, we would not even have electricity in our homes, which was also mastered only after the surprising unifying discovery in the nineteenth century that electricity and magnetism are fundamentally the same.

The view that there is one all-encompassing reality laid out there in front of our eyes, as it were, underlies the ancient Greek conception of the cosmos. In *Why the World Does Not Exist* I argued that this conception, the very idea of metaphysics as a theory of absolutely everything which exists, has to be dismissed. It is as misguided as the Aristotelian doctrine of the five elements or the medieval theory of the four humors, according to which health and illness derive from different humor flows in our bodies.

Brain research can have a disillusioning effect. It should have relieved humanity of the superstitious notion that a soul dwells somewhere within the skull or that a mind is burrowing around in our brain or trapped by it. The British philosopher Gilbert Ryle

(1900–1976) nicely summed up this whole syndrome of nonsense in his book *The Concept of Mind*, with his famous phrase of the "ghost in the machine."[8]

The evolutionary biologist and proud atheist Richard Dawkins explains this kind of superstitious belief in souls with his claim that there is a "native dualism" of body and soul and a "native teleology" entrenched in us human beings: "The idea that there is a *me* perched somewhere behind my eyes and capable, at least in fiction, of migrating into somebody else's head, is deeply ingrained in me and in every other human being."[9] Furthermore, "childish teleology" "assigns purpose to everything,"[10] a misperception in which Dawkins recognizes one of the origins of religion, which for him, as the famous title of his book already states, is merely a *God Delusion*.

Dawkins is right insofar as it is in fact not a self that is situated behind our eyes but, rather, a brain. The overall idea of an animating psychic substance is refuted by modern biology, since it has become clear that we can understand the chemistry of life without recourse to a vital force. And why should there be another vital force alongside of the chemistry of life (in the sense of biological life)? Such ideas are rendered obsolete by modern science, an insight that is quite important for our image of the self. My attack on neurocentrism and naturalistic metaphysics is not an attack on the more modest view according to which we have to take natural science seriously. Of course, the heavenly bodies are not driven around ethereal spheres by some kind of world soul. But none of this means that mind and brain are identical or that everything there is can be studied and explained by the natural sciences. This is just another form of superstitious overextension of one model of explanation over the entirety of the cosmos, a modern form of mythology.

Scientifically advanced brain research in fact contravenes ancient assumptions that stem from a teleological conception of the world and which are invalid within the framework of modern science's methodologically guided knowledge interest. The internal conduction of signals by neurons, for instance, goes through ion channels and hydrophobic fatty acid chains. In order to form a comprehensive picture of the working of the brain, information concerning countless other chemical details has to be gathered, and one must familiarize oneself with the function of different areas of the brain as well. This is the everyday business of neuroscience and brain research, which is as complex as it gets.

From the standpoint of this research orientation, one is not likely to come up with any plausible teleological action explanations. To say that certain neurons fire *in order to* communicate information to other neurons in a distant area of the brain is a misleading metaphorical expression that is nevertheless sometimes used in brain research, heedless of its teleological implications. Things do not happen in the organism as portrayed to our children in the classic French cartoon series *Il était une fois . . . la vie* [Once Upon a Time . . . Life]. The processes in the brain involving individual cells and neural networks do not happen because they are pursuing certain goals but only because they perform a function.

A *biological function* in an organism is not a *goal* in the sense of teleological action explanation. The description of the functional architecture of the brain in terms of the neurobiological mechanisms unearthed by brain research is not an insight into the goals and intentional actions of an actor. In the brain, no one is at home running the show. Indeed, no one is sitting in a cell and pulling a lever so that something can be diffused through a cell membrane. Synapses are not sluices that someone opens and closes. It is characteristic of this level of description to disregard ideas of origination, goal and action, since they lead to absurd (albeit amusing) picture thinking.

However, the fact that no one is at home in the functional biochemical architecture of the brain does not after all entail that no one ever carries out a plan such as buying a plane ticket, or that in reality brains and not people buy plane tickets without any purpose whatsoever. Let us begin with a scenario and then interpose another one in the middle of it, as in a film. In the first scene we see a man who is taking bread from a shelf. The second scene suddenly shows neurons firing in a specific area of the brain or another physical process within the organism – a change of perspective that is often found in movies – think of *Lucy*, for instance, or Shane Carruth's *Upstream Color*. With a catchy phrase by the German philosopher Peter Bieri (b. 1944), we can summarize the effect of such changes in point of view through a sudden cross-cutting: "All of a sudden no one who is doing anything is there anymore. All that's left is the scene of an occurrence."[11]

Finally, we should give our man a name: Larry. Larry wants to buy bread. He is doing what he is doing because he is pursuing this very goal. But, someone might want to object, is Larry's setting of a goal in reality not ultimately a biological function? His experience of setting such a goal for himself might turn out to be a kind of illusion, an explanation that comes to mind because we simply do not yet know enough about evolution and about Larry's brain.

Maybe teleological action explanation is shorthand for the real thing – that is, an explanation of certain events in the language of natural sciences, which, however, would be much less handy than our present account.

The thesis that all our teleological action explanations rest on illusions was already advocated as a response to existentialism in early postwar philosophy. And it also has a previous history in which Marx and some sociologists connected to him play a decisive role. **Structuralism** supposes that human goals are a kind of illusion engendered by the fact that individuals are determined by systemic structures. It attributes the superficial impression of freedom to institutions or anonymous power structures that, behind the backs of the participants in a given social field, see to it that we relate to each other in a certain way. I consider structuralism to be false, as well as the corrections added by the poststructuralism that succeeded it, which today still has many adherents. Neurocentrism is ultimately just a rewriting of structuralism and poststructuralism into a "scientific" key. Yet, if there are anonymous structures that guide us, we ourselves already belong to these structures and guide ourselves. In the chapter on freedom we will see that self-determination is unavoidable, however many there are who would like to believe that some kind of structure sustains us and frees us from the anxiety-inducing thought that we are forced to be free by our own nature as agents.

2

Consciousness

Let us begin our tour through our self-conception with the fundamental concept of consciousness, the notion at the center of the philosophy of consciousness. The advantage and disadvantage of consciousness is that we are all familiar with it as an everyday phenomenon. As soon as we wake up from dreamless sleep, but also while we dream, we are conscious. Nothing could matter to us, nothing would be present to us as thinkers, believers or perceivers, if we were not consciously experiencing something. Consciousness is at the very heart of our self-conception and, despite the familiarity of the phenomena of consciousness, the concept of consciousness immediately poses many difficulties. Soon one must face up to the fact that consciousness is a really strange phenomenon after all.

Just ask yourself the question as to what happens when you become conscious of the fact that you exist as an animal with a human mind on this particular planet? Following a good old idea of the philosopher Friedrich Wilhelm Joseph Schelling (1775–1854), the astonishment of consciousness is today still nicely expressed with the beautiful metaphor that, in the human being, nature opens her eyes, as it were. Against this backdrop, for instance, the American philosopher Thomas Nagel (b. 1937), in his book *Mind and Cosmos*, maintains that present-day science will never be able to address this question appropriately.[1] For Nagel, the idea of a cosmos gradually becoming aware of itself in conscious creatures belonging to it cannot be accounted for in terms of our contemporary materialistic world-view. Let us speak here of **the cosmological riddle of consciousness**. It derives from the impression that consciousness adds something fundamental to nature precisely because, in consciousness, nature somehow begins to become aware of itself via one of its products.

The cosmological riddle of consciousness should not be equated

47

with what Chalmers has called *the hard problem of conscious-ness*, which I have already addressed above (p. 26). Notice that Chalmers's problem was already formulated in particularly clear terms by Gottfried Wilhelm Leibniz (1646–1716). The hard prob-lem consists in the fact that it seems to be a complete mystery how material things (such as neurons or even all the areas of the brain together) can have an inner life at all. Why do we experience the firing of neurons in any specific way? Chalmers considers this problem a hard one because he supposes that we cannot resolve it with the scientific methods developed to this point, which have a quarrel with consciousness – a claim with which many, admittedly, do not concur.

A crucial point on which much hinges in his reflections is the thought experiment of the *philosophical zombie*. A **philosophical zombie** is an exact physical replica of a human being – let us say, of Chalmers himself. Furthermore, this exact replica behaves exactly as he does – with one key difference, namely that it does not have a consciousness, and thus no one is home in this organism, as one might aptly put it. Chalmers considers philosophical zombies in purely logical terms and takes them to be metaphysically possible, though many others do not. In my view, all that matters is that philosophical zombies are not biologically possible, as everything which functions in the way in which Chalmers's brain does and accordingly has the kind of neurochemistry we find within his skull will be conscious. The question as to whether philosophi-cal zombies contain a hidden contradiction cannot be resolved, either scientifically or philosophically, as science deals not with possible worlds but with our natural environment, and philosophi-cal thought experiments about the structure of nature really have cognitive value only if we can cash them out with respect to nature, as we find it. Nature, as we find it, does not contain philosophical zombies.

Usually, both the cosmological riddle and the hard problem are invoked as evidence for the notion that the philosophy of con-sciousness is a particularly pressing field. It seems as if the natural sciences were about to provide us with the solution to almost all problems concerning the universe with the exception of conscious-ness. Consciousness is the last remaining mystery, or so the story goes if we accept that there is a cosmological riddle or a hard problem.

In order to get a sense of what is at stake, let us take a step back and proceed gradually. What is consciousness and how do we know anything about it?

We wake up in the morning and slowly come to consciousness. In the course of doing so, we sometimes recall our dreams, and thus the fact that we were also somehow conscious in our dream state. As we go about our daily business, various things, processes and persons continually come into focus and receive our attention: the coffee machine, the toothbrush, the commute to work, our boss. We feel somewhat tired in the morning, refreshed after a shower, angry when we feel that we are treated unfairly, delighted when someone delivers good news to us. We experience all of this consciously, while we do not consciously experience the growing of our fingernails or hair, for instance. Some processes that concern us are experienced, they are consciously available; other processes constitutively remain in the unconscious background, such as the growing of fingernails and digestion.

Most of what happens to us every day and a good deal of what we do is processed on an unconscious level, even when it comes to activities of which we can easily become conscious. We open the car door without noticing how exactly this is done. We move our fingers – for instance, to type out these lines. We are not conscious for the most part of the vast majority of processes within our organism: the digestion of a glass of water, the circulation of blood flow to the liver, or the firing of countless neurons that enable us to move our fingers, to be angry with someone or to recognize this page in front of our eyes as an expression of intentionally formed thoughts. Only a few of the impressions processed by our organism pass through the *narrowness of consciousness*, as psychologists called this around the turn of the twentieth century. Considered in terms of the whole organism, conscious processes, experiences, are only the tip of an iceberg that protrudes from the deep ocean of purely natural, unconscious processes.

We have thus already come to know a key feature of consciousness: we are familiar with consciousness; the fact that we find ourselves in the state of consciousness is quite well known to us. Philosophers commonly nail this point down by speaking of an *internal perspective* or the *standpoint of the first person* – that is, the standpoint of the self. The **standpoint of the first person** consists in the fact that we are familiar with consciousness precisely and only because each of us is conscious. Consciousness is available from within, and it can certainly only be experienced from within. Knowing that one is conscious is first-hand knowledge, if anything is.

Consciousness thus lies quite close to us, as long as we are conscious. For this reason, it is natural to highlight this by speaking of "my" or "your" consciousness. Let us call this the **possession condition**, which means that consciousness is always someone's consciousness. I have my consciousness, you have your consciousness. I cannot be directly familiar with your consciousness any more than you can be with mine, because I would have to become you, or you would have to become me, for either of us to be directly familiar with each other's consciousness. As the philosopher Michael Patrick Lynch sums up this point in a discussion of the right to privacy in the digital age: "part of what makes your individual mind *your* mind is that you have a degree of privileged access to your mental states."[2]

Consciousness has other features which seem to make it very special among the phenomena we encounter in our life. In a sense, one can only get to know one's consciousness from within, as it were. You have to *be* conscious in order to be acquainted with that fact. The object I know about when I know that I am conscious – i.e., myself as a conscious subject – is at the same time the subject which knows this. One can only become conscious through one's own consciousness – so it seems, at any rate. We can describe this idea as the *privacy of consciousness* – that is, the assumption that each person can attain immediate consciousness only of his or her own consciousness.

Of course, I can be conscious, in a certain sense, of the fact that Martha has a stomach ache, that she is thus consciously experiencing a stomach ache. Even then I still do not experience her stomach ache, regardless of how vividly I imagine it – and regardless of how much I suffer in thinking of Martha's stomach ache. Suffering in imagining someone else's pain is not feeling someone else's pain. The two pains are still numerically different. Hence it stands to reason that consciousness of other consciousness, of other minds, is only *indirectly* accessible to us, while we are *directly* present to ourselves in our own consciousness, so long as it exists.

Considered from the standpoint of the first person, it very quickly seems as if we are stuck in our consciousness, so to speak, each of us in our own one. In this context, the influential American philosopher of consciousness Daniel Dennett speaks of the *Cartesian theater*, by which he means, as the name suggests, that this idea ultimately dates back to Descartes.

Strictly speaking, the implied historical claim is incorrect. In reality René Descartes sets out from the special status of consciousness precisely in order to argue that we cannot be encapsulated in our consciousness. That is the real goal of the reflections in his famous *Meditations on First Philosophy*, in which, proceeding from the mind's capacity for self-knowledge, he concludes that there are objective truths that are independent of and knowable by the human mind. But over the last hundred years it has become typical in the philosophy of consciousness in the English-speaking world to present Descartes as a bogeyman. I leave it open to what extent this strangely reflects a cultural divide or even geopolitical circumstances separating Great Britain from its nearest continent. As a matter of fact, the idea of the Cartesian theater which Dennett rightly attacks is much more widespread in the history of English philosophy, as it is basically the definitive idea of so-called British empiricism – that is, roughly the philosophies of John Locke, David Hume and George Berkeley – but thereby hangs a tale.

What Dennett means by the "Cartesian theater" and what he justly criticizes can be easily understood. Hitherto we approached consciousness by way of the internal perspective. From that vantage point it seems as if there is a stage on which appears everything of which we become conscious: our boss, our anger, our delight, our visual field, the sometimes annoying ambient noise in the background, and so forth. I am the only one directly aware or conscious of that stage, whereas you are aware of your own stage. If one approaches the issue in this way, the question immediately arises as to who is observing what is playing out on the stage. Who is witnessing the spectacle? And the obvious answer to this question is: I am or you are, insofar as you are also an "I" – that is, someone who illuminates his or her own mental inner space attentively and observes what is happening there. It thus seems obvious to look for whoever is controlling consciousness from within. In this way we are led to the much criticized idea of a homunculus – that is, a little person in our mind or head who observes the subjective, mental state.

I see something that you do not see!

The word "homunculus" stems from Latin and means "little man." The **homunculus fallacy** consists in imagining that our consciousness is a purely private stage on which something proceeds that a self observes and that cannot ever be observed by anyone else from an outside perspective. The private stage, the Cartesian theater, is in principle sealed off from anyone but the self forced to observe and control it. The idea of the homunculus is by no means a recent invention. It is rather ancient and extends over

millennia of the mind's self-examination. Recently, neuroscientists
and philosophers have regularly pointed out that in reality there is
no ego or self. What they mean (or at any rate what they should
mean by such a claim) is that there is no homunculus. At the very
least, neuroscience has not been able to identify any brain area as
the neural correlate of consciousness – that is, as the area which
is always active whenever consciousness takes place. There are
various hypotheses which try to explain the problem away by
identifying consciousness with a different kind of structure realized by the brain – that is, not with one specific area. For instance,
the global workspace model propounded by the neuroscientists
Bernard Baars, Stanislas Dehaene and Jean-Pierre Changeux is
roughly the idea that consciousness is more a firing-pattern which
connects different areas of the brain than the activity of one area or
a bunch of areas. In this case, consciousness could not be identified
with any specific subregion of the brain. Yet, the real incoherence
of the homunculus cannot be revealed in this way, as even the
global workspace model is immediately open to a homuncularistic
interpretation. In addition to any such model, the idea has to be
ruled out that, whatever corresponds to consciousness in the brain
or the brain's activity, it cannot have the form of a homunculus, of
an observer of an internal scene. It is important to bear in mind that
the idea of a tiny spectator who is sitting in our head was rejected
in philosophy a long time ago, for instance, in Plato's *Theaetetus*
and Aristotle's *On the Soul*. Dennett is right in calling attention
to the fact that belief in the homunculus is still widespread even
where the Cartesian theater has been officially rejected. He calls
this position "Cartesian materialism." You do not have to believe
in an immaterial soul in order to be entangled in the homunculus
fallacy. The fallacy does not go away whatever neuroscience tells
us about the brain, as any neuroscientific discovery concerning the
neural correlates of the conscious mind will be open to various
interpretations.

In his wonderful polemical book *Dreams of a Spirit-Seer*,
Immanuel Kant argues not merely against the superstitious belief
in spirits of his age but also against a belief that is widespread up
to the present day, namely the belief "that my thinking Ego [*Ich*] is
in a place which differs from the places of other parts of that body
which belongs to me."[3] Kant adds that "no experience" teaches
me "to shut up my ego into a microscopically small place in my
brain."[4] He derisively compares this to the idea that the human
soul is located in an "indescribably small . . . abode" in the brain
and perceives things there

as does the spider in the centre of its web. The nerves of the brain push or shake it, and cause thereby that not this immediate impression, but the one which is made upon quite remote parts of the body, is represented as an object which is present outside of the brain. From this seat it moves the ropes and levers of the whole machinery, causing arbitrary movements at will. Such propositions can be proved only very superficially or not at all, and as the nature of the soul is, indeed, not well enough known, they can be just as weakly combatted.[5]

Kant's spider in the center of its web is the homunculus, and it is easy to see how the idea of such a spider has a materialistic equivalent such as various possible interpretations of the global workspace model and certainly the brute identification of consciousness with the brain. In our era, neuroscience has been accompanied by new avatars of the homunculus and the spider in the web. The homunculus fallacy is correlated with the idea that we can never have direct access to the external world but can only construct mental images that originate in the brain and have little or nothing to do with things "out there" – an idea that Kant likewise already attacks in *Dreams of a Spirit-Seer*. Such an idea assumes that these mental images are seen by someone and are somehow taken to be representations of the external world. Thus one conjures the homunculus, even if perhaps in the scientific-sounding form of a certain area of the brain or even the entire brain. As the German philosopher Geert Keil (b. 1963) remarks in a similar context: "In the neurosciences, a few authors now view the homunculus-hypothesis as a legitimate research program, namely as the search for an area of the brain that carries out operations of central control and integration."[6]

It can be made clear with a simple example that, in the case of the homunculus and the Cartesian theater, we are dealing with an obvious error – even if it is to some extent very well hidden. Let us suppose that I am looking right at a statue of the Buddha. According to the homunculus model, the statue of the Buddha makes its appearance in my Cartesian theater in the form of a consciously processed mental representation directly available to me but not to you. One could connect this to the fact that I see the statue from a certain perspective. It seems distorted to me in terms of perspective, depending on my vantage point, and I know that it must appear differently in your Cartesian theater, since you must stand somewhere else in order to see the statue (I am standing here already). *I see something that you do not see.*

The statue thus appears in my Cartesian theater, and I see it

– that is, my self sees it – there. But now the question immediately arises as to how I actually know that there is a statue of the Buddha which appears onstage in my theater, on the one hand, and in your theater, on the other hand, and yet at the same time also still appears differently to each of us. What do I know about how exactly the statue appears to you? Are you perhaps an expert on such statues and do you thus experience certain details in a completely different way than I do? Do you even experience that thing as a Buddha statue? It seems as if you could not if you did not know anything about Buddha statues.

One can further complicate the issue by placing a dog, a cat or a goldfish in a bowl in front of the statue of the Buddha. Does a statue of the Buddha now appear on the mental stage of these animals? Can a statue of the Buddha appear to something that has no conception of the Buddha or even of statues at all?

One is caught in the many tentacles of the homunculus fallacy if one concludes on the basis of this thought experiment that one could only know that a Buddha statue is standing there by becoming conscious of a mental representation which might or might not be about a Buddha statue or which is of a Buddha statue for me and of something else for the cat. If this implies that the statue appears on my internal stage, then I will not be conscious of the same statue as you are and I will not be conscious of the things a dog, a cat or a goldfish are when put in front of what I perceive as a Buddha statue. Hence, the question: What, if anything, is out there? And what does "out there" mean here? If it refers to reality without anyone present, without anyone looking at it in such a way that she perceives it as being a certain way, is it even any particular way?

If we take dolphins or bats into consideration, things become even weirder. Thomas Nagel wrote one of the most influential philosophical essays of the last fifty years on this topic, entitled "What is it Like to be a Bat?"[7] In this, Nagel invites us to imagine what it would be like to receive sonar signals from our environment and live the life of a bat. But it is simply not possible to shift ourselves into this perspective. This is also true for the underwater perceptions of dolphins, for the sensitivity of snakes to temperature, or for the spectacular capacity of bees to perceive properties of light in the sky which turn the sky for them into a very detailed map by which they can travel incredible distances and still find their way back to their hive. Let us thus place what a few of us human beings consider to be a statue of the Buddha in a pit full of snakes and bats (a scene familiar to us from the *Indiana Jones* films). No statue of the Buddha will appear in the consciousness of snakes and bats. What is it that appears to them? Something evidently does, which we can conclude from their perception-based behavior with respect to the object we experience as a Buddha statue. We do not really know, since we have no access to such an alien consciousness from an internal perspective.

A very nice illustration of the pitfalls of the homunculus idea can be found in *Doctor Who*, one of the most successful TV series of all time, which has been on the air for more than fifty years. In the most recent season 8 (2014), episode 2 bears the title "Into the Dalek." Daleks are murderous cyborgs whose only aim is to annihilate all lifeforms other than Daleks. They consist of a neurobiological structure (a brain) which is embedded in a tank-like war machine. Their most commonly used saying is "Exterminate!" They are pure killers. Originally they were mutant neural networks set into war machines controlled by their neural activity. Daleks are thus something akin to what neurocentrism today considers us human beings to be: brains embedded in non-conscious machines functional only in the struggle for survival between species and fundamentally, if not exclusively, driven by their own egoism.

The Daleks are the main adversaries of the protagonist of the series, the Doctor, whom one could interpret as a philosophically trained critic of ideology. As "Into the Dalek" unfolds, the Doctor is shrunken into a nano-sized version of himself and climbs into a Dalek that had surprisingly began to engage in moral deliberations, which is extremely uncharacteristic for Daleks. This is why the humans wonder what is going on, as they do not trust the fact that an actual ethical conversion has taken hold of a Dalek. The Doctor is transported onto a spaceship by the name of "Aristotle," whose crew captured this remarkable Dalek. Incidentally, it is interesting in this context that Aristotle, with his book *On the Soul*, can be viewed as the originator of the homunculus fallacy.[8] Even though he ultimately overcomes the fallacy, he is one of the first to point it out. Perhaps the name of the spaceship on which the homunculus scene occurs alludes to this.

In any case, the Doctor climbs into the Dalek's skull. We then see that the Dalek brain has an eye in front of which a film is playing that consists partly of memory images and partly of images of the external world that it receives through the outstretched lens of the Dalek's body machine, which each Dalek operates as a kind of eye in addition to its internal eye. A brain is situated in the Dalek with an eye installed that watches a movie theater hidden from the view of others. This immediately raises the question of whether there is an even smaller Dalek in the Dalek's brain, and so forth, which is one of the problems with the homunculus fallacy. One simply needs too many homunculi (infinitely many) to solve this self-created problem. We cannot solve the problem as to how an observer observes the scenes of which we are conscious by introducing an observer who in turn can be observed. In this way, we create the Dalek problem of always having to bring in another smaller Dalek, who watches a Dalek one level up watching a Dalek one level up, and so on *ad infinitum*.

Neuronal thunderstorms and the arena of consciousness

Of course, one can simply insist on the fact that the brain or some region of the brain is in fact a homunculus. Yet, this brute assumption does not explain anything but simply takes a myth at face value. Another option, which is only slightly better, can be introduced with recourse to the issue of the Buddha statue. The problem with the idea that our consciousness is a private stage, exclusively accessible and intimately familiar to each individual, consists in the fact that, on this model, it is hard to see how one could ever make sense of our perceptions of things belonging to the external world. If anything, perception is a form of consciousness. If consciousness always shields us from reality or from things "out there," this would also be true of perception. Yet, this turns us into Daleks; it pushes perception entirely into our head so that it begins to look reasonable that we never know what is really "out there," since all we are acquainted with in perception are glimpses of the consciousness movie played in the brain's internal home theater. But, then, how could we so much as know that things "out there" are even approximately as they appear on our private screen? Indeed, how could we know that there are any things "out there" at all?

The only reason that seems to speak in favor of this explanatory model is that, in a sense, each of us really does see something different when we stand before a Buddha statue, whereas other animals do not even get to see one. In addition, some other animals have entirely different sensory modalities and sensations we cannot even imagine. This almost immediately leads to the position of **neuroconstructivism** – that is, to the view which denies that we directly perceive reality and the things in it and holds instead that we can only ever perceive mental images or representations that the brain has constructed on the basis of sense-impressions of which we never become aware as such. The sensory registration takes place below the threshold of conscious experience but is turned into conscious experience via non-conscious neural channels of information-processing which result in mental images, but not in direct perceptions of the external world.

All of this can be made to sound very scientific. But this should not mislead us. Neuroconstructivism must also suppose that there is something "out there" which is portrayed in my theater of consciousness as a Buddha statue which shows up differently in the mental realm of a snake. Thus, according to neuroconstructivism, there had better be something that appears to be a Buddha statue to me and appears to be X to a snake and to be Y to a bat (X and Y are placeholders here for something that we human beings can never fully picture to ourselves). This raises the perfectly legitimate question: What's "out there" then? The neuroconstructivist replies: "A physical object or an enormous mass of physical objects are out there: some kind of electromagnetic swirl, which we upload through *our* sensory receptors and which other animals simply upload through *their* sensory receptors onto their mental user interface, their consciousness." Here, you can fill in your favorite metaphysical picture of physical reality out there which is supposed to explain how physical states carrying information can affect our nerve endings.

But does such an obvious seeming and scientifically informed response provide much help at this point? No it does not! The entire thought experiment simply amounts to the claim that we can only ever attain consciousness of physical objects (including electrons, photons, electromagnetic fields) because they make an impression on our private mental screen. Indeed, to this point, we have not been provided with any reason for the claim that we can somehow be directly conscious of anything, that we can perceive things "out there" at all. Here, the strategy of the neuroconstructivist is usually to be content with the thought that we cannot perceive electrons, photons, etc., but that we must infer their existence by means of methods, experiments and models. We *infer* that the objects underlying our perception of a Buddha statue as well as the X and Y of bats and snakes are a certain way.

Yet what about our consciousness of the experiments, the measurements, the instruments and our theoretical understanding of electrons? Where does any of this come from? If it is impossible consciously to take note of anything without uploading it onto our purely private mental user interface, then this also holds for everything which we can ever know about things "out there," in the external world. But then we do not even perceive measurement instruments or brains, hands, etc. Thus, we do not get through to things by means of our scientific experiments, as we do not get through to our scientific experiments.

If consciousness is literally nothing but a neurochemical process within our skull, through which a theater in the head is set in motion, which might or might not depict the external world to some degree, how do we even know that there really is an "out there" that our mental images are connected to in any relevant way whatsoever? At this point, we cannot backpedal to the claim that we discovered any of this via scientific experiment, since we would have conducted these in our internal "consciousness movie," too. Yet, an imaginary experiment is not an experiment. Ludwig Wittgenstein (1889–1951) formulated a series of fitting metaphors for this problem in §265 of his *Philosophical Investigations*: "(As if someone were to buy several copies of the morning paper to assure himself that what it said was true.) Looking up a table in the imagination is no more looking up a table than the image of the result of an imagined experiment is the result of an experiment."[9] It would amount to a contradiction to believe on the one hand that we can only ever attain consciousness of anything by projecting it onto our own screen, and on the other hand to proceed as though we know this because we attained consciousness of something that does and cannot appear on our own screen. The neuroconstructivist suffers from a split mind: by trying to withdraw himself into his most private realm of conscious experience he first loses touch with reality, which he smuggles back into the picture by secretly leaving the private home of his consciousness in order to conduct experiments in the real world . . .

Contrary to the overly complicated – and fundamentally misguided – theory construction of the neuroconstructivist, it is most natural to suppose that I see a red cup when I turn my head to the left because there actually is a red cup over there to the left and actually a coat hanger over there to the right. Cups and coat hangers are not just lying around in our consciousness; rather, they are in living rooms or clothing stores. There is also no room for all the things I perceive on an everyday basis in my brain. Where in my brain should I fit my office in which I am working right now? And don't tell me my office is in my mind, as my mind is not the kind of place where you could store all those books, the wood of my floors and the pictures on my wall.

Buddha, the snake and the bat – again

Sometimes, neuroconstructivists invoke the epistemology and view of the mind you find in Immanuel Kant. However, Kant was much more consistent than neuroconstructivism. In particular, Kant saw through the contradiction in which neuroconstructivism is continually entangled. In one of his major works, the *Critique of Pure Reason*, he is concerned with demonstrating, among other things, that the identification of the bearer of our thought processes with any kind of thing (be it an immaterial soul or the brain) is a fallacy that imposes itself on us in the realm of self-consciousness and self-knowledge, a fallacy which he is eager to expose. Kant chose the term "paralogism" (from Greek for fallacy) for this specific fallacy. According to Kant, **paralogism** is the misguided belief that the bearer of the capacity for thought must be a thing that one can find somewhere in the external world: an immaterial soul that is difficult to detect or just a property or activity of the brain, or even a cluster of brain regions actively creating a neural symphony that cannot be precisely localized. A paralogism identifies the thinking subject with an object in the external world.

Kant is especially aware of the fact that we cannot even in principle *scientifically* solve the problem of the Buddha statue, which appears to one human being in a certain way but to other human beings or other animals in a completely different way. If consciousness were really a private user interface upon which constructed mental images appear, science alone would be of no help to us, since it would only describe what appears in the theater of consciousness. It would just pile one layer of appearances onto another one. The kind of objectivity on the basis of which any science proceeds would not be possible at all. If we are all trapped in our experiential bubbles, we cannot even succeed in inferring that there are such things or phenomena as electromagnetic fields by interpreting data we receive from our measuring instruments, as we could never perceive these instruments as they are in themselves.

How does Kant approach the problem of the Buddha statue? He starts with the unproblematic assumption that a Buddha statue appears *to us*. He then can add that an X appears to the snake, a Y to the bat. He could call the Buddha statue, the X and the Y "appearances" and write a list of appearances:

Appearance 1   the Buddha statue (human representation)
Appearance 2   X (snake's representation)
Appearance 3   Y (bat's representation).

Roughly speaking, his term for what is there independently of appearances and which we can only ever hope to access via inferences on the basis of what is immediately available to us is the "thing-in-itself." Kant's absolutely central thesis, without which his entire edifice of thought collapses, and which he very consistently argues for, is that we can neither perceive nor know the thing-in-itself or things-in-themselves. **Kant's main thesis**, that we can perceive and know only appearances but not things-in-themselves, is called **transcendental idealism**. Thus Kant writes:

> No subtle reflection is required to make the following remark, but rather one can assume that the commonest understanding might make it, even if in its own way, through an obscure distinction of the power of judgment that it calls feeling: that all representations that come to us without our choice (like those of sense) give us objects to cognize only as they affect us, so that what they might be in themselves remains unknown to us; hence that as regards this species of representations, even with the most strenuous attention and distinctness that the understanding might add to them, we can attain merely to the cognition of *appearances*, never to *things in themselves*.[10]

One can illustrate Kant's thought here as follows: imagine that your only active sensory modality as your contact with the external world was touch. Indeed, it is already sufficient for the thought experiment to close your eyes and attempt to concentrate only on your sense of touch. Now imagine that someone were to touch you gently on the top of your hand with a certain object (let's say a matchbox). On the basis of your tactile sensation alone, it is very unlikely that you could tell the touch of a matchbox from the touch of any other object with a similar kind of structure. The tactile and the visual registration of a matchbox hang together for you only if you have seen matchboxes or have received information about them from people who had already seen matchboxes. If no one had ever seen matchboxes, no one could come to know that there are matchboxes on the basis of tactile sensory information alone. Whatever theories you would formulate about the thing "out there" – the thing-in-itself – on the basis of your sense of touch – the appearances – your descriptions would still be quite different than what you would give if you could see the thing "out there." Kant extends this line of thought to all of our senses and believes in particular that space and time are forms of our intuition that quite possibly have nothing to do with how things are in themselves. For him, space and time are, as it were, ways in which reality looks for the eye, not ways for reality to be.

Surfing on the wave of neuro-Kantianism

Of course, there is plenty of room for disagreement with Kant's transcendental idealism, and I, for one, do not believe that it is true. What is important here is that Kant would certainly have protested had he known how popular it is in our time to attribute to him the thesis that we only construct our world mentally, and that this is because our nervous system processes certain stimuli internally in the way it does. This is precisely a paralogism, an identification of the functions of thought with objects "out there" (such as brains or brain regions). Kant would have had countless objections to precisely this thesis, although it became fashionable in nineteenth-century physiology to construct neuroconstructivism in the wake of Kant. Thus, for instance, the famous German physiologist and physicist Hermann von Helmholtz (1821–1894) wrote in 1855:

> That the mode of our perceptions is conditioned by the nature of our senses just as much as it is by external things is quite evidently brought to light by the aforementioned facts, and is of the utmost significance for the theory of our cognitive capacity. The very thing that, in recent times, sensory physiology has established through experience, Kant already sought to do earlier for the representations of the human mind in general by explaining the share that the particular innate laws of the mind, the mind's organization, as it were, have in our representations.[11]

The bizarre view that Kant paved the way for neuroconstructivism has been a topos since the nineteenth century and has been extended into present-day textbooks. The Nobel prizewinning neuropsychiatrist Eric Kandel (b. 1929) writes in his standard text *Principles of Neural Science*:

> Thus we *receive* electromagnetic waves of different frequencies, but we *perceive* them as the colors red, blue and green. We receive pressure waves from objects vibrating at different frequencies, but we hear sounds, words, and music. We encounter chemical compounds floating in the air or water, but we experience them as smells and tastes.
>
> Colors, tones, smells and tastes are mental creations constructed by the brain out of sensory experience. They do not exist as such, outside the brain ... Our perceptions are not direct records of the world around us. Rather, they are constructed internally according to constraints imposed by the architecture of the nervous system and its functional abilities. The philosopher Immanuel Kant referred to these inherent brain properties as *a priori* knowledge. In Kant's view

the mind was not the passive receiver of sense impressions envisaged by empiricists. Rather the human mind was built to conform with certain preexisting conditions, such as space, time, and causality. The existence of these ideals was *independent* of any physical stimuli coming from beyond the body.[12]

Kant advocates virtually nothing of what Helmholtz and Kandel freely associate with him. He believes neither that we receive electromagnetic waves which we perceive as colors nor that space and time are pre-existing conditions, as Kandel writes. Kant distinguishes between forms of intuition (space and time) and categories (which include causality) and denies the very claim that we can know how things are in themselves through the application of categories to spatio-temporal sensations. Furthermore, Kant does not consider perceptions to be mental constructions that have anything to do with our nervous system. He argues, rather, that in principle we cannot know who or what is actually thinking inside of us. For this reason, he shies away from the identification of thinking with anything beyond the realm of thinking – again: be it with an immaterial soul or a material brain.

The thesis that the self can be identified with the brain is ruled out by Kant just as much as the thesis that we have an immaterial soul that thinks inside of us. It is reasonable to suppose that Kandel has not read Kant and that, if he has, in any case he did not understand much. From the standpoint of epistemology and the philosophical theory of perception, most of what he writes about the nature of perception and its relation to the perceived environment is confused and false.

Be that as it may, there is a line of interpretation which began shortly after Kant's death and attempts to locate Kant's term "the 'I think'" in the brain, a tradition which includes thinkers such as Schopenhauer but also in due course scientists such as Helmholtz. Kandel accepts in an uncritical way a topos of the erroneous interpretation of Kant's theory of knowledge and carries it to an extreme. He reclaims Kant for himself – whatever the motivation for this appropriation might be. What Kandel describes as a philosophical option – leaving aside the question of what Kant really thought – tends not to be advocated by contemporary epistemologists in this form, since it is connected to a whole series of quite obvious fallacies to which Kant had attempted to find an alternative.

The claim that brains construct distinct user interfaces, so that we tap into the existence of an external world only in a hopelessly mediated and distorting way, but never directly, rests on a fallacy or an error that cannot be remedied by any kind of scientific progress. If this were indeed the case, how could we even know that we only ever have mediated and distorted access to an external reality? Assessing the veridicality – i.e., the correctness or degree of distortion – of our perceptual representation of external reality presupposes an independent grasp of that reality, a grasp simply assumed but unargued for in the view according to which we perceive reality not as it is in itself, but only its shadows, as it were, constructed by and in our brains.

If consciousness boiled down to a relation between a homunculus in the mind and the show on its private stage, the appeal to science would never get us out of the quandary. The sciences could then describe only what plays out on the private stage of the individual scientist. The claim that in reality there is only a swarm of particles dancing where I believe myself to be seeing a Buddha statue, a swarm of particles that in itself has neither the color nor the form of a Buddha in any way, would be only a further representation of what might be there in itself, a random guess in the dark. We could in principle formulate only relatively wild speculative hypotheses about the external world if our entire experience were only ever a mental construct that presents images on a private, internal stage located within our skull.

Nothing is beyond our experience – or is it?

That all of this presents an enormous problem for the scientific image of the world today is relatively easy to recognize in a typical sentiment regularly expressed in this context. This view has severe effects on the common conceptions of the relation between consciousness and the brain. I am thinking here of *empiricism*. **Empiricism** (from the Greek *empeiria* = experience) is the thesis that the only source of our knowledge is experience, which in this context specifically means sense experience. This claim, which is ancient in terms of the history of philosophy, and which recurs repeatedly over millennia, is today defended in a particularly aggressive manner by people such as the popular American physicist Lawrence Krauss (b. 1954). Krauss emphasizes again and again that there is only a single scientific method. This method supposedly consists in the fact that our critical thinking can be guided by experience. He seems to understand "experience" as a combination of sense experience, measurement, and a theoretical edifice constructed from these two elements. In more precise terms,

he believes that experience with reality ensures that one makes reasonable predictions and can then prove these predictions by means
of experiments. We already adapt this method in everyday life, and
for him modern science is a way of perfecting it.[13]

Krauss bases his campaign against the world's religions on this
point, a campaign that he is currently conducting together with
Richard Dawkins. Both understand "religion" as merely irrational superstition that clings to obviously false theses concerning
nature's mode of functioning – a dangerous superstition which
stands in the way of any advance in knowledge. As a philosopher,
I am of course sympathetic to the struggle against superstition. But
one does not fight very effectively against superstition on the basis
of a very poorly established philosophical position which on closer
inspection turns out to be itself a form of superstition.

Dawkins reduces religion to "baseless and arbitrary beliefs
and injunctions, handed down the generations."[14] In addition, he
assumes that all religions are concerned with God, and that this
word is a way "to denote a supernatural creator that is 'appropriate for us to worship.'"[15] Yet from where does Dawkins receive
the supposed insight that each religion is concerned with God and
that "God" means what he thinks it does? How does he justify this
knowledge claim?

What Dawkins overlooks is the fact that the world's religions
(whether they accept a God, like Judaism, Christianity and Islam,
or whether they are polytheistic, like Hinduism, or ultimately
atheistic, as are some versions of Buddhism) emerged in an era
when the modern conception of nature did not yet exist. How is
the author of the Book of Genesis in the Bible supposed to arrive
at the thought that God is a super*natural* creator when he never
had the concept of nature to begin with, which Dawkins anachronistically projects into the past? The anachronistic contrasting of a
scientific and a supernatural explanation of natural occurrences
pervades the historically uninformed neo-atheism that is advanced
by Dawkins.

His simple-minded model of the critique of religion has admittedly
already been around for centuries. However, from a perspective
that is both historically informed and critical of actual textual
sources – a perspective that has long been adopted by academic
theology and religious studies – it is simply an unfounded and
arbitrary belief that religion generally is what Dawkins imagines
it to be. His account of religion does not stand the test of religious
studies, theology, sociology or the philosophy of religion. It is not
scientifically backed up by any discipline based on actual empirical

and conceptual engagement with the phenomena grouped under the heading of "religion." What he says about religion is, thus, unscientific by any respectable standard. Since he takes his critique of religion to be the prototype of the rules for the enlightenment of humanity and its liberation from supposedly childish superstition, his critique of religion fulfills his own definition of religious superstition, even if he does not believe in God but instead replaces the latter with nature. At this point it is important to emphasize that nothing which we know about nature speaks in favor or against a specific metaphysics, be it a metaphysics according to which there is a God or one which denies this. On no minimally sophisticated account of the monotheistic divine can it be located within the realm of nature insofar as it is studied by the natural sciences. That is the point of thinking of the divine as supernatural! It simply does not belong to the natural order. Yet, this is something God or the divine shares with the conceptual setup even Dawkins has to rely on: the concepts, inferential patterns (logical rules) and truths he believes to have grasped and employed are not themselves on the same level of natural phenomena as, say, digestion or gene mutation.

The question of how we conceive of human knowledge acquisition has many far-reaching consequences and does not concern merely philosophical epistemology. Rampant empiricism – i.e., the thesis that all knowledge derives exclusively from the source of experience – means trouble. If all knowledge stemmed from experience, and we could hence never really know anything definitively – since experience could always still correct us – how could we know, for example, that one should not torture children or that political equality should be a goal of democratic politics? If empiricism were correct, how would we be supposed to know that $1 + 2 = 3$, since it is hard to see how this could be easily revised by experience? How could we know on the basis of experience that we know everything only on the basis of experience?

Rampant empiricism breaks down in the face of simple questions. If *all* knowledge really stems from the source of sense experience, what are we to make of the knowledge concerning this supposed fact? Do we know from sense experience that all knowledge stems from sense experience? One would then have to accept that experience can teach us wrongly even in regard to this claim. In principle, one would have to be able to learn through experience that we cannot learn anything through experience . . . How would this work? What kind of empirical discovery would tell us that not everything we know is through empirical discovery?

In order to delve a little bit deeper into the incoherence of rampant empiricism, we might consider another simple line of thought. Krauss and many other scientists in their philosophical moments say that all knowledge is based on experience, or is "evidence-based," as one also calls it. They point this out because they would like to draw our attention to the fact that we can err. We are susceptible to error, which is called **fallibility**. Empiricism's recommendation derives from its modest-sounding commitment to our fallibility and to its attempt to explain why we are susceptible to error, namely because we receive data from the external world that we must interpret and order in a theoretical way. If we ever wish to know anything on this basis we must eventually claim that we have arrived at our goal. We then formulate a knowledge claim. Yet we can also be deceived and corrected by experience. For that reason, one must actually be open to revisions. Empirical, experience- or evidence-based knowledge claims are defeasible; they come with the idea that they could be retracted or corrected.

Yet how could the claim to know that all knowledge stems from sense experience be corrected by sense experience? The simple answer is: it can't! The statement that all knowledge stems from sense experience is for this reason not a scientific hypothesis that can be proven or disproven. This is because, no matter how well a scientific hypothesis is established and embedded in a theory, it must remain conceivable that pieces of evidence can emerge that would reveal the hypothesis to be false. Therefore, rampant empiricism is not itself a scientific hypothesis.

To be sure, there are subtle varieties of empiricism that were articulated in the last century under the heading of "logical empiricism" in particularly impressive form by Rudolf Carnap (1891–1970) and Willard van Orman Quine (1908–2000). Thus, for instance, Carnap claims that there are truths that one cannot grasp through sense experience, while Quine corrects him to the effect that *all* knowledge is always a combination of theoretical elements and experiential data. According to Quine, there is neither pure empirical knowledge nor pure *a priori* knowledge – that is, knowledge not derived from sense experience at all. Yet all of this ultimately makes the situation philosophically subtle and complicated in such a way that Carnap and Quine are in any case not of the opinion that scientific knowledge might be a description of processes in our theater of consciousness.

However, the situation becomes even more uncomfortable for the kind of crude empiricism that Krauss propagates. In public debates, philosophers repeatedly ask him whether there is mathematical knowledge, thus for instance knowledge of the fact that 1 + 2 = 3. Since Krauss is a theoretical physicist who works with mathematical equations in his everyday research, one would hardly expect him to contest the fact that he possesses mathematical knowledge which is incomparably more complex than multiplication tables from elementary school. Krauss's answer to this question is typical. He suspects that he has been lured into a trap but persists in maintaining that he certainly does need sense experience to attain mathematical knowledge: he has to read somewhere that 1 + 2 = 3, for instance, or become informed about mathematical axioms and how mathematical symbols function.

Yet this solution has been arrived at by cheating. If I know through sense experience that there are still two bread rolls in the breadbasket (I see them lying there), this is possible because the bread rolls emit light that hits my photoreceptors. I can attain knowledge of bread rolls from sense experience because bread rolls are the kinds of things that can enter into an appropriate causal relationship with my sensory receptors. But the numbers 1, 2 and 3, as well as mathematical symbols, are not identical with signs that have been written down. When I write the number 1 down three times, thus – 1, 1, 1 – I repeat the exact same number three times, namely the number 1. There are not nine different number ones on this page, but simply nine different cases in which I have written the same number down. If I see two bread rolls lying in the breadbasket, there are actually two different things – the one bread roll and the other bread roll. In contrast, numbers can neither be seen nor measured – they can only be visualized by means of signs, which is not the same thing. The visualization or vocalization of a mathematical truth is not itself a mathematical truth, nor is the fact that at some point in my conscious life I learned a mathematical truth in some way or another. To know that 1 + 2 = 3 is not to know as such that someone taught me this or that I saw something on a piece of paper.

By the way, one can also neither see nor measure the difference and identity of things. In this context, in philosophy one speaks of the *a priori* (Latin *a priori* = in advance, independent of all experience). This means that we can have sophisticated empirical knowledge only because we employ theoretical concepts – such as cause, law of nature, identity, object, thing, consciousness – that are certainly connected to our experience, but which cannot simply be picked up by sense experience. No science is possible without some *a priori* assumptions. No scientifically respectable body of knowledge will be entirely empirical or grounded in sense experience.

Things become still more uncomfortable for the crude empiricism represented here when we return from this somewhat abstract consideration to consciousness. There may indeed be different degrees of consciousness, from complete alertness to the feeling of pain all the way to the dim consciousness of being lost in daydreams. There are also fleeting transitions such as nodding off, in many ways dangerous or simply just annoying (if one sleeps through one's train stop or has to stay awake through a boring lecture, which is part of everyday academic life). Here, the empiricist idea that we know through sense experience that we are conscious bears pathological features, since it inherently includes the possibility of a misinterpretation and could thus at any time reveal the fact that we are not really conscious. If my way of knowing that I am conscious right now is a kind of hypothesis fumbling on the basis of sense experience, there could be a way for me to be wrong about this. But being conscious and wondering whether one might not be conscious borders on a symptom of mental illness. Fortunately it is not the case that at any time in my conscious life I might fear undergoing the experience of not being conscious at all. It seems as if, at the very least, one could not be deceived regarding the question as to whether one is actually conscious. This insight is encapsulated in Descartes' most famous statement: "I think, therefore I am," the cogito. The **Cartesian cogito** amounts to the claim that, as long as we are conscious, we cannot be deceived about the fact that we are conscious, while we can certainly be deceived about what consciousness consists in, which Descartes does not deny.

Krauss sometimes discusses this topic with the previously mentioned philosopher of consciousness Daniel Dennett and even admits that consciousness is a difficult problem. At the same time, however, he believes (as does Dennett) that future neuroscientists will eventually find a solution. But how, one wonders, are we supposed to be informed by sense experience, and thus in an empirical manner, that we are conscious? Could it be revealed that this is false? Could experiments persuade you that you are not conscious right now?

In the nineteenth century, the French neurologist Jules Cotard (1840–1889) discovered an illness that is named after him, the Cotard syndrome, in which afflicted patients profess that they are dead and do not exist. A strict empiricist would have to assume that patients suffering from Cotard syndrome are perhaps right and really are dead. They would then be zombies and *World War Z* could soon break out. Yet of course they are not dead, and even the idea that they might be is odd. Patients who suffer from Cotard syndrome cannot be right, because they obviously still have a living body and are conscious. They suffer from a neurological disorder that requires a treatment to allow them to return once more to a healthy consciousness, which then helps them to realize that they have been conscious and alive all along.

As we can see, it is a ridiculous idea to suppose that it could one day come to light that we have no consciousness at all. Whoever sincerely claims that he is not conscious is examined with good reason so that it can be discovered what illness he is suffering from or whether he is an ingeniously constructed android. Since such androids do not exist at present, all that remains is the presumption that one cannot deny that one is conscious without at the same time being conscious. As I have already emphasized, this does not imply that one learns about the nature or the necessary biochemical preconditions for consciousness through introspection. At any rate, no one, not even Descartes, claimed that this was the case! Even though we are infallible in believing that we are conscious when we are, this does not mean that we are also infallible with respect to what consciousness is. However, the self-intimating aspect of consciousness at least rules out a number of verdicts, such as the ultimately pathological denial of the very existence of consciousness.

Of course, we can have false ideas of what it means to be conscious. In this regard, we are susceptible to error. It is simply a different matter to know *that one is conscious* and to know *what consciousness is*. There are indeed scientific disciplines designed to give us a better grasp of consciousness, including philosophy. In any event, this should never mislead us into believing that no one was ever conscious or that we are just not conscious, since these "findings" would clearly imply that – to put it mildly – something has gone wrong in the process of theory construction.

Faith, love, hope – are they all just illusions?

Our present culture is very fond of the fear that we are in fact not really conscious at all. The fear of losing one's own consciousness while fully conscious is expressed in zombie films and television series such as *The Walking Dead* or in the classic movie *Awakenings* from 1990. The latter is the film adaptation of a book by the same title written by the famous neurologist Oliver Sacks (1933–2015). The book documents a real case that transpired in New York. Sacks succeeded in waking up, as it were, some victims of the epidemic *Encephalitis lethargica* from their nearly complete unconsciousness. Unfortunately, this worked for only a short period of time, which is portrayed as the tragic story it is in the movie (with Robin Williams and Robert de Niro in the starring roles).

Surprisingly, there are philosophers who believe that we are not conscious, because they believe that the term "consciousness," strictly speaking, does not really refer to anything. I am thinking here of the position of so-called *eliminative materialism*, which is advocated with especial verve by the neurophilosophers Patricia Churchland (b. 1943) and Paul Churchland (b. 1942), both of whom taught at the University of California in San Diego until recently. **Eliminative materialism** claims that our mental states are on the whole illusory, because in reality there are only material states and processes in the universe, such as the information-processing states in the brain studied by cognitive science and neurobiology.

In a well-known essay Paul Churchland sets out to eliminate mental states as we believe we know them. Roughly, he proceeds as follows. First he points out that there is such a thing as an *everyday psychology*, which he dubs "folk psychology." We talk of human beings as conscious, say that they have opinions, that they are rational or irrational, unconsciously repress feelings, have good intentions, and so forth. We all have our own unique views of consciousness and continually imagine how other human beings perceive us and feel about us and the things surrounding us. At this stage of the argument Churchland assumes that folk psychology is an empirical theory like any other. This already betrays an empiricist assumption in that he views our account of consciousness as an empirical theory.

On his view, we attribute mental states to ourselves and others because we have a certain theory of such states that we derive from our experience. In contemporary psychology and cognitive science this is called a "theory of mind": the capacity to form assumptions about other minds and thus about the feelings, intentions, hopes and beliefs of others. According to Churchland, we have constructed folk psychology on the empirically shaky ground of somewhat naïve theorizing about the mental states of others. In particular, he maintains that folk psychology has made no progress over the millennia (an unargued assumption which happens to be false).

To sum up, Churchland begins with the twofold assumption that our everyday psychology is a folk psychology, which he regards as

discover anything whatsoever about consciousness without help from the neurosciences, a project that has been given the name of "neurophilosophy."[18] To ponder concepts such as "propositional attitude" and their embeddedness in other concepts such as perception, knowledge, belief, and so forth, and to analyze them firmly with arguments, is thus not supposed to further the state of knowledge, although the philosophy of mind has done this for millennia.

But could we be conscious without having propositional attitudes? Consciousness is obviously a quite complicated affair. In particular, it is not self-evidently certain which phenomena, processes and states we associate with consciousness. But it is certain that we cannot even imagine what it would be like to be conscious without having propositional attitudes. For instance, let us consider an everyday case, such as sitting on a train and listening to music. We look around us, observe other passengers and, while doing so, pay attention to the music, but sometimes we forget about it and our thoughts wander from one topic to another. Such everyday situations have been described in literature by means of the well-known narrative technique of the *stream of consciousness*. This was also very humorously front and center in the brilliant British comedy series *Peep Show*, in which we can hear the protagonists' inner monologue and hence get a voyeuristic look into their inner lives, into their consciousness.

With the help of our imagination, let us thus climb aboard a typical stream of consciousness while on the train. As soon as we begin to describe what we consciously experience in this situation we will ascribe propositional attitudes to ourselves: we pay attention to the music, look around the train and spot an individual who seems interesting. We try not to stare at that person, since there are many reasons to look around at our fellow commuters discreetly, although these reasons can mostly be traced back to the fact that we are not sure which propositional attitudes the interesting person there in the front might have if we were to stare at them for too long. The whole situation would no longer make sense at all; strictly speaking, it could not happen if there were actually no propositional attitudes. Human consciousness, as we are familiar with it from our own experience, would not exist without hopes, convictions, opinions, doubts, intentions, and so forth. Sociologists speak here of communication as a form of **double contingency**, which in simple terms means that human beings always develop their beliefs by comparing them to the beliefs which they ascribe to other human beings, and vice versa.

This quite obvious insight is eagerly denied, however, within neurocentrism's framework of interpretation. That is already remarkable in itself. This poses a decisive question: Why would anyone wish to deny that there really are hopes, convictions, opinions, doubts and intentions? What lies concealed behind the illusion that a great part of our consciousness is an illusion?

Accepting the claim that propositional attitudes, and thus an essential aspect of our consciousness, are an illusory affair, a kind of folklore that is supposed to be eliminated by the amazing, evidence-based future technologies based on futuristic neuroscientific discoveries, is a philosophical thesis. If one probes more closely, one soon realizes that it rests on untenable assumptions. These assumptions are a matter of not one, but a whole series of errors, many of which we still have to identify and, well, eliminate. It is better to eliminate the errors of eliminative materialism than to eliminate consciousness.

Yet these errors have in the meanwhile come to shape the everyday self-images of many human beings in economically advanced industrial societies, since they are considered to be progressive and scientific. We should all like to be progressive and scientific if the alternative is superstition, ignorance and manipulation. But the problem is that the errors of neurocentrism are precisely superstition, ignorance and manipulation, though these facts are to some extent well concealed. The errors become evident only when one takes the time to question the image of the world that stands behind them, all the way to its underlying assumptions. That holds true for any superstition which prevails at a given time. Unreason is always disguised, or else it would not be as effective as it unfortunately is. How is it possible to gloss over the quite obviously absurd claim that we do not have any propositional attitudes?

Various strategies are employed to this end. A common strategy that is not of much philosophical interest simply appeals to scientific facts. This strategy maintains that the accumulation of comprehensive knowledge of the human brain and of the neurobiology of human cognition will eventually lead to a realization of the fact that we do not have any propositional attitudes. Of course, for the most part this is not expressed very clearly or distinctly. Instead, for instance, there is research into what causes human beings to fall in love, to vote, or to act morally, in the most general sense of acting in a minimally altruistic manner. The normal answer to the question of why someone acts altruistically does not appeal to scientific findings, however. For thousands of years the question has been posed as to why human beings have regard for other human beings and live in communities instead of roaming the forests as solitary loners. For a long time now, we have heard myriad answers to questions such as that concerning the origin of morality. Almost the entire history of thinking about these topics, from Plato to Nietzsche and beyond, is ignored in favor of the naïve and much refused assumption that moral behavior is tantamount to altruistic behavior. However, the actual history of philosophy has a lot to teach us in the area of self-knowledge, which has certainly not been made obsolete by modern science. Ignoring history does not make it go away.

An altruist is lodged in every ego

An answer to the question why human beings are not simply merciless egotistical predators – although they can act this way! – is that they have the capacity to recognize that other human beings should be respected. For other human beings lead a conscious life, too. To lead a conscious life means to experience oneself as the subjective center of events, to experience oneself as a self or an "I." To modify slightly a proposal by Daniel Dennett: to be someone, to experience oneself as a self, is to be the rationalizing "center of narrative gravity." What often goes unnoticed is the remarkable feature that at the center of being is our potential of being able to understand that there are other such centers apart from our own. To be a conscious self is immediately to be in contact with the fact that we are not the only centers. Anyone who is really a practical egotist and tries to get rid of the presence of other minds at the core of her very being turns out to suffer from one of the manifold psychological disorders associated with an exaggerated sense of self.

As I am conscious right now of being conscious, I can easily remind myself that at this very moment there is a child in Shanghai for whom nothing is more important than a certain toy, which in contrast would not be of interest to me. It is a characteristic feature of conscious human life to know that others are consciously alive, too, and that different things matter to them just as different things matter to us at different stages on our life's way (and even at different moments in a single day). Without the capacity to recognize that different things can matter to different people or to ourselves over the course of a single day (or even a single hour), we would indeed be no one at all.

Thomas Nagel rightly considers this insight into the inevitable presence of otherness at the rational core of our centers of narrative gravity to be the basis of **ethics**. By *ethics*, I understand the systematic reflection on the foundation of the principles for our action in light of the fact that we are capable of good and evil (of morally recommended and morally prohibited action). In his books *The Possibility of Altruism* and *The View from Nowhere*, Nagel distinguishes two categories: the subjective and the objective. The "subjective" is his name for our thinking that is bound to a conscious standpoint. Insofar as we are conscious, we experience everything from a subjective standpoint. This holds true not only for our perspectival sensorily based perceptions but also for all of our beliefs, insofar as these too are embedded in a personal network of beliefs that we do not survey in one fell swoop. It is for this reason that we can entertain contradictory beliefs, because we do not have an overview of everything that we actually believe and assume.

A simple demonstration: I am absolutely positive that almost any reader of these lines (at least anyone who has read from the beginning up to this sentence) agrees that more than seven people in India have seen a tree more than once in their life. Furthermore, any reader believes that more than eight people in New York City have noticed the Empire State Building. Until this moment, you have probably never explicitly formulated this belief. And for the same reason we can also change our beliefs if we realize that some of our beliefs are actually incompatible with others that we also hold. Our beliefs do not continually flutter around in our conscious interior life; they are not like birds in an aviary, as Plato put it in his dialogue *Theaetetus*. This means that our belief-system is not itself an occurring thought or conscious stream but, rather, something which consists largely of a logical network of presuppositions, inferences we can spontaneously draw in order to travel through the logical space of our beliefs, as well as contradictory assumptions isolated from each other precisely because we did consider all of them together as we formed them. In other words, most of our beliefs are unconscious and non-objectively entertained. To hold a belief is not to be conscious of that belief. Even though we can become conscious of some of our beliefs, we are never in a position to survey them completely. This is why our rationality is subjective to the extent to which it can operate only on a limited data set we consciously process.

In contrast, "the objective" consists in the realization that we are part of a context which to a large extent is completely independent of what we suppose about it. Regardless of how much power we ascribe to our thoughts and our linguistically coded theoretical constructs, we all know that most facts are simply what they are no matter what opinions we have and no matter what perspectives we adopt. Reality and our belief system do not simply match each other. On the contrary, given that there are many belief systems apart from my own, I can know with absolute certainty that my belief system is nothing like an adequate representation of reality as a whole. To know anything about our beliefs is to know that we do not know everything. Hence there is an ideal of objectivity that consists in describing a reality which is abstracted from ourselves – from our interests and our perspectival consciousness. Admittedly, we do not always attain this ideal, and in the interpersonal realm it is perhaps even unattainable in principle, for which reason it is part and parcel of ethics to realize that our contexts for action are never ideally constructed. The ethical dimension for evaluating our actions is formed from this weighing up of subjective and objective perspectives on facts.

Every consciousness must recognize the fact that other consciousnesses exist independently of one's own. Even if one wishes to be a completely ruthless egotist, as Lorne Malvo from the brilliant *Fargo* series does, one must acknowledge these facts, since otherwise one cannot successfully pursue one's own goals. Human beings can only be egotistical if they understand that others are conscious, too. Altruism, a mindset characterized by regard for others, which initially seems to be contrary to egoism, is based on the potential for realizing that others are conscious, too. If I have even one reason for not using someone merely as a means for my egotistical ends, then the reason for this is precisely that the other has conscious experience and unconscious beliefs, too: he or she feels pain, hopes for something, wishes for and avoids things, and believes certain things. People and other animals are not merely tools like screwdrivers. In order to be egotistical in a meaningful, goal-oriented way, we must have taken the standpoints of others into consideration, since otherwise we cannot understand their motives or use them for our purposes. There would be no egoism without this decentering. The potential for altruism is thus based on it. Altruism is made possible by egoism. Whether one likes it or not, others are conscious, too, and pursue goals, and thus already fundamentally deserve ethically relevant consideration. The egotist recognizes this but acts according to her wish to disrespect that very fact by taking it into consideration in her strategic plan to make use of others whatever their intentions. One should not, however, conclude from this that we only act ethically when we are somehow like Mother Teresa and sacrifice our life for others. Egoism is not evil per se, nor is altruism good per se. They are both aspects of ethical action that reciprocally condition each other. If we reproach someone for egoism, we really mean that this person is pursuing a poor balance of egoism and altruism – for instance, by merely pretending to do something for others while their own interests secretly prevail. However, the problem here is one of fraudulent intent rather than egoism. Since each of us only lives once, we have a right and an obligation consciously to lead this life as our life. We are entitled to egoism, but this does not mean that egomania is the right mental profile.

In light of this, it is ethically convenient simply to deny the consciousness of others. However, it does not work. If one denies the consciousness of others (including of other conscious animals), one avoids recognizing the fact that others are living beings able to feel pain who can also suffer from the cruel actions and injustice that human beings perpetrate on each other. When one succeeds in eliminating the standpoint of the subjective and replacing it with a purely objective standpoint, such as the standpoint of a neurobiology of the human mind that is supposedly attainable someday in either the near or the distant future, one is thus freed of the burden of being bothered by the claims of human freedom. The irony in this is that one can regard the fantasy of a completely objective description of reality, in which no subjective experience occurs any longer, as very egotistical. All ethical claims, which rest on the fact that there is conscious life which harbors propositional attitudes, are thus removed from one's image of the world. If we array ourselves against consciousness and instead conceive of ourselves as neurocomputers, it makes it easier for us to ignore the fact that actually we are not neurocomputers. It is a relief to envision one's own freedom in this way and then ultimately delegate it to our neurochemistry. Yet all of this is just a kind of self-blinding. It is an ethical stance which sells itself as purely objective, non-ethical scientific insight.

The Churchlands are only too happy to gloss over this. This takes the form of complaisant affirmations such as that family life and canoeing are important, or that they still like going into nature as though into a museum and how they marvel at the indigenous peoples of Canada, and so forth.[19] Whether one sympathizes with such declarations or not, it remains the case that human society is structured by linguistically coded propositional attitudes. Such attitudes are not annoying vestiges of a pre-technological era, and they will not be changed by any neurobiological discovery. No possible medical or technological advancement of human nature will ever make it the case that we can get rid of "folk psychology," let alone of propositional attitudes. What is more, ethics requires that we do not even desire to overcome the ethical condition of human agency. We ought to be ethical.

The subjective and the objective are interrelated. Without subjective standpoints we would not have any beliefs, or any networks of beliefs, which distinguish us as persons from one another and make our different life projects possible. It is a condition of possibility of our ethical life that we regularly disconnect from ourselves and can visualize how others perceive us – which we constantly do. Even scientific objectivity is attained only by our conscious striving for it, which of course does not imply that it is not really there. To claim that everything is subjective or that everything is objective is equally absurd.

Davidson's dog and Derrida's cat

At this point, at the very latest, some among you will have asked how things stand with other animal species besides the human being. For surely they, too, have consciousness, while up to this point I have been speaking almost exclusively of human beings only. In no way would I want to deny that other animal species have consciousness, too, and from this formulation you can infer without further ado that I evidently consider the human being to be an animal among other animal species. Despite the fact that it is as hard as it gets to find a precise cut-off point in the animal kingdom which would separate conscious from non-conscious life, I assume that lots of animals belonging to different branches of evolution are conscious. Some life forms might turn out be automata, mechanical data machines of self-replication in open systems. Yet this does not apply across the board, and this is all that matters at this point in the argument.

"Human being," or to express it better in this context, *Homo sapiens*, is among other things a name for a specific kind of animal. Carl Linnaeus (1707–1778), who in his *Systema naturae* introduced the species name *Homo sapiens*, cites as the human being's characteristic feature the famous ancient precept "Know thyself!" (*nosce te ipsum*)[20] The capacity for self-knowledge presupposed by this precept is, according to Linnaeus, precisely what makes us "*sapiens*," a living being that is capable of wisdom.

This notion has an important history. In his famous defense speech before the Athenian jury, which Plato composed as *The Apology of Socrates*, Socrates recounts that the Delphic Oracle called him the wisest of human beings.[21] The Oracle calls for universal self-knowledge. Its precept "know thyself" was a great theme of ancient Greek literature and philosophy. Wisdom is based on self-knowledge, for which reason Linnaeus defines the human being as *Homo sapiens*, since the Latin verb *sapere* means "to be knowledgeable." However, Linnaeus' classification applies not to every kind of knowing but, in particular, to the specifically human form of self-knowledge that makes wisdom possible. The possibility of wisdom is anchored in the fact that human beings live their life in accordance with a symbolic representation of what that means. Ever since Socrates and Linnaeus, the human being, as we know it in modernity, has been explicitly defined via its capacity for wisdom. Philosophy is notoriously the activity we engage in when we reflect upon that very capacity, as philosophy is literally the love of wisdom. We distinguish ourselves from other human beings, from inanimate nature and from other animals by ascribing different mental states, the absence of mental states or different kinds of mental states to these entities respectively.

Other animal species live a conscious life as well. We even ascribe propositional attitudes to them. One could not imagine any documentation of animals that would not describe how a lion lurks in ambush or how a herd of gazelles runs away in terror because they have sensed the lion. Of course, our practice of ascribing propositional attitudes in us to the animal realm around us is in part problematic, since we ascribe certain attitudes to animal species that we have come to prefer for historical reasons and deny that other animal species have these attitudes. Most of us consider our domestic animals to be friendlier than poisonous snakes in the Amazon jungle, and almost anyone holds that dolphins are nicer than sharks (which can be dangerous when confronted with orcas, which happen to be much more dangerous to humans than sharks). Yet we also do this in the case of human animals when we ascribe only to our enemies motives such as envy, ruthless egoism or other flaws, for instance, while in contrast we ascribe goodwill and commendable altruism to our friends (or those whom we consider to be friends). Which form or what degree of biological organization must be present for one justifiably to ascribe consciousness to an organism is in fact not yet clear. This remains an important and open question, since there are of course (neuro)biological bases as well as necessary preconditions for consciousness of which we do not yet know enough to be able to say precisely which living beings are really conscious. In fact, to discover this is an important task for neurobiology in the future, as well as to spell out the consequences of future discoveries in this field for ethics and philosophy in general.

In any event, one should never get carried away in denying consciousness to all other animal species, although of course this is quite convenient if one wants to ease one's conscience concerning the slaughterhouses and other torture chambers for animals that are dedicated to medical progress for humans.

However, there is an interesting line of thought that problematizes the ascription of propositional attitudes to the animal realm beyond us. It was pioneered by the American philosopher Donald Davidson (1917–2003), to whom we are indebted for important contributions to the philosophy of mind. Unfortunately, his writings range from being partly cryptic to completely incomprehensible, although fortunately his basic ideas have often been reconstructed, more or less intelligibly, by other authors.

Davidson, at any rate, is (in)famous for the fact that he denies our form of consciousness to other animal species, since he considers our form of consciousness to be linguistically structured through and through. His line of thought runs roughly as follows.[22] Assume that you come home and your dog is already standing at the front door wagging its tail and yelping. Ordinarily, we interpret this as the dog's delight in the fact that we are home. As the comedian Jerry Seinfeld once said, all of this boosts our self-confidence. A dog, according to Seinfeld, is an animal that is always impressed all over again at the fact that we manage to go away and then return home, and yet somehow also see to it that it is fed. The dog has no idea how we do this and continually looks up to us, impressed – an admiration that, in contrast, we encounter in our children only until they understand how to care for themselves. Then the whole enchantment of the supposedly mysterious power of adults goes up in smoke and it is revealed that they, too, are normal people. The greatest episode of this insight is called "puberty," a process that to my knowledge has never been attested to in the case of domestic animals . . .

However, an ethically relevant respect for other animal species does not stem from the fact that they have particularly subtle networks of propositional attitudes. Otherwise, we would never have a reason to respect infants, small children or developmentally disabled adults in ethically relevant ways. Thus, even if some Davidsonian argument successfully established that other animals have no propositional attitudes (which is extremely doubtful), this would not entail that they are mere objects not worthy of ethical attention, as the same argument would apply to our own children too.

Davidson invites us to imagine what is really going on in the dog. When we say that our dog *is delighted that we are coming home*, this is much more problematic than we initially imagine. This becomes clearer when we imagine that both our seventeen-year-old daughter and our dog are at home when we arrive. Let us assume that our daughter is also delighted to see us. She thus knows what it means for someone to come home: one must unlock the door, one must have been somewhere else, in a city or in the country, for example, one must have gotten around in a vehicle or on foot, and so forth. In addition, our daughter understands the process in a certain way: she is delighted that we are coming home, because we promised her something. She knows that we are coming home, because it is the end of the workday, and so forth.

Davidson thus focuses on the "fine-grainedness" of our beliefs. We are not simply delighted when someone comes home, but, rather, our delight belongs to a network of changing attitudes. In contrast, it is to some extent plausible to believe that the dog is always simply delighted – unless it is so ill and feeble that it does not wake up when we arrive. The dog's delight over the fact that we are coming home perhaps never actually has to do with the explicit content of coming home. What we call "coming home" is something that the dog does not know at all, as it is questionable that the dog believes that he is at home and that someone is coming home in anything like the way we believe this.

Davidson concludes from this that, in any case, the dog is by no means delighted by the fact that we are arriving home in the same way that our daughter is. Let us think it through a little more deeply and ask whether a dog can be delighted that grandma is calling on the phone. The answer to this is surely no, since a dog has no idea what a telephone call is. At best, a dog is delighted by the ringing of a telephone, insofar as it resembles the sound of a doorbell. Dogs are not delighted by telephone calls from grandmothers, in the same way that they do not hope that Scarlett Johansson's next film will be good.

These simple reflections on the consciousness of other animal species, incidentally, are by no means superfluous even though they might seem to be self-evident to many readers. Geert Keil points out that the principle of guilt which prevails in our criminal justice system ("No punishment without guilt") does not belong "to the earliest achievements of Western legal history. In rural France it was common into the seventeenth century to apprehend and to punish animals in court because of alleged crimes."[23] The world of human experience is continually in contact with the rest of the animal realm. We hunt, kill and breed animals. We are stung by mosquitoes, observed by seagulls, dwelt in by microorganisms, and so forth. We naturally ascribe propositional attitudes to other kinds of animals with good reason, as we live in the same realm with them all the time (our bodies happen to be complex breeding grounds of many animals we do not notice in our everyday lives unless we are doctors or biologists, say). Our own body is indeed more like a zoo than a closed system controlled by a conscious ego running the show. That much has been established by biology over the last hundred and fifty years. Our body is not just one organism but an entire ecosystem.

Indeed, Davidson rightly points out how easily we fall prey to false ideas of the inner life of other animals because we describe their behavior in a language that is tailored to our form of life. In our association with other animal species, we tend toward **anthropomorphism** – that is, toward the projection of our form of life onto other animal species. Our beliefs are fine-grained and differentiated in a way that reflects millennia of cultural and intellectual history. Thus the human mind, as we know it, has a history. We share some episodes of this history with other animal species, especially with those kinds of animals that we have explicitly integrated as domesticated ones into our form of life.

Yet a much greater divide persists between us and our animal friends than one imagines in our at least somewhat partially animal-friendly moments. The French philosopher Jacques Derrida (1930–2004) makes this clear in reference to a situation he found himself in one morning as he stood naked in front of his cat and met her gaze. At the time, he reacted as though another person had seen him naked, until it became clear to him that the cat did not even recognize that he was naked, in any case not in the sense in which he spontaneously felt exposed in front of her.[24]

Our feeling of shame belongs to our form of life; it is embedded in our human ideas of how we should live together. To be sure, cats and other animals live among us, but they share our form of life only in a very limited way. Of course, the reverse also holds, as we share the cat's form of life only in a very limited way. Our vocabulary, designed to describe mental processes in our fellow human beings, is certainly not able to describe in an adequate and fine-grained enough way what it is like when cats slink through a city park at night and hunt mice. We cannot even imagine this, since for us there would simply be no sense in hunting mice in a city park at night and then carrying them home between our teeth.

Tasty consciousness

Many other living beings definitely have components of consciousness that remain for the most part unintelligible to us, insofar as we simply do not know what it is like or how it feels to undergo certain experiences. That also holds true even for members of one's own species. When I was a child, I always asked myself how it was possible for other people to like different dishes than I did. How could it be that someone did not always consider spaghetti with tomato sauce and a glass of lemonade to be delicious but instead preferred foie gras, for instance, and a glass of champagne?

If something tastes good to one, it is hard to really imagine what it would be like not to enjoy the very same-tasting thing. For that to happen, one must have already had the peculiar experience that one's own taste changes over the course of life and that one can of course also deliberately cultivate it. For the most part, we do not experience taste as a neutral fact that we then further evaluate as to whether we assess it as good or bad. Taste is experienced as good or bad; it is not a neutral fact in the world, as it were. Something always tastes more or less good to us. But how do we know what it is like not to enjoy something that we do enjoy or, conversely, to enjoy something that just appears repulsive to us?

Recent philosophy of consciousness has coined the term *qualia* in this context. **Qualia** (from the Latin *qualis* = qualitatively constituted in some way; singular: *quale*) are the contents of conscious, purely subjective experiences. They are ways in which we experience things. Examples of qualia are impressions of color and sensations of taste or sensitivity to heat, for instance.

We have thus already learned of two facets that are associated with consciousness. We can distinguish them conceptually as follows.

1   The first facet consists in the fact that we can be *conscious of something*. "Intentionality" stems from the Latin verb *intendere*, which means to extend or stretch outward. **Intentional consciousness** consists in our reference to something typically different from consciousness. A prime example of intentional consciousness is conscious perception. When I perceive a tree

in front of me, my consciousness "stretches out" to the tree and is, thereby, of the tree. We are able to focus consciously on something and think about it. We extend our consciousness, as it were, by directing our attention to it. With a different emphasis, this has recently also been characterized by the philosopher Ned Block as *access consciousness* – that is, consciousness that has an attentive access to states of information.

2   The second facet is associated with our internal perspective. In this context, one speaks of **phenomenal consciousness** – that is, of our subjective, conscious experience. The contents of this experience are the already mentioned qualia.

The concept of consciousness, which incidentally has many more additional aspects (and is for that reason probably a whole meshwork of concepts), inclines us to conflate intentional and phenomenal consciousness. For instance, one might suppose that we are able intentionally to focus on our percepts. I can easily focus on my experience of taste while drinking a good red wine, thus I must be able to focus consciously on this experience. One thereby turns the taste of red wine into a private object – that is, an object that only the person who experiences the taste can observe, as if my taste of wine was a secret object, hidden from your view. How do I know whether the wine really tastes to others exactly as it does to me? Certainly, they may tell me that it tastes good to them, too. Perhaps they agree with me when I emphasize the note of vanilla. But if it makes sense that one is not able to have experiences of taste without at the same time also evaluating them, then one can also experience the vanilla note of a red wine differently, even if different people publicly agree that a vanilla note is present. Are my and your vanilla notes even comparable in any way? How could I ever be in a position to know how vanilla or red wine taste to you?

Perhaps you are acquainted with a similar phenomenon, the **problem of the inverted spectrum**. Ned Block succinctly summarizes the problem as follows. Could it not be the case that "the things we both call red look to you the way the things we both call green look to me?"[25]

This line of thought poses a particularly intricate riddle if one pursues it a little further. Experiences of color are no more neutral than those of taste. Colors please or displease us, too. We do not simply just notice them and then evaluate them, but we already experience them with a view toward evaluation. We sense them immediately as cold or warm, agreeable or bothersome.

Furthermore, we also learn to see colors we might not have consciously noticed and can become better at distinguishing them.
If one now adds to the account the fact that our visual field is
colored through and through, it stands to reason that in fact the
entire reality perceived through our sense of sight perhaps appears
completely different to me than it does to you. Even if we agree
that blue dice are lying there in front of us, my experience of blue
is perhaps so fundamentally different from yours that we are not
really speaking about the same blue dice after all. How do we
know we are not basically constantly talking past each other even
in the most mundane situations, say, where we search for the red
pair of keys in the living room?

At this point, everything hinges on what is meant when one
speaks of the vanilla note of a red wine or of the blue of a pair of
dice. Does one aim at an *objective* common property of red wine or
of dice, or at our individual *subjective* sensations? In the first case,
one would have to have an intentional consciousness of these properties. In the second case, one would have to have a phenomenal
consciousness that consists in experiencing qualia. One can pin this
difference down in the following way: intentional consciousness *is
related* to properties of commonly present objects, while qualia are
ways in which we *experience* something. To relate to something
and to experience something is not the same thing. Hence, we now
have a conceptual distinction in our hands, the distinction between
intentional and *phenomenal consciousness*, which can help us to
avoid many confusions widespread in our contemporary scientific
and everyday culture.

The intelligence of the robot vacuum cleaner

All of this now perhaps seems almost so self-evident that you are
asking yourself why it is worth talking about. However, there are
many reasons for our overlooking the difference between intentional and phenomenal consciousness all too easily in important
contexts. Let us take the example of artificial intelligence and thus
the question of whether computers, smartphones and robots can
think intelligently.

The topic of artificial intelligence has occupied the philosophy of
consciousness since early modernity – it did not first become viru-
lent with the emergence of the computer. Descartes already posed
the question of how he could know that people are passing in front
of his window and not merely robots (or, as one said in those days,

automata): ". . . I see the men themselves . . . yet do I see any more than hats and coats which could conceal automata? I *judge* that they are men. And so something which I thought I was seeing with my eyes is in fact grasped solely by the faculty of judgment which is in my mind."[26] What if there were perfectly constructed humanoid robots which we could not distinguish from humans with the naked eye, such as in the movie and HBO series *Westworld*? If one thinks here again of *Doctor Who*, all kinds of scenarios can be imagined in which this could be relevant. Of course, one can also think of *Blade Runner*, zombie films, the Swedish television series *Real Humans* – or one among the countless products of literary fiction that treat this topic. One could also include classical works of literature such as those by E. T. A. Hoffmann and Heinrich von Kleist. Would we not attribute consciousness without further ado to humanoid robots, especially if they could have an intelligent conversation with us? It is even reported that many people over the course of time got the impression that their model of a robot vacuum cleaner such as the iRobot Roomba possesses its own conscious will – indeed, that it has a personality.[27]

Let us now pose the question as to whether we would actually consider humanoid robots to be conscious if they had only intentional consciousness but entirely lacked phenomenal consciousness. Of course, this already presupposes that they could have intentional consciousness, which I will provisionally accept for the following line of thought. In this case, they might well provide all kinds of accurate reports by processing information given to them on the basis of reality-tracking devices such as photosensors. Perhaps through an internal analysis of the chemical composition of the aforementioned red wine such a robot would even be able correctly to express the fact that the wine reveals a note of vanilla. In our era of digital revolution, it is particularly easy to imagine robots with an improved version of intentional consciousness – a consciousness upgrade – for example, being equipped with greater cognitive processing power in certain areas. Standard commercially available computers have for a long time played better chess or Nine Men's Morris than most human beings. Yet would all of this actually justify us in characterizing robots as "conscious"?

I do not believe so. Let us suppose that the left cheek of an otherwise perfectly humanoid robot (a hubot from the series *Real Humans* or a robot from Spielberg's *Artificial Intelligence*) suddenly fell off and it then had a similar appearance to the robot in the first episode of the eighth season of *Doctor Who*. We would be looking at a rusty primitive mechanism in its interior. It would then naturally seem reasonable to suppose that the robot does not have any phenomenal consciousness: it does not have experiences; it does not feel in any way. It is just a robot that is operated by means of a rather crude mechanism. If it now tells us that it sees blue dice, it could still utter a true statement or give an accurate account of there being blue dice. But, since it has no experience of blue at all, something essential would be missing from its perception, namely consciousness. And even if there are cases of unconscious perception (also in humans, such as cases of blindsight), they are not the standard cases for which we designed our mentalistic vocabulary. In any case, a purely intentional machine would not be conscious in the way that we are. But could the robot have phenomenal consciousness despite that? How do we know for sure that it does not?

At this point, it is important to recall that consciousness, as we know it, simply has necessary biological preconditions – which I would not wish to call into question at any point. A rather crude mechanism which does not consist of the relevant organic material that would need to be assumed as a precondition for phenomenal consciousness (lacking neurons and other kinds of cells) could not sustain any phenomenal consciousness for biological reasons. In fact, our phenomenal consciousness emerged over the course of evolution, which does not merely mean – and it is important to bear this in mind – that the human mind is on the whole an evolutionary phenomenon. Neurobiology and cognitive science do not completely cover the investigation of the mind, since they have for their focus only some of the necessary conditions for the presence of consciousness and other mental phenomena (such as the relevant wetware and crude cognitive computational power).

When we speak about colors, tastes or other qualia, we speak about something that one has to experience to be able really to know what one is talking about. It is not enough to be able to give accurate reports about such things. The relevant phenomenal fine-grainedness is simply lacking in any artificially constructed robot, regardless of how sophisticated the robot's vocabulary might be when it analyzes how a red wine tastes. A sommelier machine is just not a sommelier, even if a sommelier machine might sometimes be better at its job than an actual sommelier.[28]

Human consciousness is not a set of general rules that we can translate completely into algorithms or model in some other way. Computers are much better at processing information with the aid of algorithms than we ourselves are. What distinguishes us in this area is that we are not like Mr Spock from *Star Trek* and we do not approach everything logically and unemotionally. In part, we have irrational feelings, which include not only much maligned forms of anxiety but also our capacity to fall in love or enjoy drinking wine. The human being is neither merely an *animal rationale* nor simply an *animal irrationalis* but, rather, a being which creates self-images that can prove to be illusory and celebrates and cultivates them in concert with others, changing them if they turn out to be harmful. For this reason, we even have the right to pursue cultured absurdity, irony and illusions as well, so long as no one is harmed who for their part would like to pursue their own illusions.

A simple example of this is our everyday relation to material goods. We purchase all sorts of things, and we typically have the illusory impression of finding precisely the right thing that we sought, which satisfies our need. As soon as we own a thing or have consumed it, we again desire something else. This quite insatiable desire for material goods has been critically put to the test again and again, from Buddha to Marx and all the way to psychoanalysis and contemporary behavorial economics, with its discovery of the manifold biases underlying our exchange of goods. One must see through desire as a source of illusions. However, we cannot give up these illusions entirely, since we only come to be anyone at all through them. To live is to suffer from illusions; it is not a way of calculating our survival chances by becoming smarter. An utterly uninterested intentional consciousness not worried by illusions simply would not exist in the way that we do. It is no accident that for thousands of years we have been surrounded by beautiful things onto which we project our consciousness, even though we all know that it is an illusion, for instance, that gold has a value in itself that is greater than the value of peanuts.

The term "consciousness" refers to a combination of intentional and phenomenal elements. Phenomenal consciousness in part is grounded in facts discoverable with recourse to the theory of evolution. If one were to think that pure intentionality – that is, the fact that some system regularly gives accurate reports – could count as consciousness independently of phenomenal consciousness, this would be as though one believed that water molecules could also consist only of hydrogen and not, for instance, of the right combination of hydrogen and oxygen. Pure water molecules just are H_2O molecules. H alone is far from being water.

Strange Days – *the noise of consciousness*

It turns out that there is something wrong with the idea of dividing consciousness as we know it into two halves. Or, rather, it is perfectly fine to offer a conceptual analysis of the term "consciousness" in different aspects, but this should not mislead us into thinking that we actually have a hold on what a truncated form of consciousness, such as a purely intentional artificial intelligence, would look like. At the very least, it is highly questionable to assume that the form of representation we ascribe to a vacuum cleaner deserves the title of consciousness of any sort.

Let us now take up a thought experiment that starts from the other side and imagine what it would be like to possess only phenomenal but no intentional consciousness. In Kathryn Bigelow's science-fiction thriller *Strange Days* there is a particularly good illustration of what it would be like to be reduced to one's phenomenal consciousness. The movie transports us to a dystopian future that plays out – as is typical – in Los Angeles, the city of film itself. In the futuristic vision of *Strange Days* there are virtual reality engines with which one can record a human being's phenomenal consciousness and then experience what it is like to be them, like a multimodal, multidimensional movie. A VR device is strapped to one's head, and one then lives through exactly what the person experienced during the recording process.

Now, the arc of suspense revolves around a recording which circulates in LA's underground and on which one can see that the police murdered a black hip-hop star, a fact which could trigger a revolt, for which reason the murderers (who happen to be white police officers) attempt to get hold of the neuromovie. In the course of doing so, they employ a horrible method: the device with which the consciousness films are recorded and played back can also be used to fry a brain, so to speak. Those afflicted in such a manner end up in an irreversable condition, suffering from a completely chaotic flickering of data – their experience is forever like the flickering screen of an old television in the days when broadcasting closed down for the night. It is impossible for their phenomenal consciousness to stretch out to any real pattern external to the flickering they experience, and hence no one can get through to them anymore. In one scene this experience is shown from a first-person perspective, which leaves a quite horrifying impression.

Some forms of psychotic experience, other pathological mental states or the state of intoxication triggered by psychoactive drugs maybe come close to such a jumble of data. But we can also just try to imagine our consciousness being dissolved into a pure, temporal impressionism in which we no longer perceive any objects but experience only flowing colors and other impressions – as if one were standing too close to a late Monet or a pointillist painting.

The great Scottish philosopher David Hume (1711–1776) distinguished between *impressions* and *ideas* in order to classify forms of internal experience. On his understanding, an *impression* was a jumble of data, while an *idea* emerges from a more stable organization of one's jumble of data. Ideas are objectifications out of impressions; they help us discern real patterns (information) in the data with which we are confronted as sensuous creatures.

Impressionist painting ultimately traces back to Hume's distinction. It illustrates ideas on the basis of impressions, for which reason one must move to an appropriate distance from the painting so that the objects it presents emerge from the jumble of color. If, sitting at my writing desk, I quickly turn my head a little to the left and try to avoid too much focus on specific objects, I see blurred red, blue, black, flecks of light, and so forth. But as soon as I fix my gaze on the fleeting impressions I immediately recognize books, a glass of water, pens, and other things. The perfection of the presentation of our impressions is certainly a great theme of modern painting. Hume's helpful distinction corresponds to our distinction of phenomenal consciousness (impressions) and intentional consciousness (ideas).

If our consciousness were only a stream of experience similar to the state of intoxication, a pure jumble of data, we could no longer communicate with each other. We would not be able to distinguish our impressions from what causes them and to which we can intentionally refer. Our waking consciousness is not ordinarily impressionistic in such a way that upon closer inspection everything looks blurred. If things were always like that, we would no longer have impressions of anything. We would merge with our impressions and would no longer be present as consciously acting agents capable of making up our minds, so to speak. If we had just impressions, but no ideas, impressions would not even be classifiable by us – for instance, as an impression of red or one of pain. A pure jumble of data, without any intentional order, cannot be observed or consciously experienced by anyone, since everyone who observes must also classify. One could not register pure data without any order; strictly speaking, such data does not exist at all. It is not the case that our consciousness consists of two layers, one pure data layer of sensory registration and a second one of explicit, reflective recognition or objectification. The level described by cognitive science or vision science, for instance, does not tell us anything about how our consciousness works. It rather gives us a model of how non-conscious processes of information-processing can be accounted for in a scientific theory. Whatever the outcomes of such an investigation, they will always only unearth necessary preconditions for consciousness but never reveal the whole thing. This is a sense in which all natural sciences of the mind are and will forever remain reductionist in outlook, as they have no room for conscious experience. Actual conscious experience is not governed by any idealized laws. This does not mean that we are not able to work out scientific theories of aspects of the mind. However, these aspects of the mind are not "out there" in reality, causally interacting with each other as so many levels of physical organization. This is just a misguided projection of criteria of successful theorizing onto an external, natural world.

Phenomenal and intentional consciousness thus work together in actual consciousness. If one separates them from each other, one is left with a fundamentally unintelligible image of consciousness – as though our consciousness were either a vacuum-cleaning robot or an unfortunate hippie who cannot come down from a LSD trip. The realization that neither describes the normal case lies behind a much cited and rightly celebrated formulation of Kant's, which we can simply call **Kant's insight**: "Thoughts without content are empty, intuitions without concepts are blind."[29] What is potentially misleading in this formulation, however, is that Kant links intentionality to concepts and phenomenal consciousness to intuitions. In turn, this makes it seem all too plausible somehow to privilege reflectively competent users of concepts such as us humans and to presume that other kinds of animals have a lesser form of consciousness or no consciousness at all, as they do not possess an explicit grasp of concepts. As, for instance, the philosopher Tyler Burge has shown in detail in his major book *Origins of Objectivity*, one must guard against this. Of course, other kinds of animals and human infants have concepts too, even if they are not linguistically represented by them and are thus characterized by a different degree of fine-grainedness. In order to be able to have concepts and to classify impressions, one is not required also to be able to classify these concepts linguistically. To be sure, we human beings can do this – on the basis of our language we are quite successful in classifying reality. Yet it does not follow from this that it is only us who are able to classify, while all the other animals, on the contrary, could be reduced to being hungry impression machines, as it were.

According to Kant, our thoughts would have no content if we did not have impressions (what he calls "sensation" [*Empfindung*]). If we had only impressions but no stabilizing concepts, our impressions would be blind intuitions, since we would no longer be able to cognize anything, to discern real patterns of experience. A pure jumble of data does not even consist of green spots in one's field of vision; it consists only of pure ineffable experiences. As soon as one sees green spots, one already has intentional consciousness of something, namely of green spots.

Kant also describes the state of pure, jumbled data that is psychotically blurred in similar terms to what we witnessed in *Strange Days*. As in the movie, such consciousness would be "less than a dream."[30] For even in dreams we still dream of something. In our dreams, the sequence of representations is indeed occasionally quite odd, as is well known; one jumps from one sequence to another and has quite indefinite sensations. Also, our sensory modalities are reduced in dreams, as we usually do not have the impression of tasting or feeling anything (think of the dream of an orgasm, which is not typically accompanied by the real deal). However, one does not dream merely in tastes, tones and colors. Dreams are not pure symphonies of sensation but forms of conscious experience.

Let us call the thesis that consciousness is exclusively intentional **consciousness rationalism**. The corresponding other extreme which reduces consciousness to its phenomenal aspect is **consciousness empiricism**. Both mistakes repeatedly arise up to the present day in the sciences that are concerned with consciousness. They form the basis for different varieties of neurocentrism.

While the one takes us ultimately to be purely rational quasi-computers (biologically implemented artificial intelligence, as it were), the other views us as experience and desire machines. This is the postmodern version of the ancient Christian doctrine that the human being wavers between God and animal. The mistake of the ancient as well as the postmodern doctrine consists in the fact that these two extremes – the purely rational God and the purely emotional desiring animal – simply do not exist and at any rate have nothing to do with the reality of human consciousness as we know it, even though they are characteristic of the human mind's fantasies about itself.

A representative example of consciousness rationalism is an approach advocated by Daniel Dennett. In his highly regarded book *The Intentional Stance*, he spells out his (in)famous **thesis of the intentional stance**: this thesis amounts to the claim that every system which we can successfully describe as intentional

is intentional. For him, then, intentionality is in the eye of the
beholder, but not out there. Of course, it is not merely arbitrary to
describe a system in intentional jargon. Yet, the reality underlying
the phenomena itself for Dennett constitutively differs from the
illusory potential of the intentional stance. Let us again consider
Davidson's dog. We can predict that the dog will bark and wag
its tail when it hears Davidson coming home. We can accordingly
express ourselves as follows: the dog is delighted because it knows
that Davison is coming home. We thus ascribe propositional attitudes to it. But we could also carry out a scientific investigation
and merely describe how the sound waves affect the dog's sensory receptors, which trigger further processes. In this descriptive
account, which Dennett calls the *physical stance*, we do not employ
any intentional vocabulary. For Dennett, the physical account is
ultimately better off when it comes to the description of reality as
it is in itself, whereas the intentional stance is pragmatically useful
and probably forever indispensable, as it helps us to navigate
the otherwise overly complex social world of human intentional
behavior.

Dennett argues that everything which we can successfully
describe as intentional is in fact intentional. Accordingly, even
computer programs can be intentional, since we can say that our
computer beat us in chess or that our smartphone is "smart"
and thus intelligent, because it keeps certain things in mind for
us and is much better at solving certain problems than we are.
Dennett thereby supports a crass version of consciousness rationalism, and thus it is also no wonder that he attempts to deny that
there are qualia. This leads him to **qualia eliminativism**, the thesis
that in reality there are no qualia, which results in the following conception of consciousness: "Conscious human minds are
more-or-less serial virtual machines implemented – inefficiently
– on the parallel hardware that evolution has provided for us."[31]
For Dennett, whether or not we are robots is not really relevant.
Physically we are indeed like a vacuum-cleaning robot, because we
then detach ourselves from the fact that we have intentional and
phenomenal consciousness and take only physically describable
processes into account. For Dennett, we are agents who reciprocally describe each other in the intentional stance, virtual programs
who exist only because and for as long as we reciprocally describe
each other in the intentional stance. Consciousness is then a kind
of useful fiction, since the ascription of consciousness helps us
to predict behavior correctly to some extent. This fiction would
vanish if we had sufficient physical or neuroscientific knowledge at

our disposal at all times, so that we no longer had to envision other human beings as intentional systems.

The absurdity of this position is exposed if we realize that it amounts to the claim that no one would ever have been conscious had no one described or experienced themselves as conscious, and the real question is how it is possible for Dennett to arrive at this idea. Obviously, this model is oriented by science fiction rather than by consciousness. Many positions in contemporary philosophy of consciousness generally suffer from scientism. **Scientism** is the claim that only knowledge which is arrived at by natural scientific research and accepted by a group of scientific experts counts as genuine knowledge. Since we have only a relatively small degree of scientific knowledge concerning the neurobiological foundations of consciousness, scientistic philosophers and scientists alike tend to compensate for their ignorance by considering science fiction to be an anticipation of future scientific knowledge. We know comparatively little about the neurobiology of consciousness, because research on the brain is still a relatively new science whose subject matter is almost infinitely complex by human standards. What complicates matters is that we currently have no idea as to whether there is extraterrestrial conscious life and, if there is, what kind of neurobiological foundations such beings might have. In addition, the brain is not just a network of neurons, as there are other cells there as well as chemical processes which do not function in a digital manner according to a binary code. Here every comparison to less complex systems we fully understand fails us entirely, so that it is precisely these areas that are a welcome hunting ground for science-fiction philosophy.

We know much more about the human mind and human consciousness than about their biological foundations. This sometimes bothers natural scientists and their philosophical PR spokespeople, because they might have to admit that the ancient Greek tragedians, Augustine, Hildegard von Bingen, the Buddha, Solomon, Lao-tzu, Sappho or Shakespeare already knew more about consciousness and the mind than most of our contemporaries (which happens to be true . . .).

But then one can no longer speak in a contemptuous tone of folk psychology and treat it at best as a useful virtual machine – that is, as a somewhat useful fiction. The self-knowledge of the human mind has long been much further advanced than the best scientific study of the neurobiological foundations of consciousness. To the extent to which scientists suffering from scientism intend to make a claim on advancement of knowledge in all areas, this fact has long been a thorn in their sides. Hence, the mind's actually progressive history of self-understanding since the dawn of language and writing is either simply suppressed or reinterpreted, in short, as a continuation of biological evolution by other means, as is propagated by Richard Dawkins and repeated by Dennett. However, what a genetic mutation or an environmental adaptation in the realm of nature, which includes us too, is supposed to have to do with Shakespeare or differential calculus is not immediately apparent.

What Mary still doesn't know

Once again, the underlying problem can be illustrated with the help of an easily understandable and much discussed thought experiment that goes back to the Australian philosopher Frank Cameron Jackson (b. 1943).[32] Jackson imagines a scientist by the name of Mary. She lives in the future and knows everything that can be known about nature with the methods of the ensemble of the best natural sciences. Maybe in Mary's future the attempt to reduce all other natural sciences to physics will be successful. The theory that expects something like this to occur is called **physicalism**, which claims that all knowledge of nature is physical knowledge.

One way of supporting physicalism is to rely on the assumption that everything that exists in nature consists of elementary particles whose behavior is accounted for by natural laws. This can be characterized as **microfundamentalism**. Since, according to this thesis, neurons or DNA consist of elementary particles as well, one might believe that in the future all biological (and thus also neurobiological) facts could be expressed in the language of physics. Of course, at the moment physicalism is at best a wildly speculative hypothesis. In any case, upon closer examination, physicalism is a quite unscientific presumption, and it boggles the mind as to how this presumption could be scientifically proven. It is certainly not a consequence of physics as we know it and, for instance, it is incompatible with many interpretations of quantum mechanics. In any event, we have nothing even close to scientific evidence for microfundamentalism. Rather, the very existence of different levels of complexity in various physical and biological systems (just to mention those broad categories) clearly speaks against it on the level of an adequate description of the universe itself.

Be that as it may, the idea we pursue is that Mary knows everything that there is to know about nature, and she expresses this exclusively in the language of physics (in mathematical equations). However, Mary is not entirely perfect because she suffers from total color blindness. She sees only shades of gray – that is, degrees of lightness and darkness. She lives in a world that is completely black and white. Incidentally, a case in which this happened to a painter, of all people, has been documented and studied.[33] Other cases have been documented as well. Mary has thus never seen colors. But she knows that people speak of experiences involving colors and use words such as "green" and "red." She obviously knows, in addition, that these people call something "green" when their sensory receptors process information after being activated by electromagnetic waves in the range of 497 to 530 nm.

At this point, Jackson offers a litmus test for physicalism: Does Mary know everything or is her knowledge lacking in some way? His answer is that in fact Mary does not know everything. To be sure, she has every conceivable bit of physical information at her disposal, but nevertheless there are some things she does not know – for instance, what the green of the Colombian jungle looks like. She does indeed know that the Colombian jungle is overwhelmingly green (which she can figure out from measurements). But in knowing this she knows nothing about my experience of green during my first landing in Colombia, except that my rods and cones were activated while I had intact visual brain areas. If she were to have an operation that subsequently enabled her to see colors (which, given her omniscience regarding physics, should pose no problem to her!), she would come to know something about nature that she did not know before, to wit, what the green of the Colombian jungle looks like. Jackson concludes from this that physicalism is false. This is called the **knowledge argument**, since it is supposed to prove that not everything about nature can be *known* in terms of physics, from which it follows that physicalism is wrong.

Many objections have been raised against this. In particular, the physicalist could indeed say that what is at stake is real knowledge about nature, which for different reasons just would not include knowledge about color experience based on having it. Yet, regardless of the question as to whether it effectively refutes physicalism, Jackson's knowledge argument has revealed an essential aspect of phenomenal consciousness. Let us stick here to the example of colors, whose nature is still widely debated in contemporary philosophy. One can even claim that modernity is a quarrel over colors, because since early modern physics the tendency has been to think that the universe is colorless, that colors are only a kind of

illusory symphony in our organism that is played on the keyboard
of our nerve fibers by electromagnetic waves.

In any case, we know that whenever we have an experience of
color a physical event has occurred: photons must have hit our
sensory receptors (whatever this might mean). In the case of *visible* light, of course, a spectrum of electromagnetic radiation is
experienced by us as being a certain way. Infrared and ultraviolet
radiation are perceived by us not as colors but as heat (if, for
instance, one is sweating in an infrared sauna), so that the entire
spectrum of physical light is not visible.

But how do we know that visible light is a spectrum of electromagnetic radiation? And why do we distinguish this spectrum
from other spectra? To put it quite simply: because we have experiences of color. Had we never perceived color, the thought would
never have entered our heads that certain parts of nature can be
described in such a way that visible light is a natural phenomenon.
Our access to the physical realm is always inexorably mediated by
our grasp of objects available to us in a phenomenal format.

Let us call this line of thought, in distinction to the knowledge
argument, **the indispensability thesis**. This thesis claims that our
subjective standpoint remains unaffected however the very best
science progresses in the future. Our subjective standpoint is
simply a condition for our access to the ideal of absolute objectivity. This certainly does not mean that we cannot achieve absolute
objectivity in the sense of a grasp of how things are and would
have been had we never been around to notice. It just means that
our ways of coming to know these kinds of things presupposes
that our thoughts be anchored in our conscious experience. We
have to sense colors and tastes in order to be able to arrive at the
thought that they represent excerpts from a physical reality, which
has in itself different structures than those which characterize the
experiential sphere of colors and tastes. Our theories are always
irreducibly established on the basis of data that we subjectively
experience as phenomena. In any case, one always has first to
master the instruments to gather data on what is not directly
accessible to our senses. To this end, one must use the senses as
well as the vocabulary that we employ to orient ourselves in the
"lifeworld," as Edmund Husserl (1859–1938) called the shared
experienced world in his famous late piece from 1936 *The Crisis
of European Sciences and Transcendental Phenomenology*. We
cannot escape from the lifeworld – but why would this even be
desirable in the first place? The fact that our thought about the
human mind relies inexorably on the continued existence of sub-

jective standpoints fortunately does not make it impossible for us to grasp how things are in mind-independent reality. On the contrary, the fact that we are capable of working out theories of natural necessary conditions for certain events to take place is as much a fact about human consciousness as is its subjectivity. Subjectivity does not stand between us and the world.

The discovery of the universe in a monastery

Our classification of nature into visible and invisible processes depends on the fact that we have experientially grounded knowledge, without which we would not classify nature in this way at all. Physical classifications for this reason are a long way from being independent of the human subject, as is often pretended, and are only in part objective. The language of physics trivially reflects our knowledge interests, as there are many physical facts no one cares about. Let me just repeat that this does not mean that physics is not objective or that we do not know anything about physical reality as it is in itself.

It should be pointed out, though, that the contemporary physicalist image of the world is firmly built upon the well-established hypothesis that, within our cosmic horizon, and thus within nature as observable to us, nothing in space-time moves faster than light. As one of Einstein's famous discoveries shows, in this respect the speed of light is the absolute limit for all movement. Nothing within space-time is diffused faster than those electromagnetic waves which we call "light." This has been tested, and many revolutionary discoveries of modern physics follow from this hypothesis.

So far, so good. Yet one might wonder why living beings whose survival depends to a large extent on a sense of sight that functions halfway decently have developed a physics in which everything hinges on space-time and the diffusion of light. Our physics takes its starting point from our position on our planet and attempts from that vantage point to reveal the universe on both a large and a small scale. Crucial advances were made by instruments such as the microscope and the telescope: the microscope led to evidence that matter is composed of smaller units, and thus to the discovery of a micro-world, about which ancient philosophers had already speculated. In more recent times, the telescope led to the Big Bang theory. Edwin Hubble (1889–1953), after whom the Hubble telescope is named, first discovered in the 1920s that there were additional galaxies besides the Milky Way. He is considered as one of the discoverers of the expanding universe as well.

Incidentally, the fact that the Big Bang theory, as well as the theory of the expanding universe – aside from an anticipation in Immanuel Kant's work on the universe (in his *Universal Natural History and Theory of Heaven* of 1755) – can be traced back to the Belgian priest and theologian Georges Lemaître (1894–1966), who had already formulated both theories some years before Hubble, is quite conveniently ignored by many popular physicalists. Remarkably, Einstein initially rejected Lemaître's Big Bang theory because it struck him as too strongly influenced by the Christian doctrine of creation, while the Catholic Church accepted Lemaître into the Pontifical Academy of Sciences for his discoveries. In one word, the Catholic Church accepted the Big Bang theory before the scientific community did.

This does not fit in so well with the historical misrepresentation attempted by some ideologues of science today, according to which modern science, above all physics, is supposed to have taken up the battle with religious superstition. Time and again one reads that Galileo or even Giordano Bruno – who in the sixteenth century already taught that the universe is infinitely large – were persecuted by the Church and concludes from this that theology and the Church stood in the way of progress as they stuck to their superstitions. But one then fails to note the fact that Isaac Newton considered the universe to be a sensorium of God (whatever exactly that might mean), that Bruno was and remained a Dominican who did not believe that his insight into the infinity of the universe would lead to atheism, and that Newton happened to be a creationist who calculated the age of the universe on the basis of the Bible. Newton was neither a physicalist nor any other kind of materialist. One fails to note the fact that the Big Bang theory was discovered by a monk, that Kant was deeply religious, and so forth. Error and superstition, accordingly, do not necessarily result from the fact that someone is religious, and these are by no means found only among religious people. Religion and science are not distinguished as easily from one another as are superstition and reason.

If one would like to view this historical misrepresentation in its pure form, one should watch the first episode of the remake of the popular documentary series *Cosmos*. The original version by Carl Sagan (1934–1996), which ran in the 1980s, made a large contribution in the United States to the dissemination of the scientific image of the world. The remake, whose first season ran in 2014 as *Cosmos: A Spacetime Odyssey*, was hosted by Neil deGrasse Tyson (b. 1958). In the first episode, every conceivable error concerning Giordano Bruno, the Catholic Church and medieval "Italy" is on display, illustrated with the help of the Hollywood machinery of Seth MacFarlane (the creator of *Family Guy*). The remake is basically pure propaganda shot through with scientific fact (as most propaganda is!), and one might ask who is really supposed to profit from such historical nonsense. Bruno is presented as a stereotypical hero of science, who travels through medieval Europe and is persecuted by the powers of darkness. This image of the Middle Ages, which is prominent in the United States (think of *Game of Thrones*), and by which the United States continues to distinguish itself from Europe (or its fantasies of Europe), is about as accurate as Terry Gilliam's *Monty Python and the Holy Grail* (1975) or *Jabberwocky* (1977).

Let us return to consciousness. The crucial realization is that our knowledge of our own experience, thus our subjective knowledge, cannot be eliminated, improved or ignored by employing the language of physics. Like any other language, one understands this language only to the extent to which the technical vocabulary in which it is conveyed is understood. And this vocabulary includes words such as "color" or "time." Our understanding of the meaning of these words is naturally enriched by our discovery of which processes in the universe are connected to experiences of color or to our awareness of time. Yet it by no means follows from this that we could disregard our experiences of color or our awareness of time. Physical time and the time we experience are simply not the same, even though they are related to each other. However, the relation between physical and experiential time is not itself an object of scientific investigation. Even if psychology can reveal something about the experience of time, there is still a gap between Proust and empirical psychology which in principle cannot be closed.

That time passes is not something that can be physically understood. It has been a mystery of physics up to the present day just how there can be an "arrow of time" directed from the past into the future. In popular accounts, one sometimes reads that this is supposed to be explained by **entropy** – in simple terms, by the law that disorder always increases in physical systems. An ice cube has a specific order. If one puts it into lukewarm water, which is disordered relative to the ice cube's order, in time it takes on the disorder of its surroundings and melts. Sometimes physicists even let themselves get carried away and explain the always increasing disorder of a nursery as a case of entropy. My explanation of an untidy nursery is better, however: nurseries typically go from order to disorder because children do not respect our need for order. Children throw toys around, which is not a problem of physics – and thus not a case of entropy – but at most an issue for pedagogy, psychology or sociology.

Be that as it may, if one wishes to explain the orientation of time (the arrow of time) by means of entropy, one fails on a conceptual level, as one hides the notion of time passing in the notion of entropy. If entropy means that disorder is followed by order, then this presupposes that time passes and does not explain it. Recourse to entropy is only a pseudo-explanation which obscures the fact that one does not understand our awareness of time. On the other hand, it is of course not a good idea to say that everything is literally happening at the same time or that we will never understand how an irreversible timeline oriented from the past to the future could possibly exist. Even if the physical discoveries concerning time – in particular, relativity theory – are indeed spectacular breakthroughs with major impact on our understanding of our awareness of time, they cannot replace that very awareness or fundamentally explain it. How physical time and our awareness of time are connected is still a mystery that must be addressed by the philosophy of time.

Sensations are not the subtitles to a Chinese movie

Let us go back to Jackson's knowledge argument. In my view, Jackson misjudges the scope of his thought experiment. He believes that he has refuted physicalism, but at the same time he sacrifices his hard-won insight on the altar of scientism, which is the real problem. In particular, Jackson additionally believes that qualia do not have any causal power in the universe. That now sounds somewhat overblown and once more obscures how erroneous it is. Hence we must proceed a bit further into his argumentative presuppositions.

Epiphenomenalism generally speaking is the thesis that mental states and processes as a whole have no causal effects on processes in the universe. Epiphenomenalists consider mental states to be pure concomitant features. Epiphenomenalism thus admittedly accepts that there are mental states and processes (at least). But it denies that they causally impact natural occurrences (a shame, since this spoils everything). The American philosopher John Searle (b. 1932), who manifestly rejects epiphenomenalism, brought things to a head with the following ironical description: "The brain is just a total mechanical hunk of junk, like a car engine only wetter, and ... it functions by absolutely straightforward mechanical connections."[34] Just picture in some detail what this way of thinking amounts to. If you are thirsty in the middle of the summer and your tongue is almost stuck to the roof of your mouth, you will try everything in your power to get your hands on a cold drink. You are conscious of an already unbearable thirst; your tongue and your throat feel dry. Now you make your way to the nearest kiosk. While doing so, you imagine how something like a bottle of Coke, a can of iced tea, or just a glass of cold water will be emptied in a few gulps. You stand before the refrigerated shelf and reach, anything but timidly, for a bottle of orange juice, say, which you had not even thought of before, but which evokes memories of a beautiful summer evening last year. One could even narrate this short story, which is not very demanding in literary terms, as an inner monologue, in which you as the first-person narrator chronologically describe your mental representations. One agony thus follows the next: thirst, joyful anticipation, the odd feeling that the individual mental representations of the beverage evoke in you, and finally the cold drink that runs down your throat.

Epiphenomenalism claims that none of this has anything to do with what actually happens in reality. In reality, what takes place is that your organism is deployed into internal states of information, which ultimately traces back to the fact that certain patterns of neurons are firing. This firing of neurons triggers all of the impressions that manifest as qualia to you while in the mode of consciousness. Yet regardless of how it feels, your organism moves to the kiosk, guided only by the laws of nature. Photons are deflected by the kiosk (otherwise it would be invisible) that are again picked up by your organism and, mediated by processes that appear to be unbelievably complicated, lead to the fact that you are drawn to the kiosk.

The actual causal story could never really be told in full detail, since it contains a virtual infinity of information: all of the elementary particles of which you, the kiosk and your surroundings consist, and because of which your organism moves. Basically, on this line of thinking, the whole universe can be traced back to the fact that a chain of events takes place, which is supposed to lead in a strict causal sense (and thus, above all, without alternative and of necessity) from one cause to an effect that is in turn another cause of another effect, and so on. Thus qualia come about as mere side-effects which do not contribute anything to what really happens.

Qualia are not supposed to be causes that lead to effects in their train; rather, they are only an incidental rush of sensations. Just as the English subtitles to a Chinese movie do not contribute anything to the movie's plot (indeed, they do not belong to the world of the movie but are just there for us because we do not understand Chinese well enough), so qualia simply run alongside what really happens.

Infected by a common case of Darwinitis, Jackson wonders how the existence of epiphenomenal qualia can be made compatible with the theory of evolution. If qualia do not contribute anything to the survival of the organism, why are they around? Why is there consciousness at all, if things could have taken place without it? Were microbes or bacteria not enough? Would it not be enough for survival, much better or at least as good, if we human beings had no feelings of pain, or if the organism dealt with everything unconsciously – not merely digestion or the growth of fingernails, but simply everything? At this point, Jackson surmises that qualia "are a byproduct of certain brain processes that are highly conducive to survival."[35]

His other example for such evolutionary byproducts speaks volumes. Polar bears are weighed down by an extremely heavy coat. One could ask what evolutionary advantage is entailed by such a heavy coat, as it apparently makes survival harder (carry that around!). It quickly becomes apparent that a heavy coat is hardly an advantage, since their weight slows one down (although polar bears actually are alarmingly fast, up to 30 km/h!). In any case, one must somehow compensate for such a heavy coat (with strong muscles, for instance). However, according to Jackson, the fact that the polar bear's coat is heavy is simply a byproduct of the fact that the coat keeps the animal warm. This is the case for many qualities that emerged in the course of evolution. One must choose the right aspects in the description of a phenotype if one is to carry out a successful zoological study. What Jackson thus claims is that qualia should not play any real role in a zoological study. They are more akin to the heaviness of the coat than to the fact that such a coat keeps the creature warm.

Epiphenomenalism here is in line with the tradition of early modern thought. Descartes above all is (in)famous for his thesis that animals are fundamentally automatons, and Julien Offray de La Mettrie (1709–1751) developed a corresponding image of the human being in his book *Man a Machine*. Jackson slyly suggests that a large part of our behavior is not guided at all by the fact that we have qualitative experiences, a few of which we avoid (usually, pain, at least aside from S&M play and self-destructive behavior) and others at which we aim (usually, the satisfaction of desires and inclinations of all kinds). However, these qualia must never be seen to interfere with the mechanism of what happens, otherwise one would no longer be an epiphenomenalist.

Behind this whole debate over epiphenomenalism lies the belief that the universe is causally closed and does not actually contain any qualia. In the background is the idea that everything which happens in nature is determined by the laws of nature. Each event in space-time follows upon another event in space-time according to the laws of nature, to which there are no exceptions. This thesis is known as **determinism** and is examined in detail in the chapter on freedom that concludes this book.

At this point, I expect that some readers would like to object to such an image of causation and the laws of nature being modified, if not superseded, by quantum physics (or more sophisticated philosophical theories of causation, for that matter). Yet whatever kind of causality holds at the quantum level is irrelevant to our investigation to the extent to which it remains unclear how consciousness and the quantum level are related. To be sure, there is speculation over the fact that processes occur in so-called microtubules (certain protein structures that are found in cells) that can be described in terms of quantum mechanics, through which consciousness might be generated. For instance, a version of this has been proposed by the famous British mathematician Sir Roger Penrose (b. 1931). But, strictly speaking, the retreat to genuine or putative chance and indeterminacy in physically describable nature does not contribute anything to the understanding of the mind. There is no such thing as a quantum theory of consciousness, as the kind of object actually characterized by quantum theory is precisely not conscious mental activity or intentional thought but, rather, anonymous processes subject to laws of nature which differ from classical mechanical laws – that's all.

The idea that we are situated in an enormous container, in which lumps of matter that are invisible to the naked eye move to and fro according to inviolable natural laws that can be mathematically formulated, is indeed for many reasons a kind of fairy tale. Let us give this idea a name, too: **the fairy tale of the container**. This fairy tale draws on a world-view that rests on numerous unsupported claims. Again, at best it is a philosophical interpretation of physics, but never an actual result of physics per se.

Contemporary theoretical physics invites all manner of speculation. In particular, with regard to the various hypotheses of the multiverse, the question arises as to whether there are universal laws of nature that prevail everywhere in the space-time continuum, or whether there might not be universes which cannot even be conceived of in terms of space-time as we know it (or believe to know it). For an overview of the often wildly metaphysical conjectures at the frontiers of physical knowledge, I recommend Brian Greene's *The Hidden Reality: Parallel Universes and the Deep Laws of the Cosmos*.[36]

In my earlier book *Why the World Does Not Exist* I argued for the claim that it is absurd, in any case, to believe that there is an all-encompassing world that includes everything which really exists. There simply is no such thing as an all-encompassing singular reality. To believe in reality as a whole, or in the world, is the remainder of an ancient idea that arose among us human beings a couple of thousand years ago as a side-effect of the misguided impression that our habitat (earth) is somehow enclosed by a sphere. This impression has still not completely fizzled out. In our time, it takes the shape of the notion that the (physical) universe is all there is and that the universe is some kind of total sum or matter/energy spread out in a certain way according to laws of nature forged in a ridiculously small amount of time right after the Big Bang (fill in the details with your favorite overall cosmology).

I leave all of this aside, since in any case I do not think that wandering conceptually into the depths of the cosmos is particularly helpful if we want to understand whether our thirst on a hot summer afternoon offers a genuine contribution to what happens on earth. However, it is important to bear in mind that our overall conception of reality as a whole (if any) has immediate consequences for our conception of ourselves as minded creatures within that whole.

A large part of human life (which includes ethics and politics) can only be understood when we take the reality of qualia into account. If I want to explain, for example, why Hans went to the kiosk, I will not be able to avoid mentioning that he was thirsty. Surely there might be numerous other reasons why he went to the kiosk: he wanted to meet Joe, who works there; he hoped that Josephine, with whom he is secretly in love, would be there; he wanted to buy a magazine. No external description of his behavior, let alone a description of the distribution of mass/matter/energy in some region of the universe, will be a better account of why Hans does what he does than the account which rightly mentions his motivations. And Hans would have no motivations to do anything whatsoever if he were not an animal of a specific kind endowed with sensibilities which provide him with a constantly changing flow of qualia.

The idea that the universe is nothing but an "interlocking mechanism,"[37] as Keil has fittingly called it, and that our qualia or even our consciousness as a whole contribute nothing in causal terms to the cosmic works, in reality just provides an imaginary relief. It is an attempt to avoid confronting the complexity of human action. If it makes no difference whether Hans is on his way to get a soda, or to see Joe or Josephine, one has already taken the easy way out of human action explanation. The situation is continually complicated by our qualia, and indeed for everyone involved.

What if Hans, for instance, is a closet homosexual, since he has the misfortune of coming from a corner of a city that is homophobic and does not want to admit that he really likes Joe rather than Josephine? A psychoanalyst would be delighted to investigate this and would perhaps surmise that it is no accident that Hans is convinced that he likes Josephine, since her name is similar to Joe, the name of the real object of his affection.

The image of the world as a universe that is completely structured according to laws of nature, a view often called determinism, is an unproven hypothesis in almost every regard. The claim that everything which happens does so because there are laws of nature does not follow from the fact that there are laws of nature. When humans speculate, they quickly tend to get lost in metaphysical ideas about reality as a whole. The idea that there is just one world which may or may not be identical with the (physical) universe is metaphysical poppycock, no better than the idea that we live on a planet which is encompassed by a cluster of spheres which revolve around us according to the wishes of the gods. When faced with the infinite, events in everyday life seem overwhelmingly negligible. Yet this impression is only an effect of our perspective, and it does not give us the truth about whether human freedom or even human consciousness is an illusion. In a nutshell, we should not get lost in our ideas of the vast, maybe infinite regions of the universe hitherto undiscovered and feel small and unimportant compared to such a conception. The impression that our innermost mental states contribute nothing to what is going on in causal terms is really a form of conceptual or philosophical mild form of depression.

God's-eye view

In the absence of further elucidation, the question of how the human mind or human consciousness in general actually fits in with nature or the universe is not well formulated. On closer inspection, it is about as meaningful as the question as to whether the moon is a square root. All kinds of things can be imagined in regards to it, yet one should not be fooled by one's own imagination. The question concerning the relation of nature and mind ordinarily draws on far too many assumptions. For the most part, it proceeds from an image of the world and of the human being that can be exposed as providing imaginary relief.

In modernity, one finds, on the one hand, the representation of a universe without mind, which one then, on the other hand, complements with mind. The mind, as it were, illuminates blind nature without anyone knowing how this works. As a result, the universe, or nature, feels like a "cold place to call home," as Wolfram Hogrebe puts it.[38] That is, the naturalistic world-view still describes one's own abode, one's home, but robs this place of all its magic, which gives the impression that things have a firm, entrenched structure, albeit one which does not respect our craving for meaning. One's home is retained, but it is now as cold as the apparently black and sepulchral space outside our atmosphere.

The human mind produces images of itself. It thus transports us from the internal perspective of our everyday experience to the bird's-eye view. This is also the origin of the ancient idea that God is a kind of all-seeing eye, which in real historical terms leads to Google's image of the human being, something that is compellingly presented in Dave Eggers's novel *The Circle*. One major problem with God, indeed, was that one did not easily measure up to his omniscience. Google is a bit more helpful, even though it serves the same type of imaginary function of giving a determinate place to everything and of imagining that someone must know where and how things are.

Currently, there is a new ideology on the horizon attached to the notion of the infosphere. It sometimes seems as though many of us would like nothing more than actually to be perpetually observed and controlled, as this corresponds to the age-old fantasy of a God who takes away our freedom and forces us to obey his laws. But, for the most part, an actual God is no longer welcome today in our modern scientifically oriented society, since he is traditionally described as supremely free and a rather fearsome guy (one does not want to run into him in the desert, as the poor prophets do).

With an actual God, freedom would again be in play – at least for him.

In ideological terms, human freedom is a potentially disruptive factor: if I am free to choose my own search engine, Google's profits might decrease. The tendency to form monopolies is constitutive of present-day market conditions. To be sure, we all want to have a choice (one does not want to see only sausages and pickles on the supermarket shelves, as in good old socialism). From a business perspective, it would be best for all consumers always to choose only a single product and hence not really to have a choice at all. Hence the fantasy to make humanity computable and to restrict freedom in favor of clearly marked paths. Humanity still quarrels over who is adopting the real bird's-eye view, over whom or what is considered its God: science, technology, progress, Google or, for the more classically minded, a personal actual God. In all these cases, the frame of mind, the fundamental fantasy, remains the same – that is, the fantasy of a God's- or bird's-eye view which knows that everything is always already in order and guarantees that nothing goes unnoticed.

3

Self-Consciousness

Having dealt with some crucial aspects of consciousness naturally leads us to our next major topic: self-consciousness. In examining consciousness, we have adopted an odd perspective. We were not only conscious of certain kinds of things in our environment, as usual, but we also consciously reflected on consciousness. Most of us are not normally worried about this every day, and nobody spends her entire conscious life dedicated to the fact that she has a conscious life – with the possible exception of the truly enlightened, if such there be. Yet, it is desirable to spend some time reflecting on consciousness, at least in a context in which we are looking for a mark of the mental and deem consciousness special in that regard. Tyler Burge, a leading American philosopher of mind, nicely sums up the relevance of self-consciousness thus: "The claim that one has a conception of mind-independent entities *as* mind-independent entails that one has a concept of mind. An ability to hold that physical entities are independent of one's mind, and everyone else's mind, requires a capacity for self-consciousness."[1] Thus, to know that some things are real, and that other things are products of our minds, presupposes a grasp of the concept of consciousness and, therefore, self-consciousness. Self-consciousness is a central feature of our lives without which we would constantly confuse perception and hallucination, "inner" mental states and objects "out there."

One of the most remarkable facts of consciousness is that one cannot really deny that one is conscious while being conscious. Admittedly, we have already seen how some have attempted to do precisely this. This insight into the irreducibility of consciousness even lurks behind what is probably the most famous sentence of modern philosophy, namely Descartes' infinitely cited "I think, therefore I am." In his *Meditations on First Philosophy*, he expresses this thought as follows:

110

Thinking? At last I have discovered it – thought; this alone is insep-
arable from me. I am, I exist – that is certain. But for how long? For as
long as I am thinking. For it could be that were I totally to cease from
thinking, I should totally cease to exist. At present I am not admit-
ting anything except what is necessarily true. I am, then, in the strict
sense only a thing that thinks; that is, I am a mind, or intelligence, or
intellect, or reason – words whose meaning I have been ignorant of
until now. But for all that I am a thing which is real and which truly
exists. But what kind of thing? As I have just said – a thinking thing.[2]

One easily falls prey to a conceptual confusion on the basis of
this citation. The confusion consists in mistaking the fact that,
while one cannot be deceived about one's being conscious, one
can be very much deceived by one's opinions about consciousness.
Consciousness itself is not generally or in all cases the best guide to
the nature of consciousness. For instance, my conscious experience
of colors brings with it many riddles that cannot be solved simply
by observing my consciousness by staring at colors. As long as one
is conscious it cannot be doubted *that* one is conscious, from which
it does not follow that one thus has indubitable knowledge of the
nature of consciousness. It is actually quite difficult to distinguish
the contribution of consciousness in conscious experience from the
contribution of mind-independent reality, which is why there is
philosophy.

Hence, for centuries the following reasonable objection has been
raised again and again against the Cartesian cogito: Descartes reifies consciousness; he thus makes it into a thing or a substance,
the thinking substance (*res cogitans*). This objection, which was
formulated in especially clear terms by Kant, then by Fichte and,
later, above all by Husserl and the philosophical movement known
as phenomenology which followed him, draws our attention to
the fact that Descartes conflates the certainty that we cannot be
deceived about whether we are conscious with the claim that we
thus also have insight into a particularly spectacular thing in the
universe: consciousness. To be more precise, the objection runs as
follows. Descartes conflates an *epistemological* insight, an insight
that characterizes our form of cognition (our infallibility with
regard to our being conscious) with a *metaphysical* insight into the
structure of the universe.

Yet this fallacy secretly forms the basis even for neurocentrism.
Neurocentrism departs from the assumption that there is a thing,
consciousness, whose properties have to be more precisely investigated so that we might eventually answer the question of how
this thing relates to material things in the universe, above all to

our brain. Neurocentrism's response is that consciousness is not something in addition to the brain-thing, and for this reason neurocentrism identifies consciousness with it. It turns consciousness into a brain-thing. It thereby fares no better than Descartes' identification of consciousness with a consciousness-thing.

The question of how the brain and consciousness are related to each other was incidentally also already formulated by Descartes. He thought that contact between immaterial consciousness (*mens*) or soul (*animus*) takes place in the pineal gland (a part of the vertebrate brain involved in the production of melatonin in the sleep–wake cycle).

Following Descartes, two major options concerning the mind–brain relationship were offered. **Dualism** claims that, along with brain-things, there is also a consciousness-thing in the universe, while **monism** denies this. **Neuromonism** claims that the consciousness-thing is identical either to the entire brain or to some areas of the brain and their activities. However, both positions presuppose that consciousness is a thing in the universe, which is the crucial mistake.

Self-consciousness is consciousness of consciousness. We could not be concerned with this fact without at the same time being conscious: we are conscious while we concern ourselves with consciousness. Self-consciousness is a special state that deserves some scrutiny, as it promises to be a key element for our understanding of human consciousness.

Despite its special status, self-consciousness is a much more mundane phenomenon than one might initially suppose. We continually take a stance toward our own mental states, toward our thoughts, without explicitly reflecting on the fact that we are reflecting on our consciousness. Our stream of consciousness does not simply run like subtitles beneath our actions, as though we were sometimes additionally focusing our mind's eye on the processes in our consciousness.[3] Since Kant, many philosophers of the past and present have pointed out that our consciousness would thus oddly be made into something unconscious. For this reason, to the present day the Kantian view that there is actually no consciousness without self-consciousness is widespread, as consciousness and self-consciousness seem to be somehow inextricably interwoven. In any event, if consciousness were only accidentally related to self-consciousness, it would be hard to account for the fact that we constantly experience consciousness itself in experiencing anything through consciousness. This is why it is not hard to focus on consciousness, as it is already present and available for further reflection. It makes no sense to assume that consciousness is like any old object out there in the world, as it is the only object which makes itself known to us as knowers without mediation by consciousness. Consciousness is available to consciousness without a further consciousness mediating between consciousness and consciousness. If this were not the case, we could never achieve consciousness of consciousness. This would destroy the entire discipline of a philosophy of mind or any other knowledge of ourselves as minded creatures.

Let us make things a bit more concrete. We continually evaluate the thoughts and impressions that we consciously experience. They do not suddenly appear in the obscure field of our consciousness and then vanish again, but they are immediately consciously experienced by us in such a way that they bear a stamp. For instance, it occurs to us that we still have to write an email to a friend. As this occurs to us, we feel immediately ashamed that we have not yet replied. Perhaps it thus dawns on us that we really do not wish to reply to her at all, since her last email had strange undertones. In any case, our friendship is on shaky ground and we would prefer not to reply. The consciousness of the fact that we have not written a reply, which can suddenly arise in the midst of an entirely normal situation, implies that we go around evaluating our thoughts – we are ashamed – without being able actively and consciously to control them. For its part, shame comes in many shapes and sizes, if you will. There are degrees of shame, which shrewd observers of the inner lives of human beings have illuminated in countless novels. Our conscious experience is always at the same time an experience of our conscious experience in light of certain aesthetical, ethical or purely biological values. If you become aware of a lion running toward you, this perceptual experience should trigger flight behavior. The conscious experience of a lion is judged in a certain way if it provokes the right response in you. This is self-consciousness in action.

Of course, we can be delighted or annoyed by a thought or a sense-impression. We experience a beautiful sunrise and are delighted by it. Perhaps it is connected to memories of other sunrises. We enjoy the taste of a brioche. We are annoyed by the watered-down coffee we have purchased at the train station. We clench our fist in our trouser pocket when considering that our favorite sports team is about to lose again, and so forth.

A large part of our emotional world, thus, has the form of self-consciousness. This does not mean that we explore our inner world from an internal vantage point; rather, it means that intentional

and phenomenal consciousness are fundamentally intertwined. As
mentally more or less healthy human beings, we do not have any
states of consciousness without their already appearing to us to be
evaluated in a certain way. On this basis, it becomes clear why our
moral values are connected to our world of emotions, since we first
become capable of morality when we are conscious that others are
conscious too and experience this structure as a system of values
that is to be perpetually calibrated anew.

How history can expand our consciousness

The modern history of research into self-consciousness reaches
a major peak in Marcel Proust's epoch-making masterpiece *In
Search of Lost Time*. Literature, perhaps paradigmatically narrative literature and poetry, has for millennia contributed to our
achievement of a better understanding of consciousness. In the
course of the mind's history, humanity has become more conscious, if you will, insofar as for thousands of years we have no
longer merely had attitudes toward our natural environment and
vague attitudes toward ourselves and others. Rather, at the latest
since the advanced cultures in Mesopotamia, a subtle language has
developed that enables us not merely to explore the fine-grainedness of our consciousness but to deepen it. It is hardly an accident
that the scientific discipline of psychology, which, to the present
day, has continually vacillated between the natural sciences and the
humanities, emerged in the second half of the nineteenth century in
the wake of the literary ascendancy of self-exploration. Nietzsche,
for instance, was able at this time to be simultaneously one of the
best writers in the German language (as both a prose stylist and
a lyrical poet) and a critical psychologist of our moral attitudes,
just as Freud around the same period achieved breakthroughs
in psychoanalysis and developed a profound understanding of
mythology, art and literature, to which even someone like Eric
Kandel has recently called attention.[4] Freud too was a first-rate
writer, which is certainly a major part of his cultural impact
beyond academia.

The history of the mind is thus among other things a history of
the expansion and transformation of consciousness. Consciousness
is not a thing that was always already precisely exactly what it is.
We do not discover it in nature as we do neutrons, chestnuts and
rainstorms. "Consciousness" is a concept that belongs to our self-
portrait – that is, the word "consciousness" does not simply pick

a natural kind or object in nature. Consciousness is connected to natural phenomena (no human consciousness without a functioning brain), but it is neither identical nor in any other meaningful way reducible to them.

We describe ourselves as conscious living beings with minds and thus produce a certain image of ourselves. Consciousness is not a reality that exists completely independently of how we form a concept of it. This makes it different from a crater on the moon, for example. Of course, other living beings, or even children who have not yet been culturally socialized, also have states of consciousness, such as impressions of color, auditory impressions and impressions of taste. However, whether one can identify Yves Klein blue on first sight in a museum, and knows how to bring a framework of allusions to the history of art to bear on it or not, makes a crucial difference even on the level of conscious perception. This cultural and historical potential for classifying sense-impressions fundamentally changes our consciousness. There is a gradual and progressive formation of consciousness – again a great theme in literature – which was treated in the genre of the *Bildungsroman*, from which arose Hegel's *Phenomenology of Spirit*. Hegel's great work examines the formation of consciousness in a philosophical way by investigating different forms or shapes of consciousness that have become differentiated over the course of millennia. His basic idea is precisely that consciousness itself can change according to our conception of it. This is why there can be such a thing as psychotherapy where you can learn to change your consciousness by changing your concept of it. If you realize, for instance, that certain negative thoughts come to your mind only because you belittle the role played by your conscious experience of social situations, you are in a position literally to change your consciousness for the better. The concept of consciousness is connected to that of self-consciousness, which for its part can have a history in which new facets that were not there before are cultivated.

The findings of paleoanthropology, which are popular today and supposedly obtained in a strictly scientific manner, often invite people to make big claims about everything that our ancestors in caves experienced and how morality and civilization are supposed to have gradually developed in the savannah, making it seem as though one might have a glimpse into the inner life of our prehistoric ancestors. For instance, such a glimpse might be obtained by forming ideas of how tool use, burial rites and inner life are related. But even tool use has a history and is embedded within the history of the mind. There is no overall relation between tool use and the mind, as there is no stable entity called "the mind." What we share with our minded ancestors is only the capacity to create self-images and not necessarily the same self-images. As a matter of fact, without written documents or oral evidence we cannot know anything about the minds of our ancestors. Visual imagery is insufficient as long as one knows nothing about the function of the images, for which reason the impressive cave paintings of our ancestors will forever remain a fundamental mystery to us, since we simply do not have any reliable evidence that would enable us to figure out what was really going on. Any substantial hypothesis (be it a reading of cave painting as art, maps or religion) is unsubstantiated, albeit amusing, speculation.

Depending on how one envisions the manner in which a subtle inner life arose in preliterate epochs, it can be surprising to discover what level the first literary works of advanced Mesopotamian cultures reached – for instance, the *Epic of Gilgamesh* or the lyric poetry (in the form of temple hymns) of the Assyrian high-priestess En-Hedu-Anna, who wrote in the third millennium BC (in the area of present-day Iraq, the cradle of advanced culture) and who was possibly the first person (at least, as far as I know) to sign her name to a literary text.

The first written evidence of advanced cultures certainly did not fall from heaven but, rather, suggests that it was preceded by a long prehistory of self-conscious inner life, which is accompanied by complex self-depictions that were orally transmitted and refined over a long span of time – as with the Homeric epics the *Iliad* and the *Odyssey*, or the much longer Indian epics *Mahabharata* and *Bhagavad Gita*. One should also not overestimate our "Western" subjectivity and capacity for self-depiction and self-knowledge, just because we happen to live at this moment and are proud of the way in which our technological achievements have been arranged.

Unfortunately, there is a widespread tendency to look anachronistically for contemporary forms of self-consciousness in the scenes depicted in cave paintings, although it must have been clear, at the latest since sociology emerged in the nineteenth century, that there is a history of self-consciousness. This idea was first formulated quite clearly by the post-Kantian philosophers Fichte, Schelling and Hegel, the so-called German Idealists. It forms the core of Hegel's *Phenomenology of Spirit*, in which he wants to establish that the human mind, *Geist*, considered as a whole, has a history that cannot be understood if one conceives of it as a continuation of biological relations to the external, natural world by means of consciousness.

Unfortunately this history – like every other real history – does not simply proceed in such a way that we always make further progress in ways that leave a trace. That literary works or languages fade into oblivion is enough to cause self-consciousness to regress to stages that have long been rendered obsolete. A reason for this lies simply in human freedom, which likewise consists in being able to forget, overlook or repress something.

However, it is crucial that we are not simply conscious but that we also have a consciousness of consciousness, even in everyday contexts. We do not know this merely because we take up attitudes to our own beliefs, wishes, feelings or sense-impressions, attitudes that we cultivate and develop. We can become wine connoisseurs and gourmets. We can learn to recognize Yves Klein blue at first sight. We can become judo masters. We can classify a brief sequence of chords as typical of Beethoven or Nirvana. We can familiarize ourselves with our own patterns of reaction, and so forth. In addition to all of this, we are immediately conscious of the fact that others are conscious. Consciousness of the fact that others are conscious is just as primordial a fact as consciousness of ourselves. To borrow a term from Martin Heidegger: consciousness and consciousness of the consciousness of others are equi-primordial [*gleichursprünglich*]. Self-consciousness is not only directed toward ourselves as individuals but is already structurally connected to the consciousness of others. The judgments belonging to our consciously experienced attitudes (such as being delighted or ashamed about something) are oriented to our expectation that others take up attitudes to our attitudes. From the outset, we experience ourselves in social contexts and do not first need to find our way into them by leaving our own private Cartesian theater behind. Each of us experiences this primordial sociality of consciousness, for instance, in the well-known phenomenon of being only too happy to share wonderful experiences (such as a trip abroad or a visit to a museum), since only in this way can one expect confirmation of the structure of these experiences. We cultivate our consciousness in light of the criterion of the consciousness of others, a criterion that has already been inscribed into our inner life the moment that we are able to put anything at all into language. This is actually quite obvious, insofar as we must have learned the rules of our language from others, which already imposes a discipline on our individual consciousness so that we are no longer able arbitrarily to let our thoughts wander (like a small child who calls everything that pleases it and is to its liking "mama" or everything that moves "car").

Our consciousness of the fact that others are conscious was recognized as primary by Kant and then recognized even more explicitly as the basis for human society by Fichte and Hegel after him. Marx and the founding fathers of sociology and psychology have contributed to this idea in their own respective ways. Contemporary feminist theories, in particular Judith Butler's gender performativity theory, are also based on this idea, and Butler quite explicitly invokes Hegel.

In times of neurocentrism, the capacity to attain consciousness of the fact that others are conscious is called a "theory of mind," which is a misleading expression, since the word "theory" is here used in an improper way. Since the 1990s, it has also been believed that the biological basis for this phenomenon has been discovered. So-called mirror neurons are accordingly supposed to see to it that we reproduce, as it were, the behavior and feelings of others through the firing of neurons and the internal simulation of the conscious attitudes of others. One feels a shadow of pain, so to speak, for a person writhing on the ground, because certain neurons emerged and lasted in the course of evolution (in other words, random genetic mutation, not history, is supposed to explain the vagaries of self-consciousness).

I am certainly not in the business of denying that there are mirror neurons, nor do I even want to deny that, without them, we would not have been able to attain either self-consciousness or the consciousness that others are conscious. No more do I deny that important biological foundations of human mental states have ultimately emerged through random genetic mutation – that is, not in a goal-directed or planned way – and were then selected due to environmental pressure. That there are conscious living beings on our planet, and perhaps elsewhere, too, is a matter of chance, when viewed from the perspective of the universe. That is, there are no particular reasons for it. However, from the perspective of the universe there is no particular reason for anything whatsoever; in the universe, there simply is what there is.

All this means, though, is that we are able to form an image of the universe and its sheer infinite expanses, in which we, with our consciousness and the needs and values associated with it, play no constitutive role. The universe, understood in this way, is of course not concerned about us. For all we know, the processes that result in the emergence of species, which we call "evolution," are not consciously or intentionally guided. There is no deeper biological reason for the fact that beings like us exist beyond the fact that animals like us are simply here now and the fact that our biological emergence was possible, because certain functional structures were selected in time immemorial and were passed on through reproduction. Our existence as animals and its continuation depend on our adaptation to an extremely fragile natural environment, an adaptation that can come to an end at any time as a result of a natural or humanly created catastrophe. The universe, our planet or nature will not see to it that we survive when the composition of our atmosphere changes (whether because of man-made global warming, a meteor crashing into earth, or a volcanic eruption) in such a way that we can no longer breathe. Yet, none of this speaks in favor of an identification of mind and brain.

Insofar as human beings are prone to misjudge their own position as minded, historical animals because they do not know much about the universe, the progress of our discoveries in the field of neurobiology is obviously conducive to progress in self-knowledge. Whether one believes that the sun shines so that we may see, or that the fact that we are conscious and self-conscious is a kind of symphony of the mind which is arranged for the glory of God, who literally views the performance "down here" from a distance, is in fact quite beside the point. Yet it would be a misunderstanding if one thought that all of our recently acquired neurobiological knowledge would give us a better understanding of self-consciousness than what was at the disposal of En-Hedu-Anna, for instance, or Homer and Sophocles, Nagarjuna, Jane Austen, Augustine, Hildegard von Bingen, George Sand, Hegel, Bettina von Arnim or Marx. Knowing more about the neurobiological conditions of the mind contributes to self-understanding. However, the biological perspective also obscures the historical dimension of self-consciousness.

Why reducing the mind to its neurobiological conditions is prone to misunderstandings is revealed by a now already familiar line of thought. Indeed, we have seen that we know how impressions of color are associated with electromagnetic waves only because we have impressions of color and learn to distinguish them (*the indispensability thesis*). Impressions of color do not disappear with our increasing knowledge of electromagnetic waves. Our experience always remains its own dimension, without which we would have no access at all to the scientific facts and processes that are associated with it.

Monads in the mill

The indispensability of subjective experience becomes clearer with a helpful distinction from John Searle. In his book *The Rediscovery of Mind*, he refers to the fact that our experience is **ontologically subjective** – i.e., that consciousness can be described from an internal perspective in which we also experience colors, feelings and so forth. He distinguishes **ontologically objective facts** – i.e., facts that one can describe in such a way that no consciousness is involved in their existence – from what is ontologically subjective. For example, if one describes a chemical reaction, one thus describes an ontologically objective fact. Consciousness, in contradistinction to chemical reactions, is ontologically subjective; it would not take place without anyone noticing that it takes place.

At this point, Searle adds a decisive insight by referring to the fact that consciousness is nevertheless **epistemically objective**. This means that claims to truth can be formulated about what consciousness is, which in turn means that one can get consciousness right or wrong. The fact that consciousness is ontologically subjective, hence, does not imply that we cannot be wrong about it. It means simply that the facts of consciousness are subjective, not that our beliefs about it are not truth-apt.

Yet, when it comes to consciousness, that which is formulated in terms of truth claims is and remains irreducibly ontologically subjective. The confusion to which many who want to deny consciousness fall victim, according to Searle, can be attributed to the fact that they do not understand that something can be epistemically objective and ontologically subjective at the same time. There is simply no reason to consider our consciousness only from the ontologically objective perspective.

One source of the contemporary, neurocentric alienation of self-consciousness from itself can be identified as follows. We have learned that many phenomena which we experience every day prove to be entirely different than we had previously thought. As we obtain more precise knowledge of the universe, it begins to look like a strange place. Let us once again take the example of sunrises. As a matter of fact, when one thinks that one sees the upper edge of the sun on the horizon, this is actually a perception not of the sun but of a chemically induced reflection of it, comparable to a Fata Morgana, which is made possible by the chemical composition of the atmosphere. Besides, the sun does not rise in the literal sense of an upward movement. Therefore, in a certain sense there are no sunrises. At any rate, some express themselves in such a fashion, and something similar holds true for the horizon or for the blue sky, two effects that are not ontologically objective. There is no blue sphere above our heads screening us off from the cosmos – at least, not in the sense in which one might interpret the phenomenon of a blue sky before knowing anything about the atmosphere. The ontologically objective facts about celestial bodies and our atmosphere make the situation seem as though events such as sunrises turn out to be a mere semblance, a kind of illusion.

But this distinction between objective reality and subjective appearance does not apply to the case of consciousness. Consciousness cannot be an illusion in this way. Rather, consciousness is the source of illusions as well as of perceptions, and so on. Without consciousness, we would neither deceive ourselves nor ever have true beliefs. Consciousness is simply the standpoint from which something appears to us, and we cannot dispense with this standpoint, since then no one would actually be there any more to be able still to recognize anything.

We would not even know what we should be looking for in the brain, for instance, or in the traces of our species' biological past, if we were not already familiar with what it means to be conscious or self-conscious. Our fallible acquaintance with consciousness – i.e., self-consciousness – is an indispensable requisite for any further inquiry into the nature of consciousness. This is what the famous German philosopher Gottfried Wilhelm Leibniz had in mind with his **metaphor of the mill**, which has been a hot topic up to the present day. It is actually one of the earliest modern formulations of the so-called **hard problem of consciousness.** In §17 of his short text *Monadology* (1714), he claims that one could not explain our subjective impressions *"in terms of mechanical reasons"* – that is, "through shapes and motions" that are at work in our organism.[5] To be sure, Leibniz could not yet know much about the precise structure of the physiology of our brain. Nevertheless, the misleading metaphor of a mill can easily be replaced by any other kind of machine (be it a network of neurons or a silicon-based computer).

Leibniz imagines being able to climb into a thought machine, thus into the brain. He compares this with going into a mill and claims: "Assuming that, when inspecting its interior, we will only find parts that push one another, and we will never find anything to explain a perception."[6] From this he draws the quite unjustified conclusion that the human mind does not have any internal complexity at all, but is just a monad (from the ancient Greek *monas* = a unit). The famous Nobel prizewinning physicist Erwin Schrödinger (1887–1961) goes further in *Mind and Matter*, and in opposition to "Leibniz's fearful doctrine of monads"[7] even believes that ". . . in truth there is only *one* mind. That is the doctrine of the Upanishads. And not only of the Upanishads. The mystically experienced union with God regularly entails this attitude unless it is opposed by strong existing prejudices; and this means that it is less easily accepted in the West than in the East."[8] Admittedly, one can hardly take this thesis seriously, either scientifically or philosophically, without extensive justification. Schrödinger himself probably also suspected this, which is why he immunized himself from critique by "the West." However, locating a thought in the West or the East has no philosophical purchase power. Where does the mysterious East in which strong prejudices are less common begin? Am I more spiritual than anyone in London or New York because I live east of them? Might I be a Far-Eastern thinker for Californians or for Indians, should they ever travel east on their way to meet me? Is there more consciousness of unity in Germany than in France, because Germany lies to the east of France? Were the Californian hippies so "spiritual" because they resided so far to the west that they almost made it to the Far East?

Schrödinger, like many before and after him, unfortunately falls prey to **Euro-Hinduism**, a view that spread out in the wake of German Romanticism. It is the idea that there is a greater and truer mystical consciousness of unity in India – as though it were harder for Indian citizens to understand that their neighbors had consciousnesses of their own! The pseudo-mystical idea to which Schrödinger adheres (which of course originates in what he would call the "West") is in his case a consequence of the fact that he is not able to solve the hard problem of consciousness, which he formulates in neuro-constructivist terms right at the beginning of his book:

> The world is a construct of our sensations, perceptions, memories. It is convenient to regard it as existing objectively on its own. But it certainly does not become manifest by its mere existence. Its becoming manifest is conditional on very special goings-on in very special parts of this very world, namely on certain events that happen in a brain. That is an inordinately peculiar kind of implication.[9]

This is, in fact, "an inordinately peculiar kind of implication," though not in itself but in the eye of the misguided beholder Erwin Schrödinger, who works out an incoherent account of the nature of consciousness: if (1) the world is a construct of our sensations and (2) the world includes the brain, then the brain is also a construct of our sensations. But how then is the brain supposed to form the basis for these constructions if it is thus something that is not itself constructed from its sensations? How is such an impossible miracle supposed to happen?

Leibniz and Schrödinger both overlook the fact that, when something does not function in a purely mechanical way, like clockwork, we are still a long way from being able to conclude that it does not possess any internal complexity. One cannot oppose mind and matter as one does the simple and the complex. Here it is enough, as Brigitte Falkenburg (b. 1953), a German philosopher and physicist, emphasizes, to point out that mental phenomena are structured in a different way than physical phenomena, which is why the true statements that one can utter respectively concerning both cannot be consolidated into a single theoretical discipline. Mind and matter are both complex in their own way. For this reason, Falkenburg adheres, within new parameters, to Leibniz's thesis that the mental and the corporeal are fundamentally measured according to different standards, that they are thus incommensurable.[10]

It is not my concern to champion Leibniz over Schrödinger or Falkenburg over both. I consider Leibniz's theory of consciousness to be false, since he goes so far as to think that everything which exists fundamentally has a kind of consciousness. This position is known as **panpsychism**, which, it should be noted, has had many adherents up to the present day who defend it with impressive precision. Among others, Chalmers comes close to such a position. He goes so far as to entertain the notion that, wherever information-processing is going on, experience might also be present. For this reason, he considers it to be an "open question" as to whether a thermostat could be conscious (even if its consciousness has to be fairly dull).[11]

The real open question at this point is probably just how much must have gone wrong if one no longer knows whether thermostats, photoelectric sensors, lightbulbs and rainstorms, contrary to our expectations, might somehow be conscious. Obviously, such things are not conscious, and any other claims can only be the result of false premises or muddled conceptions.

The metaphor of the mill nevertheless contains a glimmer of truth. What it reveals is that the description of mechanical or, rather, quasi-mechanical (chemical) processes that run their course while we are conscious or self-conscious, and which must be somehow connected with consciousness and self-consciousness, follows different principles than the description of consciousness and self-consciousness. If I am speaking about ion channels and neural networks, this will presuppose completely different considerations than if I am speaking about self-consciousness. Self-consciousness is embedded in social contexts. In the case of brain processes, however, there are no social contexts; rather, an internal processing of information takes place, if one may even put it in these terms. A variety of people participate in genuine social interaction who never turn up in my brain. It is not as though I absorb them into myself. That is, consciousness which is socially interactive and directed outward cannot be captured by concentrating on the description of processes in the brain. Once again, in the words of Wolfram Hogrebe's aphorism: "Spirit is outside but breaks through inside."[12]

Bio is not always better than techno

The thesis that some contents of our consciousness are located outside of our skull is called **externalism**. One important version of externalism is **social externalism**, which amounts to the claim that some contents of our consciousness exist only as a result of our contact with another consciousness. The most radical version of this thesis is **social interactionism**, which claims that we would not be conscious at all without such contact, an idea that harks back to George Herbert Mead (1863–1931) and was recently restated by the renowned psychologist German Wolfgang Prinz (b. 1942), in his book *Open Minds: The Social Making of Agency and Intentionality*.[13]

A founding father of externalism, the recently deceased American philosopher Hilary Putnam (1926–2016), was one of the most important postwar philosophers. He is well known for being at least an indirect influence on the *Matrix* trilogy of films. In the first chapter of his book *Reason, Truth and History*, entitled "Brains in a Vat," he sketches out a dystopian vision of the possibility that we are all just brains which are electrically stimulated, so that we are led to believe in the illusion of a reality independent of ourselves.[14] This idea is taken up and put into action by the *Matrix* films. Putnam is also one of the first to have suggested that the brain be envisioned as a computer, on which consciousness or the mind in general runs like a piece of software. This thesis is also known as **machine state functionalism**.

Putnam originally introduced externalism into the philosophy of language and then went on to employ it fruitfully in the philosophy of consciousness. One of the central questions of the philosophy of language is how it is possible for our words to mean anything at all. The things that we name and the states of affairs of which we speak do not cry out to be named and carved up in the way we refer to them in our natural languages. This is why different natural languages can exist. It has been pointed out that many claims about the human mind and its relationship to the natural environment – which for the most part is characterized as an "external world" – are in part based on quite confused claims about the meaning of our words. Putnam has repeatedly posed the question in his books as to which implicit or explicit theory of the meaning of linguistic expressions guides our reflections on ourselves as minded animals. This illuminating approach has led to far-reaching insights, particularly to the fact that almost no one who has worked with such insights for a while says to themselves "I am a brain."

Putnam uses the now overused example of the meaning of the term "water," a consideration which led him to externalism. Let us pose what appears to be the easiest question of all: What does the term "water" mean? The answer, as easy as it is superficial, is that "water" means water. "Water" refers to water. But this is by no means self-evident. That is to say, if we were living in the Matrix, if I were thus identical to my brain, which is not in Germany at all but somewhere on a space station and has been electrically stimulated there from the beginning of time, the issue with water would pose a genuine problem. If that were the case, I would never have seen real water. Every time I had had the opportunity to think about water, the machines inputted thoughts of water into me, and when, perhaps, I thought that I was a child who had been taught the meaning of "water," that was all just a radical illusion. I was never in contact with water, and maybe in reality there is no water (who knows what my brain on that space station out there in the real world outside of the Matrix is made of!).

As a brain in the Matrix, everything that I know about "water" I know only from my own imagination, from my hallucinations that the machines I am plugged into actually produce. This sounds horrific, and one quickly sees that in such a scenario we could never really be sure of anything, not even of the meaning of our most simple words. All of our seeming knowledge would consist of illusory impressions that the machines feed us – perhaps only in order to keep our brains intact. A brain that has beautiful dreams can potentially be better preserved than a brain which also knows that it will be forever misused as just a source of energy by machines, and in the midst of such thoughts would probably gradually sink into a lasting depression before finally drowning in its sorrows.

All of this sounds dreadful. It sounds even more dreadful when it becomes clear that neurocentrism would have us believe, in all seriousness, that in fact *we* are essentially brains in a vat. According to neurocentrism, we are indeed brains that are enclosed within our skulls. Evolution is supposed to guide our thoughts, since everything we consider to be true only seems plausible because the bio-machines to which we are connected pursue certain egotistical interests: they want to pass on their DNA and aside from that simply live on without further purpose. Neurocentrism accordingly teaches that we really are brains in a vat, which are guided by alien processes and machines – by evolution, genes, neurotransmitters, and so forth. Thus it is as if we are dealing with a bio-variant of the *Matrix*. However, bio is not always better than techno.

Of course, Putnam does not stop there. Rather, he imagines a scenario that helps him to illustrate why we cannot be brains in a vat. Imagine that you see ants crawling in front of you on the beach and executing a remarkable march back and forth. You then notice that the ants have apparently sketched a portrait of Winston Churchill in the sand. Question: Are the ants familiar with Winston Churchill and have they made a picture of him in the sand? This would be just as inconceivable as the proverbial ape who hits the keys on a typewriter at random and as a result produces a manuscript of *Macbeth*. The ants are unfamiliar with Winston Churchill and the ape is unacquainted with *Macbeth*. Nothing against ants and apes, but they are simply no more educated within our lifeworld than we fully understand theirs. What do I know of what ants experience or what they think if they communicate with each other via pheromones – that is, by way of scents? Apes are closer to us in evolutionary terms, which is why we do not hesitate to characterize some of them as humanoid – that is, similar to humans. Nevertheless, this does not mean that we can imagine what their lifeworld is like, how they experience their reality.

Ants which are crawling in the sand are simply in no position whatsoever to sketch a portrait of Winston Churchill. It would be a miracle if they knew that Churchill had even lived. How would they supposedly have obtained this information? Who would have explained this to them and how could they ever understand it?

At this point, Putnam connects his two lines of thought together. If we were brains in a vat, we would know as little about water as the ants do about Churchill and the ape about *Macbeth*. Brains in a vat are simply missing the right kind of contact with water, which consists in the fact that one has at some point actually touched, seen and drunk water. Similarly, the ants are missing the right kind of contact with Churchill, which consists in the fact that one has had history lessons on him, that one has seen him on YouTube, in TV documentaries or in books, for example.

Generally speaking, the following is the case: the poor brains in a vat know nothing of anything that goes beyond the realm of their imagination. This means that they never have a language that even remotely resembles ours. All of their words refer only to hallucinated episodes and objects. They know neither water nor land, neither friends nor elevators, nay, not even their own fingers! We only imagine that we could be such brains in a vat because we ignore the fact that our language does not continually report what is going on inside of us but speaks about the common environment in which we are situated.[15] This thesis is the **basic idea of externalism.**

To believe that the simple words which we first learn at a very young age could not have any relation to the external world but are, rather, just labels we attach to our mental imagery is again to invoke the homunculus. This would be like believing that children are effectively stuck inside their minds.

Putting aside the sinister scenario of brains in a vat for a moment, the idea that we have an interiority that no one else can access tickles our fancy. We would be perfectly happy if our whole life played out on a private stage that would not exist without us. This would give us much more control over our lives than we actually have. It would mean that the entirety of colorful reality comes to an end with our demise, as if every death were a true apocalypse in which everything hangs in the balance. But we are not that important.

How the clown attempted to get rid of omnipotence

The claim that we are brains in a vat or brains in a skull (which amounts to the same thing) is a narcissistic fantasy. Sigmund Freud (1856–1939) investigated the fundamental structures of this fantasy in a wonderful chapter of his not so wonderful book *Totem and Taboo* entitled "Animism, Magic and the Omnipotence of Thoughts." Indirectly referring to Freud, Putnam himself calls the notion that the ants might after all be sketching a portrait of Churchill a "magical theory" of linguistic meaning.[16]

Freud reminds us of a phenomenon with which we are all familiar: sometimes we think of a person, for instance, and then suddenly meet this person on a streetcar or receive an unexpected phone call from her. In general, we more or less have the experience of an unexpected meaningfulness in common. Despite its utter randomness and complexity, social life seems to have an underlying thread. In moments in which we give in to this fantasy, it is as though the chance occurrences on our planet were somehow tailored for us: when the sun suddenly and unexpectedly shines on the day of a long-awaited reunion or when it begins to thunder at the moment of a friend's death. Such experiences can of course be quite profound and leave us with the impression that it is as if there is a purpose concealed behind what are only apparently chance occurrences, that this whole show (as in *The Truman Show*) had something to do with us. If one were to carry the impression that we are at the center of a show too far, one would wind up with superstitious beliefs or, much worse, psychosis.

Freud thinks that humanity has lived for long stretches as if chance occurrences were always an expression of psychical connections, a view he calls **animism**. Today, animism is entertained even by philosophers and scientists in the form of panpsychism, or the **hypothesis of panspermia**. The former, as has already been described above, holds that everything is ultimately animate, that our mind is only a complex variant of a basic mental force that is just as real as the strong nuclear force. The latter holds that perhaps life on our planet emerged because it was floating around through the universe from primordial times in embryonic form and finally settled here.

Admittedly, Freud's own world-view does not get us much further. In particular, he claims that we are quite primitive machines that are continually beset by a stream of desires, which he calls **libido**. For him, our mental life consists essentially in organizing our pleasurable sensations in some way. According to Freud, mental life is fundamentally the attempt to achieve pleasurable feelings. On his view, it is simply the case that we are desire-machines that emerged through evolution who fool ourselves into thinking that there are purposive structures which go beyond the regulation of our libido. Hence he rejects the idea of a homunculus but goes so far in the process that he immediately suspects that we are never really a "master in . . . [our] own house."[17] If one looks a little more closely, Freud thus secretly adheres to the homunculus but turns him into a stupid puppet.

Yet he does not even stop there but shamelessly indulges in a complete exaggeration. Because, like many of his contemporaries – Nietzsche, above all – he saw through the fantasy of the omnipotence of thought as an illusion, he rashly concluded that our conscious thoughts, our "ego," as he calls the level of conscious thought, is just a complete idiot: "The ego here plays the ludicrous role of the clown in the circus, who, by his gestures, tries to convince the audience that every change in the circus ring happens as a result of his orders. But only the youngest in the audience are taken in."[18] A few things get quite mixed up here. If the ego is only supposed to be the plaything of anonymous forces, who is playing the clown? Someone is considered to be a clown precisely because others are more intelligent. It cannot be the case that someone is simply a clown insofar as he or she is actually an ego. The clown would not be a clown then and the adults would not be smarter. And who is the audience?

Freud's belief that the ego is a clown is typical of the denial or denigration of the ego or the self: like so many others, he conflates the realization that there is no homunculus with the supposed realization that there is no ego or no self – or, if you will, that both are ultimately just more or less useful fictions. But, in doing so, he overlooks the really obvious option that the ego or the self is just not a homunculus and that virtually no one who has spoken of an ego or a self in the long history of the philosophy of mind has spoken of it in such terms!

For this reason, one should draw on Freud in another way that is more fruitful. One can follow his observation that our thoughts do not have any omnipotence or magic, without concluding from this that our thoughts have no power at all and are only waves of illusion that break on an immense, wild ocean. We can call the thesis that the mind is somehow everything and already disseminated across the universe – the omnipotence of thought – **joyful animism**. Such animism is an expression of a complete overestimation of the self, which is something we can learn from Freud. The converse claim, that we are basically clowns who are witnessing a circus show that in reality has nothing to do with us, is in contrast a complete underestimation of the self. I would like to call this – recalling Hegel's apt expression – an **unhappy consciousness.**

At this point, one can see that there is a connection between the technical philosophical term "self-consciousness" and the everyday usage of the word in the sense of lacking "self-assurance." In fact, our conceptions of consciousness, and thus of our consciousness of consciousness, are linked to the value we ascribe to consciousness. Often, if not always (as Freud believes), our own feelings of self-assurance are for this reason reflected in our theorizing, when it is a matter of figuring out what the human mind is.

There is a whole series of problems that come along with self-consciousness. These problems arise as a result of the fact that it is difficult to form an exact picture of how one can genuinely have consciousness of something, on the one hand, and have consciousness of consciousness, on the other. How are consciousness and self-consciousness related?

For a start, ask yourself the following question: Can you be in a conscious state of any sort without being able to give an account of it when asked? It seems as though one always consciously experiences one's own conscious impressions and could give an account of them in some way. Such a diagnosis has led to the establishment of an entire branch of theory that is today called HOT – that is, "higher-order theory."

On closer examination, we are once again dealing here with old wine in new bottles. These ideas were spelled out for the first time in Kant's *Critique of Pure Reason* and were then developed further by those who came after him, primarily by Fichte, a virtuoso of the self [*Ich*] (who even has "ich" embedded in his last name).[19] Kant and Fichte considered the crucial distinguishing feature of our consciousness to lie in the fact that we can accompany any single conscious state with a higher-level consciousness of our consciousness. For example, I am tasting vanilla right now because I have eaten vanilla yogurt, and I can tell you this. In the same way, I see ever more letters appearing on my computer screen, feel how my fingers just move effortlessly over the keyboard, sense the contact with my desk chair and can give an account of all of these things. We can also intensify our impressions and manipulate them to a certain degree by moving to the level of self-consciousness – that is, by occupying ourselves with our own consciousness.

However, self-consciousness can also be frightening, which is quite vividly depicted in the work of the German poet Heinrich von Kleist, who was very exercised by Kant's philosophy, even having what is termed a Kant crisis which contributed to his actual suicide. Kleist wrote a wonderful short text *On the Marionette Theater*, in which he investigates the uncanny phenomenon of being unsettled by attaining a consciousness of our consciousness. In this text, a scene occurs in which two male characters are in a bathhouse and one of them (a sixteen-year-old boy) lifts his foot and thereby gestures in a manner that reminds both of a famous motif in the history of sculpture, the "Boy with Thorn." The "Boy with Thorn" is a statue of a youth who is pulling out a thorn that has pricked his foot (Freud would be delighted that a thorn should be pulled out!).

The many homoerotic and borderline pedophilic connotations of this scene are unmistakable (above all, if one thinks of

Thomas Mann's *Death in Venice*, for instance, where Gustav von Aschenbach also compares his beloved Tadzio to "Boy with Thorn"). Be that as it may, the crucial point that is emphasized by Kleist arises from the fact that the older observer of the scene irritates the youth by laughing at him and pretending not to have noticed the unwanted, natural grace of his gesture at all:

> My friend was reminded of this statue when after our swim he placed his foot on the footstool to dry it and at the same time glanced into a large mirror; he smiled and told me what a discovery he had made. And indeed I had made the same observation at the same moment; but whether it was that I wanted to test the security of his natural grace, or whether I wanted to challenge his vanity, I laughed and replied that he was imagining things. He blushed and lifted his foot a second time to show me; as one could have easily predicted, the attempt failed.[20]

A similar point is made in a brilliant episode of the American sitcom *Seinfeld*, to be found in the episode "The Chaperone" (sixth season, first episode). Elaine learns a painful lesson about grace in a job interview:

> LANDIS: Of course, Jackie O. was a great lady. Those are going to be some tough shoes to fill. Everyone loved her. She had such … grace.
> ELAINE (gushing):   Yes! Grace!
> LANDIS: Not many people have grace.
> ELAINE: Well, you know, grace is a tough one. I like to think I have a little grace … not as much as Jackie –
> LANDIS: You can't have "a little grace." You either have grace, or you … don't.
> ELAINE: O.K., fine, I have … no grace.
> LANDIS: Grace isn't something you can pick up at the market.
> ELAINE   (fed up): Alright, alright, look – I don't have grace, I don't want grace … I don't even say grace, O.K.?
> LANDIS: Thank you for coming in.
> ELAINE: Yeah, yeah, right.

If we focus our consciousness on our consciousness, our consciousness is transformed. Whether we achieve grace depends on the degree to which we are able to lose control over our gestures and let them happen without conscious access.

Concealed behind this phenomenon lies a quite general problem that was examined closely not only by Kant but also by

Fichte and Hegel after him, influencing various Romantic circles. This combination of philosophy and literature ultimately led to the great achievements of psychology in the discovery of the unconscious.

The general problem identified by all three consists in the fact that one cannot really maintain that consciousness is always accompanied by self-consciousness, as if all of our conscious states were always also simultaneously monitored by a higher, evaluating authority. The question could then immediately arise as to whether this authority is itself conscious or not. If it is conscious, there must in turn be an even higher authority that monitors it. Thus, a problematic infinite regress emerges: for any consciousness another consciousness is needed for the former to be conscious, and so on to infinity.

Now of course one could attempt the following evasive maneuver: Why shouldn't the higher authority (self-consciousness) simply be able to monitor itself? It would then have the twofold task of monitoring consciousness (or evaluating it) and also monitoring or evaluating itself in the bargain.

However, this does not work, which one can illustrate with a simple case. Try sometime to play a strategic board game – Nine Men's Morris, let us say, or chess – against yourself. Such an attempt will fail, as is well known. We cannot really play Nine Men's Morris or chess against ourselves, since it would not then make any sense to devise a complicated plan, because we could not keep it a secret from our "opponent." Something like this is the case with self-consciousness monitoring itself. Here there is a vicious circle, a circle in which an attempt is made to engender self-consciousness through an impossible form of self-monitoring. If we try to generate consciousness and self-consciousness in one act of self-monitoring, we are stuck in either a regress or a circle.

Self-consciousness in a circle

We are familiar with these structures not merely from philosophical theories of self-consciousness but also from everyday situations. Let us assume that we want to go on a diet right after a lazy holiday of overindulging in food and lying on the beach. We now experience being in a restaurant where we could order a tempting pizza. We have a choice between the extremely unsatisfying salad, which is consistent with our plans to be on a diet, and the tempting pizza.

At this point, self-consciousness comes into play and begins to evaluate our consciousness, as with the well-known image of a little angel on one shoulder and a little devil on the other. The all but clearly noticed, almost even unconscious to and fro runs its course. Eventually, a decision is made and the little devil and little angel disappear for the moment.

Whatever one makes of this, it is usually not the case that there is someone else standing behind the little devil and little angel, evaluating them in turn. And even if this were the case, if another voice were thus added and disparaged the little devil, for instance, there would not be yet another voice behind this voice. The chain comes to an end somewhere, usually with a little devil and a little angel. Thus we hear an inner voice full stop, without another commentary following it again.

The issue can be grasped even more succinctly. If consciousness only ever exists in such a way that there exists an accompanying self-consciousness that is distinct from consciousness, the question arises as to whether self-consciousness is conscious, too. Since one has assumed that consciousness could by definition always be accompanied by self-consciousness, this also holds true for self-consciousness. But then immediately there are infinitely many levels: consciousness of consciousness of consciousness, and so on. This is the infinite regress *par excellence* – that is, an infinite regress: in order to be conscious, one must be conscious of being conscious; in order to be conscious of being conscious, one must be conscious of being conscious of being conscious; and so on.

This theory does not add up. Hence, it was traditionally assumed (especially in Kant's and Fichte's influential theories of self-consciousness) that the chain terminates in sheer self-consciousness. Yet the latter was then assumed to be able to observe itself. How else would we know that self-consciousness exists at all? This is known as the **problem of circular reasoning**: self-consciousness knows about itself through itself; it is intimately acquainted with itself. Yet, this comes suspiciously close to a brute assertion which covers up the problem that we have to stop somewhere but do not really know where.

Kant clearly recognized this problem of circular reasoning: If we are self-conscious, we must already be conscious of being conscious. We cannot conjure this up from nothing and hence cannot explain it from a perspective in which we act as though we did not yet know what we are talking about. He expresses this in a somewhat complicated manner thus:

Through this I, or He, or It (the thing), which thinks, nothing further is represented than a transcendental subject of thoughts = x, which is recognized only through the thoughts that are its predicates, and about which, in abstraction, we can never have even the least concept; because of which we therefore turn in a constant circle, since we must always already avail ourselves of the representation of it at all times in order to judge anything about it.[21]

Kant here speaks of the "I, or He, or It" that is supposed to think and leaves open what this actually amounts to. He gives the following reason for this. Our representation of consciousness crucially depends on how we represent the bearer of thoughts. Who or what actually has thoughts? Who or what thinks inside of us? Kant's answer is that we can never really know this, since we must already form a representation of the bearer of thoughts before we can delve deeper into its nature. According to Kant, one cannot get behind one's own representations to find a reality of consciousness that is hidden there, whether this be an immortal soul or the brain.

Those who followed Kant were not satisfied with this conclusion. We still want to know who or what is actually the bearer of thoughts. Are *we* thinkers of thoughts or are *they* thinking in us? Georg Christoph Lichtenberg (1742–1799), a contemporary of Kant's, considered something like this when he wrote: "We are conscious of certain ideas that do not depend on us; we believe that others, at least, do depend on us. Where is the line drawn? We know only the existence of our sensations, representations, and thoughts. *It thinks*, we should say, just as one says, *it lightnings*."[22]

At this point, Fichte and Hegel had considered a strategy for resolving the problem, the strategy of **social interactionism**, with which we have already briefly familiarized ourselves. This strategy solves the problem by proceeding from the fact that there must be more than one consciousness in order for self-consciousness to exist. Fichte and Hegel maintained that we understand consciousness and self-consciousness because we perceive the consciousness of others, which then installs their self-consciousness into us, as it were, through interaction.

The basic idea is perhaps familiar to you from other contexts (pedagogy or psychology). Especially widespread is the idea that the "voice of conscience" – that is, the evaluating authority in us – develops through education. Our parents and other teachers are accordingly supposed to have installed a conscience in us. Like conscience, on this model self-consciousness would then be a social artifact.

Wolfgang Prinz has recently elaborated this line of thought in his book *Open Minds*, where he argues for the thesis that "self can emerge" only "from others."[23] Prinz goes so far as to claim systematically that none of us could have intentions without having first learned from the intentions of others: "Agency and intention, I contend, are initially perceived and understood to be operating in others, and it is only through practices of social mirroring that individuals come to apply these notions to themselves and to implement related control mechanisms for their own actions."[24] To my knowledge, this idea was first systematically elaborated by Fichte, who formulated it as follows: "The human being . . . becomes a human being only among human beings . . . *if there are to be human beings at all, there must be more than one*."[25] Fichte calls this structure *recognition*. According to him, at some point we are summoned to be a self. This summons is implemented as a steering mechanism, and in this way we attain self-consciousness.

At first sight, all of that sounds plausible; it allows us to make sense of how we internalize ideas of *who* and *how* we ought to be. Indeed, it is certainly true that we incorporate values and patterns of conduct from our social surroundings. But can we really apply this model as an account of self-consciousness? Are we self-conscious, self-aware of our own consciousness, because someone teaches us to become conscious?

Social interactionism goes too far. How is it supposed to be possible for me to recognize another person as self-conscious if I am not already, for my part, conscious and thus implicitly self-conscious? I cannot first attain consciousness, which is linked to self-consciousness, as a result of learning that others are conscious, as they summon me to be conscious. It would never be possible to upload consciousness, so to speak, to a completely unformed mind. One resolves neither the problem of the infinite regress nor the problem of circular reasoning by increasing the number of self-consciousnesses.

Hegel, who critiqued Fichte's attempt at a solution to the problem at hand in his notoriously difficult book *Phenomenology of Spirit*, was probably the first to have recognized this. Hegel's point is that we do not achieve a better understanding of self-consciousness by claiming that it exists in the plural. If we have a problem with something, it is usually no solution to multiply that thing!

Furthermore, one can ask social interactionism the following: Why can we not successfully convey self-consciousness to a stone? Probably because it does not even have *the potential for self-consciousness*. The potential to be a responsive person must already be present when one is summoned. What one learns through social interaction, in fact, are steering mechanisms and complex ideas of courses of action, roles, and much more. What one cannot learn in this way, however, is how to be conscious and self-conscious as such. Social interactionism fails at this level and, therefore, explains the existence neither of self-consciousness nor of consciousness.

But what now? Does self-consciousness perhaps not exist at all, since every attempt to render it intelligible founders on fundamental problems? We have seen that one cannot explain consciousness by means of consciousness itself. One winds up in inescapable situations – that is, in aporia – if self-consciousness is understood to be a kind of higher-level consciousness.

Consciousness is not a skeleton key for the human mind. The concept(s) of consciousness provide us with only a limited model of the human mind. This can already be seen from the fact that one runs into trouble having to explain consciousness by means of consciousness, which triggers the problems of self-consciousness already outlined above. If we wish to understand ourselves as the minded animals we are, it is not enough to notice that we are conscious. For this reason, neither the philosophy of consciousness alone nor an upgraded version enhanced by research in psychology and neuroscience is the philosopher's stone in the realm of self-knowledge.

We find ourselves in quest of ourselves. If one wants to achieve self-knowledge, it stands to reason to ask first what the self that one would like to know could be. We have now become acquainted with two candidates: consciousness and self-consciousness. Both concepts fail as candidates for answering the question of who or what we really are. They are limited explanatory elements in our self-portrait.

4

Who or What is This Thing
We Call the Self?

"The self" is a rather ominous concept that is used today in a vague manner as a name for the control center of thinking, feeling and willing. Neurocentrics often argue on behalf of the claim that there is no self, since there is no evidence of it in the brain. At the same time, some of them, such as the German philosopher of consciousness Thomas Metzinger (b. 1958), maintain that the self is a kind of simulation that the brain produces, a "transparent model of the self," as Metzinger puts it, which gives us the impression that we are looking through an "ego-tunnel" positioned behind our eyes, as it were, out into a directly accessible reality.[1]

In any case, a contradiction emerges: on the one hand, the self is not supposed to exist – which is a sensational thesis allegedly supported by brain research and the theory of evolution – but, on the other hand it certainly does exist, namely as an ego-tunnel, though not as a permanent thing. Metzinger thinks that we have a multiplicity of different self-models at our disposal, a structure that has been developed by organisms via selection in evolution's icy struggle for survival.

Now, that may well be. In any case, there can be no doubt that at some point we must reckon with an explanation from the bottom up, and thus with the claim that complex neurobiological structures such as the human brain emerged over the course of millions of years of evolution. Metzinger believes that the capacity of organisms to create self-models is "a weapon that emerged in the course of the cognitive arms race."[2] Yet, on closer inspection, he does not achieve his denial of the existence of a self, as this would lead him to a contradiction: on the one hand to claim that there is no self, and on the other hand to give an account of a self that supposedly does not exist. The only "advantage" of this account is that it can easily be embellished with technological and martial metaphors.

I like to look at the human self-model as a neurocomputational weapon, a certain data structure that the brain can activate from time to time, such as when you have to wake up in the morning and integrate your sensory perceptions with your motor behaviour. The ego machine just turns on its phenomenal self, and that is the moment when *you* come to.[3]

It is entirely correct that the self is not an object among other objects. It does not exist within the order of objects which includes rats, cats and mattresses. Whoever thinks it does deceives herself. However, one cannot rid oneself of the self by affirming that we are really no one at all on the basis of metaphors indebted to Darwinist and martial influences.[4] If the self were the organism's conscious user interface, which is experienced as a supervisory control center, a simulation through which a tunnel-like self-model emerges (what an odd account of the self!), it would exist after all.

Simulations exist no less than drops of water. The effect of a spectacular discovery that there is no self, supposedly supported by the latest research on the brain, arises from first fueling the expectation that the self has to be an object which one can look for within the skull, so that one can then come up with the discovery that no self is to be found there. But why should one expect that the self should be a spatio-temporal thing? This expectation already presupposes modern naturalism, and thus the notion that everything which exists can be scientifically researched. Despite assurances to the contrary, the concept of the self is retained, but now in the form of a simulation. The real question, however, is: What is this ominous self, really, such that one can even ask to what extent it is a simulation? And to what extent can research on the brain answer this question?

Furthermore, how does Metzinger know that he is tricked into believing in an ego-tunnel? It is as if someone described on the telephone how it feels to sit in a flight simulator. Such a description, in any case, is not a scientific perspective on inner experience. Thus it may well be that some philosophers of consciousness and some neuroscientists experience themselves as an ego-tunnel that is positioned behind their eyes. And I agree with them that this is a kind of illusion which occurs with the involvement of their brains (which holds true for every illusion that is experienced). The question as to whether such accounts of the theater of consciousness are conceptually coherent, however, cannot be delegated to brain research. The real venue here would be philosophy, which developed the concept of the self.

The reality of illusions

It has long been suspected that, in the case of the self, we could be dealing with an illusion, a position prominently advocated by no lesser figures than Buddha, David Hume and Friedrich Nietzsche. Within this tradition, Hume speaks of a *bundle theory of the self*, which is distinguished from a *substance theory*. The **bundle theory of the self** claims that we find ourselves in many states of consciousness (i.e., states of thinking, feeling and willing), but that the self is no more than the mere sum or aggregate of these states. Accordingly, the self constantly changes depending on what states are present and is nothing which exists continually. The self is thus a bundle.

The **substance theory of the self**, in contrast, holds that the self is an entity which has the experience of thinking, feeling or volition. According to the substance theory, the self is the bearer of mental states, he or she to whom something becomes manifest. It is distinct from all of its states, insofar as it can have them. A substance is the bearer of properties; it has properties. If the self is a substance, it is for example distinct from its thoughts and sensations because it is the very entity that has these thoughts and sensations. According to this theory, the self does not exhaust itself in these states but, rather, is situated at an evaluative distance from them.

The pros and cons of both theories have been pondered for thousands of years. Research on the brain is not of much help in this matter, which is concerned with the conceptual question of whether the self can be coherently conceived of as a bundle. To identify the self with the brain amounts to a form of substance theory (other substance theories identify the self with the soul or with the whole body). If one considers the self to be a simulation that the brain produces in a specific area or by synchronizing many areas, it still remains a substance, but one that is identical with parts of the brain rather than with the whole brain. Hence, if anything, research on the brain imposes a substance theory on us rather than a bundle theory.

An influential branch of contemporary philosophy of consciousness draws on so-called phenomenology, a philosophical orientation that started in the nineteenth century and was definitively elaborated by the German mathematician and philosopher Edmund Husserl. **Phenomenology** (from the Greek *to phainomenon* = what appears) is concerned with different forms of seeming, appearance, illusion, and so forth, as well as their counterparts evidence, intuition, etc. Phenomenology deals with how reality appears to us. From its inception, the self played a central role in it, insofar as the self can be conceived as something to which something else appears. My computer screen appears to me, as do a variety of other objects and subjectively experienced impressions which are all connected in one field of consciousness, which is experienced as unified over spatio-temporal distances.

Many contemporary philosophers of consciousness are affili-ated with phenomenology, even if they are at the same time naturalists – something that differentiates them from the great phenomenologists of the past such as Franz Brentano, Husserl, Heidegger, Sartre and Maurice Merleau-Ponty. In one of his influ-ential books, John Searle has built on an important basic idea of phenomenology, which he sums up very accurately as follows: "The marvellous thing about consciousness is that if you have the illusion that you're conscious then you are conscious. See, the normal appearance/reality distinction doesn't work in quite the same way for consciousness as it does for other phenomena."[5] Searle of course concedes that we can consciously deceive our-selves about all sorts of things: for example, we can believe at first sight that something is a hedgehog when it is really a cactus, or briefly think that something tastes sweet but then quickly learn better. In all of this, however, we do not deceive ourselves about the fact that we are undergoing a conscious experience. As was mentioned above, many are convinced that this is what lies behind Descartes' famous statement "I think, therefore I am," though considered in historical terms it is problematic to equate what Descartes calls "thinking" (*cogitare*) with our later concept of the self. But thereby hangs a tale.

What is crucial is that consciousness is another case that displays the typical structure of the mind in general, namely that, when it comes to the mind or spirit, even an illusion is a kind of reality. If I experience a Fata Morgana, there is of course no water where I believe to be seeing water. Nevertheless, I experience water and may perhaps rush thirstily to the water's apparent location. Even if consciousness is on the whole an illusory structure that our body, as a genetic copying machine programmed purely for self-preser-vation, produces completely unconsciously, this illusion still exists. Furthermore, it would be the decisive factor for us conscious living beings. As Searle, once again, puts it: "Consciousness is our life . . . So what's special about consciousness is that as far as human life is concerned it is pretty much the precondition of everything important."[6]

Puberty-reductionism and the toilet theory

Neurocentrism's typical strategy of claiming the territory of self-hood and self-knowledge typically consists in "naturalizing" the self – that is, incorporating it into a subject area of phenomena that can be scientifically explained and understood. In this way, the self loses its mysterious character. The **naturalization of a phenomenon** is the attempt to treat a phenomenon that can apparently not be investigated scientifically as something that, contrary to its appearance, can be scientifically articulated and researched. Here, "natural" accordingly means something like "potential object of natural scientific research," which already raises innumerable questions, since it is anything but clear what allows something to be scientifically investigated.

A slightly different concept for this explanatory procedure is *reductionism*. **Reductionism** in this context is the reduction of a concept that does not seem to be established in a scientific framework to a scientific equivalent. For a reduction to be meaningfully made, there must be a *reason for it*. In a given subject area, discoveries need to have been made that seem to entail that we can achieve a better explanation of a phenomenon only by reducing some concepts by which we characterize it into the language of science.

Accordingly, **neuroreductionism** is the reduction of a phenomenon that, at first glance, is not subject to neuroscientific explanation to a discourse capable of couching the phenomenon in relevant neurobiological terms. Puberty is a simple everyday example of such a process that could be cited here, as it offers a reason for the reduction. On the one hand, we are familiar with puberty as continuous sequence of behavioral changes: rebelliousness, fighting against parental authority, the withdrawal into a private sphere, changes in the pitch of a boy's voice, and so forth. On the other hand, all of this has to do with the concomitant phenomenon of hormonal changes associated with sexual maturation. So far, so good. A reductive explanation at this point tells us that the system of behavioral changes can be reduced to processes that can be neuroscientifically explained. If one wishes actually to explain adequately what is going on in puberty, one has to take facts about hormones and their effects on the human brain into consideration. The reductionist view claims that, in the case of puberty, one need not take anything more into consideration. Rebelliousness or criticism of authority such as parents and teachers in this perspective is nothing but a byproduct, a concomitant phenomenon of hormonal changes, and thus nothing with which one should be concerned if one is interested in the objective facts of the matter. The behavioral phenomena typical of puberty can accordingly be reduced to hormonal changes, with the result that one can leave aside changes of behavior when offering an explanation of the phenomena.

At this point, it is important to take into account a distinction that is often overlooked in public debates on these issues. There are at least two kinds of reductionism. **Ontology** (from the ancient Greek *to on* = being and *logos* = rational discourse or theory) is concerned with the question of what it means for something to exist. Correspondingly, there is an **ontological reductionism**, which claims that a phenomenon that does not appear to be natural exists only as a phenomenon, as an appearance, behind which lies a natural process and nothing else. An example of this would be the reduction of pure water to H_2O: viewed objectively, pure water is nothing but H_2O. One can, at least so the reductionist believes, ontologically reduce pure water to H_2O. Philosophers often cite as an example the reduction of perceived temperature to the average kinetic energy of particles, which allows us to bring thermodynamics to bear instead of sensations of heat. In this way, temperature can be reduced to properties of a particle system, with the result that one can leave our sensations out of the picture, in a truly ontologically objective manner. **Theory reductionism**, in contrast, is more modest and claims only that a phenomenon that can be described with non-scientific concepts can be more adequately described with scientific concepts.

If one now applies this to puberty, it is already no longer clear which form of reductionism is even in question. Does one wish to say that puberty can be described by taking hormonal changes into consideration, or does one wish to say that puberty is nothing but hormonal changes?

Neuroreductionism arrives on the scene with a typical nineteenth-century style cockiness by attempting an ontological reduction and a theory reduction at the same time. And that is precisely the problem. In the nineteenth century, neuroreductionism was advocated in its original form by Karl Vogt (1817–1895), a Swiss-German scientist who, in the middle of the century, denied the freedom of the human will in the manner that has become customary today. Vogt was notorious in his time for declaring that "Thoughts stand in the same relation to the brain as the gall does to the liver or urine does to the kidneys."[7] If one ontologically reduces puberty according to such a model, then the moodiness of a pubescent youth is nothing but hormonal fluctuation. But what is that supposed to tell us about our association with each other? Can we really deal with the behavior of our children as if it was literally nothing but hormonal fluctuation? And what about other complex forms of behavior which we classify as crime?

In his *Phenomenology of Spirit*, Hegel, in his inimitable way, anticipated and dismissed with sharp irony theses such as Vogt's. In a famous passage, he writes:

> Brain fibres and the like, when regarded as the being of Spirit, are no more than a merely hypothetical reality existing only in one's head, not the true reality which has an *outer* existence, and which can be felt and seen; when they exist *out there*, when they are seen, they are dead objects, and then no longer pass for the being of Spirit ... the Notion underlying this idea is that Reason takes itself to be *all thinghood*, even *purely objective* thinghood itself; but it is this only *in the Notion*, or only the Notion is the truth of this idea; and the purer the Notion itself is, the sillier an idea it becomes when its content is in the form, not of the Notion, but of picture-thinking ... The *depth* which Spirit brings forth from within – but only as far as its picture-thinking consciousness where it lets it remain – and the *ignorance* of this consciousness about what it really is saying, are the same conjunction of the high and the low which, in the living being, Nature naively expresses when it combines the organ of its highest fulfilment, the organ of generation, with the organ of pissing. The infinite judgment, *qua* infinite, would be the fulfilment of life that comprehends itself; the consciousness of the infinite judgment that remains at the level of picture-thinking behaves as pissing.[8]

Vogt's toilet theory of thinking, as we can now call it following Hegel, originally intended to point out to us that our thinking is not a divine spark but, rather, a natural organic process. Yet Vogt is by no means only a coarse critic of religious or theological conceptions of the soul (as was, for instance, Karl Marx) against which he marshals the brain. Vogt and other neurocentrists of his time, such as Ludwig Büchner (1824–1899, brother of the famous writer Georg Büchner), who was very much read and discussed at that time, were, incidentally, severe racists and misogynists – as were, unfortunately, the overwhelming majority of scientists and thinkers at this time, not merely the neurocentrists of the day. In his bestseller *Force and Matter: Empirico-Philosophical Studies, Intelligibly Rendered* (1855), Büchner explains (supposed) differences in behavior between the "Caucasian race" and the "other varieties inferior to" them with reference to the physiology of the brain, since according to this kind of reasoning a difference in behavior must always be reduced to a function of the brain: "The natives of Australia, in whom the superior parts of the brain are almost wanting, possess neither great intellectual capacity nor any sense of art or moral worth. All attempts of the English to civilize them have hitherto failed."[9] The following argument of Büchner's, which is still popular today in a somewhat better concealed form, is not much more pleasant: "It is known that the female sex is intellectually inferior to the male sex. Peacock found that the average weight of the male brain considerably exceeds that of the female."[10] Were these remarks not all too pathetic nonsense, they would almost border on irony, when Büchner, on the same page no less, supports his claim by citing a "Dr *Geist*" (Dr *Spirit*!) from a "hospital" who is also supposed to have proven it.

One of the major weaknesses of ontological neuroreductionism lies in the fact that it identifies social and historically variable (institutional) channels of behavior in natural terms. This is also known as **essentialism** (from the Latin *essentia* = essence) – i.e., the assumption of an immutable essence for which one is not responsible, but which one also cannot change. One cannot fundamentally change processes of the brain with only persuasive coaxing any less than one can suppress hormonal changes that way. If there were a female brain, one could do nothing about it through processes of social emancipation. Women would then be determined to behave in certain ways by their specifically grown brains. I hope none of my readers believes such crap (Trump voters and racist Brexiteers probably did not read up to this point). Given the weaknesses of all-out reductionism, it would be more advisable for neurocentrism to adopt the more modest strategy of theory reductionism. Certainly puberty can be better understood if one also explains it neuroscientifically. However, theory reductionism is not a spectacular insight and it also cannot promise to replace our traditionally developed modes of accounting for human action by the fancy neurospeak of the future.

Self is god

All of this now in fact leads us to the self, the small god upon the earth. There is much talk of the self these days. There are questions of to what extent egoism is supposed to be justified, of self-employment, and much more. The I or ego can be found in everyday application from iTunes to iRobots. Neurocentrists vacillate between identifying the self with the brain and denying its existence. Yet who or what is this self after all?

At this point, it is advisable to look at the history of mind or spirit. One of the first who substantivized the personal pronoun "I" [*Ich*] in the German language to "the self" [*das Ich*] or "this self" was a medieval philosopher who is usually referred to as Meister Eckhart (1260–1328). "Meister" (as translation of *magister*) in this case basically means professor of philosophy and theology. Meister Eckhart was accused of heresy in Cologne by the Inquisition and died during his trial in Avignon, where his main doctrines were posthumously condemned as heretical. It is precisely his concept of the self that can be cited as a reason for the fact that the ecclesiastical authorities of his time were not particularly pleased with him. Later this concept of the self was seen as the opening move of the Enlightenment, which can thus be found as early as the Middle Ages (as is so much of what is considered to be modern – that is, neither ancient nor medieval). In a famous sermon – mind you, not incriminated by the Inquisition – Meister Eckhart said:

> *Therefore I pray God that he may quit me of God*, for my unconditioned being is above God and all distinctions, insofar as we conceive God as the origin of creatures . . . If I had not been, there would have been no God: I am thus the cause of the fact that "God" exists; If I had not been, God would not be "God" . . . in bursting forth I discover that God and I are One.[11]

This is a much more radical move than cheap contemporary atheism which merely denies the existence of God. For Meister Eckhart points out that those who speak of God actually create an image of themselves. His name for this structure – which indeed is the structure of a *Geist* or a mind – is the self, the I.

Meister Eckhart developed a theory of "the agent of the soul" and hypothesized a "spark" of "the soul" in us.[12] This is connected to his theory of the self. On closer inspection, his idea is quite radical, and it rests on a simple line of thought. Suppose I pick up a coffee mug. I am now looking at my coffee mug. There thus exists a relation between me and the coffee mug, the relation of seeing. To see something means to perceive something by means of our senses. I thus perceive the coffee mug. Now let us pose the question: Am I identical to this perception or am I to be found somewhere in this perception in such a way that I can grasp my identity with an object given to me in perception? I am not the coffee mug; that much is clear. But do I come into existence by being that which perceives the coffee mug? This also does not add up, since in any case I cannot strictly be identical with that which perceives the coffee mug because I, the same thinker, can perceive many other things too. If I exist at all, I am thus someone who can perceive coffee mugs and at the same time someone who can perceive other things too. I am still myself when I perceive the lamp.

Thus I can perceive all kinds of things, and as long as I live it is an open question what I will perceive in the future. Let us assume that it is possible to perceive myself as I am perceiving a coffee mug. If self = brain, this is quite possible. I would then perceive myself in a functional magnetic resonance imaging (fMRI), for instance. To be sure, neuroscientists to this point have told us that this is not yet feasible, because the self has yet to be found. It is unclear how multiple streams of information can be incorporated into a unity at all at the level of our perception, which is known as the **binding problem**. Not to mention the question of how all the processes that are relevant for perception could be bound together in such a way that a self could be perceived in them. But let us assume for the time being that this will be solved in the future. Then I could see my self flickering in the fMRI. Yet, this self would still not be the self that we are looking for. The self perceived in the fMRI would be no more strictly identical to the perceiving self than in the case of my perception of the coffee mug. The very reason why I cannot be identical to a coffee mug I perceive counts against identifying myself with any object I can perceive by means of an fMRI! According to Meister Eckhart, then, we thinkers of thoughts are categorically distinct from any object we could ever perceive or think of.

With this basic line of thought, which I have here extended to the topic of the brain, Meister Eckhart discovered the topic of the radical non-objectivity of the self. This idea lies concealed behind the modern concept of *autonomy* – that is, our giving laws to ourselves (from the ancient Greek *autos* = self and *nomos* = law). What Meister Eckhart is saying amounts to the claim that the self cannot be strictly identical with any object that it perceives. The self only falls under laws it gives to itself; it cannot be strictly determined by the objects it perceives. Meister Eckhart proceeds so far on this basis as to consider the self "godlike," since the distinction between objects and the divine mind, in his view, is one of monotheism's fundamental insights.

If one subscribes to this line of thought and cuts God out of the picture, one quite quickly arrives at the idea that there is an all-knowing self that strives to perceive reality as a whole and to unlock its secrets. This profoundly theological model forms the basis for the early modern understanding of science, a fact which today is too often pushed aside into oblivion. The self does not merely want to be godlike, it wants to be God and hence strikes him from its world picture in order to take his place. This is how science started occupying the very position of religion. This does not mean that science is just another religion. However, it does mean that science currently occupies the position of religion, which is ultimately just as bad.

Actually to cut God out of the picture and not still remain secretly in the clutches of theology presupposes that one has developed another concept of the self, a genuinely modern one. Otherwise we will be stuck with the fantasy of a creation liberated from God. The paradox is that the early modern scientific image of the world is actually taken from Judeo-Christian-Islamic monotheism. The difference is that nature is radically emptied of God, and in the place of the divine spectator of the world-spectacle there now sits the thinking, critically examining self.

This corresponds to Max Weber's thesis of the "disenchantment of the world," which for him is by no means a specifically modern phenomenon, but which in his eyes begins with the prophets of the Old Testament, who, in the name of the newly revealed desert God, turn against the mages of neighboring polytheistic religions and in this way disenchant nature. All enchantment lies in God's hands. Nature turns into a desert, into the absence of God from his creation.

The best illustration of the theological fantasies of the scientific image of the world is found in the already mentioned new edition of the American television documentary series *Cosmos*. The narrator, the astrophysicist Neil deGrasse Tyson, presents himself as capable of swiftly moving through space-time at will in his spaceship (his vessel of imagination) so as to inform the audience about the Big Bang, quite distant galaxies, gravity, and so forth. His spaceship can also shrink down at will, doing so in order to make the universe visible at different scales of magnitude. He suggestively names it "the Ship of the Imagination," though in fact, on close examination, it reveals more about the imagination of Tyson than it does about the history of science. Granted, the scientists and their history are lucidly illustrated by means of the animated illustrations of Seth MacFarlane (the creator of the cartoon series *Family Guy*). In many regards, the series is a paradigmatic example of successful science education for the broad public and, thus, welcome in our dark times of widespread superstition and ignorance (a very serious problem for the US these days as well as for the rest of the world). We could use more of such programs on our television, but perhaps with a little less ideology.

The critical point can be grasped especially well from a scene in the first season that is concerned with the age of the planet earth. The narrator heads to the rim of the Grand Canyon with the Ship of the Imagination. In order to be able to show the audience the hidden strata where fossils can be found, he raises his hands – like Moses or a small god – whereupon the strata are parted from each other with an Old Testament-like roar and hidden treasure is uncovered. The show's production here suggests, as at many other points, that the narrator is pretty much like God, who can be present at will in all places and at all times of creation, as well as on all scales. The narrator even works miracles, since it would be a miracle if someone could stretch apart the strata of the Grand Canyon at will, or (as in another episode) increase the gravitational force in Manhattan from a g-force of 1 all the way up to a g-force of 100 and can then reduce it again to the same degree, so that water hydrants are crushed by their own mass and furniture movers are flying through the streets. The Ship of the Imagination is an example of the fantasy of the omnipotence of thought.

The thought that lies concealed behind the self often plays a role where one would least suspect it at first sight. In particular, the self comes to fruition against the background of the modern conception of absolute objectivity. **Absolute objectivity** is a vantage point from which the universe can be observed as if no intelligent observers with their species-specific conditions for knowledge were present. Absolute objectivity tries to break free from the obvious fact that no one knows anything except from a subjective standpoint. Knowledge in light of this counts as more objective the less it is marked by the fact that it is acquired from a subjective standpoint.

Thomas Nagel, whom we have already come across a number of times, has summed this up with his famous metaphor and rejection of the "view from nowhere." In *Why the World Does Not Exist*, I spoke in this connection of the "world without spectators."[13] Many believe that science should strive for absolute objectivity. Ideal knowledge would then consist in developing a world-view in which our standpoint would no longer play any role.

Neither Nagel nor I deny that we in fact succeed in dissociating from our standpoints to some extent and that we accordingly achieve objective knowledge. As already discussed above (p. 76), Nagel even considers our capacity to dissociate from ourselves as a foundation for ethics. As a matter of fact, if I want to restrict claims to ownership and to share resources with other people, I must be able to understand that objects are not simply out there so as to belong to me. Without the capacity to empathize with others and to desist from doing whatever one wants or evaluating a situation however one likes, one could never understand how any kind of ethically or politically relevant decision would be possible. At most, one could suppose that the egoistical struggle for survival of citizens or other members of communities engenders the illusion that one can renounce standpoints, just as we saw in the account of egoism above. Our capacity to examine critically the relation of interests that belongs to our beliefs is connected to our capacity for theoretical abstraction. Traditionally, this capacity is known as *reason*.

To be sure, no one can adopt the paradoxical standpoint of standpointlessness, since it contains a contradiction in itself. Hence, this standpoint can remain at best an ultimately incoherent ideal that we strive for but, in principle, can never attain. One must become conscious of this fact, since otherwise one takes on God's theological role without even noticing it.

Fichte: the almost forgotten grandmaster of the self

The topic of the self or the I is at the center of the thought of the German philosopher Johann Gottlieb Fichte (1762–1814). Fichte was made famous by Kant, who anonymously published Fichte's first work, *Attempt at a Critique of All Revelation*, with the help of his publisher, so that readers at the time believed that it was a new book by Kant himself. In the wake of this event, in 1794 Fichte obtained his first position as professor in Jena, which he eventually had to resign due to a harsh dispute over his supposed atheism. Remarkably, Fichte was a thorn in the side of Goethe, who was then the minister responsible for the University of Jena. Goethe did not think much of the idea that the self is a small god on earth, since he was instead of the opinion that the divine can be found in nature rather than in us. He thus indirectly supported the demise of Fichte in Jena.

We can already conclude from the title of his first work that it was no accident that Fichte was considered to be close to atheism. Fichte, incidentally, later became the founding rector of the Friedrich Wilhelm University, which is known today as the Humboldt University of Berlin, and was socially and politically active throughout his lifetime. As a prodigy from a poor part of the Eastern German countryside, he was from a young age promoted by a nobleman who was impressed by the young man's stunning foreign-language skills. In contemporary philosophy, Fichte still plays a role, as he was the first philosopher who established a conceptual connection between the autonomy of the self and its recognition by others. He thus also became the originator of social interactionism, discussed above (p. 124), on the basis of which he founded his philosophy of law and the state.

At any rate, Fichte is particularly well known for the fact that he took up the question of who or what the self really is. In this context, he developed his philosophical program, which he called "the science of knowledge." His basic thought is easy to understand, and throughout his career Fichte never stopped wondering why so many people apparently did not want to understand him. Fichte's writings, at first sight, are difficult or even incomprehensible, simply because he attempted to avoid unnecessary conceptual ballast or complicated debts to the history of philosophy, as he actually wanted everyone who was interested to be able to understand him. He invented a new language for philosophy based on ordinary German in order to undermine traditional authorities and to claim more territory for the radical freedom of thought. However, one must carry out a bit of translation work to reconstruct his ideas for our time.

In order to do this, let us depart from the **basic thought of the science of knowledge:** There are distinct domains of knowledge whose fundamental features we are taught in elementary school: mathematics, geography, English, physical education, and so forth. What we learn about in the course of studying these subjects are not only matters such as multiplication tables, spelling and the names of capitals. We also learn how to learn something. School is not just about collecting information; it is about collecting information about how to collect information in the future, how to become a responsible knower. Accordingly, one might ask what the common denominator for all domains of knowledge is, since all of them must have a common form that links them to one another. There seems to be an overall structure of learning something, of coming to know something. This is why Fichte departs from the assumption that all domains of knowledge are connected despite the fact that they respectively convey distinct substantive contents. Despite its distinct contents, according to Fichte, knowledge must nevertheless have a unified form.

And this is precisely Fichte's Archimedean point. His science of knowledge examines how the form and content of knowledge are connected. His basic question is actually as old as Plato's philosophy. Even today it is still lodged in our word for mathematics, since this word is derived from the ancient Greek verb *manthano*, which means "to learn." For Plato, mathematics is a matter of learning how to learn something, by gradually being led to an insight that can be taught to all human beings. He illustrates this in his dialogue *Meno*, in which an uneducated slave is taught fundamental geometrical insights in a step-by-step manner. Hence, class distinctions according to Plato and Fichte play no role when it comes to our coming to know something. As knowers or rational animals we do not differ with respect to our rationality. Fichte thus aims, as Plato did before him, to demonstrate to us human beings that we are all endowed with reason. This means that we can learn from others, because we share the capacity to know something with other human beings. This is **rationalist universalism**, which is a basic assumption of the Enlightenment.

Furthermore, Fichte supposes that the form of all knowledge stems from the fact that we have the capacity to understand. Thus, even though we aim at absolute objectivity, we must still be able to understand what we find out. That is, even the limiting case of absolute objectivity remains related to us. Against this backdrop, Fichte speaks not merely of the self or "I" [*Ich*] but of the "we" [*wir*], which Hegel took up in a much cited formulation: "'I' that is 'We' and 'We' that is 'I'."[14] What *I* know is something *we* can know. I can tell you what I know and you thereby come to know it, and vice versa. Knowledge is essentially shareable. Even in the limiting case of absolute objectivity, there is still a distinction between the self or "I" and what is not the self, between the knower and what is known.

In this context, Fichte introduces the notion of an absolute I. This just means that the self is released from or categorically distinct from what is known (the Latin term *absolutum* means nothing more than "that which is detached"). On this basis, Fichte develops three fundamental propositions, which become the supporting pillars of his philosophy of the self. These should be kept in mind when one speaks of the self today, since Fichte's basic ideas have had a lasting influence all the way to Freud and Sartre, which still resonates in our contemporary psychological vocabulary. If one disregards this history, it is all too easy to fall prey to thinking that "the self" is something so utterly familiar that we can ask whether it is an illusion or not. Fichte had to defend himself against various misunderstandings of his view throughout his lifetime and as a reaction to this came to the conclusion that "The majority of men could sooner be brought to believe themselves a piece of lava in the moon than to take themselves for a *self*."[15] As neurocentrism proves, in this respect nothing has changed since that time.

The three pillars of the science of knowledge

Let us very briefly go over the three tenets of the science of knowledge. They will help us to finally come to terms with the self (and therefore with ourselves).

The **first tenet of the science of knowledge** is: "I = I [*Ich = Ich*]."[16] Of course, that sounds trivial, but it is not. One might think that this proposition is just an instance of the claim that everything is identical to itself, that everything is what it is. Then the proposition would be a **tautology**. But consider the following:

The round square = the round square;

or

The current king of France = the current king of France.

If the round square or the current king of France are identical to themselves, then apparently there is a difference between self-identical things that exist and those that do not. There are no round squares and there is no longer a current king of France (Nicolas Sarkozy was an exception . . .). The problem does not arise for the self or "I," however, since the term "I" means nothing more than the knower. We want to develop a science of knowledge and thus think about how it is possible that different domains of knowledge are connected. "I" is the name for the fact that there is a knower. One cannot deny this. *In particular, if for some reason one might feel tempted to deny that anyone knows anything, one could not even know that there is any reason to believe this!* That is Fichte's scaled-down version of Descartes' cogito. "I think, therefore I am" becomes, in Fichte, "I = I" or "I am I." The first tenet thus guarantees that in the realm of knowledge there is at least one thing that is identical to itself: the "I" or the knower. If I know that it is raining right now in London, and then I also know that 2 + 2 = 4, I am not split into two separate beings: one who knows that it is raining, and another who knows that 2 + 2 = 4. I can be identical to myself as knower on various occasions and with respect to different contents of knowledge.

The **second tenet of the science of knowledge** is (slightly simplified): "self ≠ not-self." The second tenet expresses precisely the by now familiar idea of absolute objectivity. It tells us that we have a concept of a reality beyond ourselves. Stones, meadows, neutrinos, galaxies, mountains, and so forth, can be subsumed under the concept of a not-self. They fall within the category of objects that do not think. Fichte also calls this category "nature," which immediately led Goethe among others to raise objections, since he did not think that the self ought to be excluded from nature. Yet Fichte here has been historically triumphant, since with the second tenet he got to the bottom of the idea of nature as not-self, the idea of absolute objectivity. Nevertheless, in so doing he was not of the opinion that nature simply is what it is; rather, he thought that the concept of nature as a totality of everything that belongs to the not-self is a product of the self's abstraction. The concept of nature plays a role in our theories of reality, as it classifies some phenomena we encounter as natural and others as social or mental.

To be sure, it was Fichte's intention to save the self from nature in this way. He was interested in telling us apart from merely natural objects, to draw a principled distinction between thinkers and things. As a consequence, he completely purged nature of traces of the self, so that subsequently it was no longer evident how the self could ever belong to nature again.

This dilemma has been a concern to the present day, to the extent that, by "nature," we understand everything which we investigate from the standpoint of absolute objectivity. By definition, this excludes our subjective standpoints. The self became in this way radically opposed to nature, so that the temptation immediately arose in Fichte's wake likewise to cut it out of the picture entirely. Neurocentrism would like to explain the self away by attempting to translate everything that has the form of the self into the language of neurochemistry or evolutionary psychology. Neurocentrism is a violent way of integrating the self into nature – that is, into a domain which in principle cannot serve as a home for the self. It, thus, is a form of radical alienation of the self from its world.

Fichte struggled mightily against this – and with good reason. The conception of absolute objectivity disregards the fact that it forms nature into a unified concept. Let us follow a simple line of thought. What do protons, bosons, photons and neurons actually have in common? It is not only the fact that they all end with "ons" (otherwise we would have to add lemons to the standard model of particle physics). In addition to such particles, molecules and galaxies, the Big Bang, gravity, bacteria, tardigrades, supernovae and space-time belong to nature. Thus, again: What do all these objects, laws or facts actually have in common, such that we can actually recognize that they belong to the same realm?

And here Fichte replies: they have in common the fact that they play a role in an account from the standpoint of absolute objectivity. But that means that all of these objects, laws and facts are connected within the framework of a theory. Strictly speaking, there has been no such theory up to this point; there is no unified theory of nature that is recognized as some particular science. Physics has never achieved this. But why are we sure that there is even a unified realm of nature that we can investigate in the mode of absolute objectivity? Where do we derive our concept of nature from if not from nature itself?

The key to answering this question lies in the fact that the standpoint of absolute objectivity cannot itself be investigated at all from the standpoint of absolute objectivity. The idea of absolute objectivity is a product of abstraction that arises from the fact that we put ourselves to one side while investigating. In so doing, we do not disappear but keep ourselves out of the picture that we are forming of the actual situation we are in as thinkers of thoughts and builders of theories.

More recently, Nagel and Searle have reformulated precisely these thoughts wholly in keeping with Fichte's intention. They both refer to the fact that our ideal of objectivity is formulated from a standpoint that cannot itself be absolutely objective. The distinction between our subjective standpoint, the self, and the domain of objects under investigation from the objective standpoint, nature or the not-self, cannot be derived from the objective standpoint alone. These theories were not forged first in laboratories but in social relations, which Nagel and Searle do not foreground, but which Fichte before Marx recognized.

Notice that it does not follow from all this that absolute objectivity does not exist – i.e., that neutrinos are "socially constructed." Neutrinos actually do exist, and their hypothesis and ultimate discovery forms a fascinating chapter of the last century's history of science. However, what does follow is that it is impossible for absolute objectivity to exist independently of a context in which subjectivity plays a role. An all-encompassing, purely objective world picture, in which the self does not feature, is radically incomplete and impossible. In the first place, all-encompassing world-views are incoherent anyhow – which was the theme of my earlier book *Why the World Does Not Exist*. Yet we do not have to rehearse the arguments developed there in detail. All we need to do here is simply realize that our claims about what belongs to nature as a whole are made from a standpoint. This standpoint investigates things and states of affairs in the mode of absolute objectivity, in which we are trained by modern scientific methods. Yet these methods and thus the framework of absolute objectivity itself simply cannot be investigated by using these methods on it. There is no natural science of natural science, which is why until now there have indeed been the most absurd neurodisciplines – neuro-German studies, neurosociology or neurotheology. But there is no neuro-neuroscience, which would then have to be trumped in turn by a neuro-neuro-neuroscience. At some point or other we will always encounter ourselves as the originators of the subjective standpoint we inhabit even when engaging in dissociating from it and observing natural phenomena, as if we were not present.

With this in mind, we can now turn to the **third tenet of the science of knowledge**. One must let this dissolve on the tongue, as it were, before I can explain it in a way that is understandable for those of us native to the twenty-first century: "*In the self I oppose a divisible not-self to the divisible self.*"[17] There are three protagonists in this tenet:

1   the self
2   the divisible self
3   the divisible not-self.

The tenet sounds odd, but it is easy to reconstruct. In distinction from the divisible self, "the self" is the general circumstance that you share with me: the circumstance that we can know something. Here it is important to keep in view an important difference between *knowledge* and *representation*, which is very easily blurred today.

From Plato up to contemporary epistemology – which among other things is intensely concerned with the question of what knowledge is – one speaks of the **standard definition of knowledge**. This runs as follows: *knowledge is justified true belief*. Behind this lies the following idea, which was for the first time developed by Plato in his dialogue *Theaetetus*, the foundational text of epistemology. Ask yourself for a start whether someone can know something that is false. Can I know that Angela Merkel has seventeen index fingers? How am I then supposed to know that she only has two (at least, to this point)? This is known as a **truth condition**. It entails that one can only know something that is true. What one knows is a fact, something that is true.

Next question: Can you know something that you do not

believe at all? Suppose I were to tell you that I know that $2 + 2 = 4$. Would you answer back: Do you really believe that? And what if I were then to let you know that I am by no means convinced of it. That would be strange. Hence there has been a discussion lasting millennia about the relation and difference of knowledge, certainty and belief. One cannot know anything that one does not consider to be true with a high degree of certainty. If I know something, I should be willing to bet on it – at least under the right circumstances, in which I have no reason to question or restrict my own knowledge.

Now perhaps you will want to point out to me, however, that we are almost never absolutely certain. We often get it wrong even though we are certain that we are right. Likewise, one can persuade people that they know something which they really do not know at all – which is a condition of possibility of ideology. We often make others and ourselves believe that we know certain things we do not know, as well as that we do not know certain things we actually do know (think about the incredibly stupid US debates about evolution vs. creation or debates about climate change; of course, animal species are not created by a very powerful dude from heaven from mud, and, of course, there is man-made climate change).

The third condition for knowledge, the **justification condition**, has it that one cannot know anything which one cannot defend with good reasons as soon as legitimate doubts are raised. If I say that I know exactly where Angela Merkel is right now, and you question this claim, I can point out to you that I just saw her on live television giving a speech in Berlin or that an acquaintance of mine just called me because she saw the chancellor shopping with her bodyguards. To know something presupposes that one can provide good reasons for what one considers to be true. It also means, at the very least, to consider something that is true to be true on the basis of sound reasoning or some other kind of legitimate evidence, along with quite firm belief. In this sense, the testimony of our senses typically serves as a good reason to believe something and to claim knowledge.

Knowledge is essentially shareable. If I call my wife and ask her whether our dog is sleeping in the living room, she can take a look and confirm this. My wife then knows through simple observation (which is a good reason for her knowledge) that the dog is sleeping in the living room. Knowledge is shareable and communicable. Fichte refers to this aspect of knowledge as "the divisible" or "shareable self." If I tell you what I know, you can thereby come to know it yourself. We can share knowledge.

What I cannot share with my wife, however, is her *representation* of the scene. If she goes into the living room and sees our dog there, she sees her from a particular perspective; she has particular feelings about the dog, perceives particular objects that I would perhaps not pay attention to at all, because she has other background assumptions and experiences, many of which are unconsciously processed. Our representations are embedded in a background, as Searle calls it, thus in a prevailingly unconscious concurrent repertoire of capacities and assumptions.[18] Representations are not shareable, they are private.

By a **representation** here, we can understand the psychological episode that occurs when one processes sensory impressions or calls to mind impressions that have been processed with the aid of our imagination. The concept of representation, in turn, introduces difficulties, which can be avoided if one understands representations as those pieces of information that are accessible to an individual on the basis of his or her specific situation considered as a whole, which includes the fact that the individual is located in a specific place at a specific time. I do not know exactly what my wife is representing and imagining as she shares her knowledge of the dog's whereabouts with me, and vice versa. Even if one knows a person very well, one cannot step into their world of imagination in this sense and perceive it by viewing it from the inside – as occurs, for instance, in *Being John Malkovich*. No one except John Malkovich can be John Malkovich. However, John Malkovich can easily share his knowledge with us by communicating it to us. In order to do this, we do not have to step into his mind and merge with him in an impossible manner.

Hence one can communicate representations but cannot literally share them. In contrast, one can both communicate and share knowledge. That simply follows from the concept of knowledge, which I would here like to summarize once more: I can know the same thing that someone else knows if both of us recognize the same state of affairs as being true on the basis of having good reasons for our recognition of the fact. We then find ourselves in the same state of knowledge. But I cannot have exactly the same representation as another person, since I would then have to be that other person.

Fichte's fundamental idea is to reject the notion that we can always only know something because we have representations that arise in us as a result of the stimulation of our nerve endings or any other kind of information-processing. Ideas structurally similar to the neurocentrism of our day circulated at his time and were employed to call our knowledge into question. Fichte points out that these arguments conflate knowledge and representation. His ultimate aim is the defense of enlightenment, knowledge and facts against the dark forces of anti-modernism, which are once more on the rise in our allegedly "post-truth" or "post-factual" era. It is simply an ideological lie that we live in a post-truth era, a lie designed to convince the people that they do not know what they actually know.

Knowledge that can be communicated and shared is universal. "The self" is Fichte's name for the universal dimension of knowledge. It is the universal knowledge subject. "The divisible self," in contrast, is Fichte's name for the fact that many thinkers can know the same thing. "The divisible not-self" is everything which one can know in the mode of absolute objectivity. You and I know the same thing (the same divisible not-self) if we know the speed of light or the mass of certain elementary particles.

One could draw on Fichte to justify contemporary scientific culture by enriching the latter with the self rather than letting it conflate the self with the brain, as it currently does – and thus with something that belongs to the category of the divisible not-self (nature) rather than to the adequate category of a thinker. Even so, one would then be on the cusp of the beginning of the nineteenth century, regressing behind neurocentrism. Yet philosophy did not end back then; rather, it was just getting started on the right track.

In the human being nature opens her eyes and sees that she exists

We now know what the self is: it is the subject of universal knowledge. To be a self means to know something and to be able to communicate it. In no way does it mean to be alone with oneself or to dwell like a homunculus in the brain. That said, it is already clear: the self is not a brain.

However, Fichte's philosophy of the self runs into problems as soon as one poses the question of how the self is actually related to nature. In Fichte's lifetime, Schelling, the major thinker of German Romanticism, formulated an all-decisive objection, the aftermath of which, incidentally, made existentialism, Marxism and modern depth psychology possible. As if that were not enough, Schelling's student Johannes Müller (1801–1858) ranks alongside Charles Darwin (if not actually on the same level) as one of the most important biologists of the nineteenth century. His formulation of the **law of specific nerve energies** is still found in neuroscience textbooks up to the present day. This law states that the objective structure of an external stimulus does not determine a sense-impression; rather, the stimulated sense organ (in other words, the respective nerve cells) is responsible for the modality in which a stimulus is processed as a perception (i.e., seeing, hearing, tasting). Considerations of this kind imposed themselves upon Müller, since he takes Schelling's objection against Fichte seriously, an objection which ultimately led to so-called *Naturphilosophie*.

Naturphilosophie poses the question of how nature must be constituted if at some point in the course of its development beings could arise who are capable of conceiving of nature's development. Reflections of this kind are today familiar under the heading of the *anthropic principle*. The **anthropic principle** (from the ancient Greek *ho anthropos* = human being) in general is the view that the observable universe is manifestly suited to the development of living beings who observe this universe. Indeed, we are such beings who have developed within the universe. This is expressed metaphorically in the claim that nature wakes up, as it were, in the human being and attains consciousness of herself, originally a Romantic metaphor, which in our times Nagel took up in his most recent book, *Mind and Cosmos*, explicitly borrowing it from Schelling.[19]

In fact, it is remarkable that we are able to understand nature at all. This can be considered simply amazing, since in any case there is no evidence that nature was literally waiting around so that living beings with minds to figure her out would develop and begin to decipher the laws of nature. That there are living beings with minds does not appear to be necessary, at any rate. That is, we can easily imagine an alternative course of evolution in which living beings like us, who attempt to conceive of nature and their own place in it, would never have emerged at all. If our own existence could not have happened, if we are contingent, there is the worry that we might not be in any position whatsoever to figure out nature. However, we only discovered that we are contingent through figuring out something about nature (in particular, evolutionary theory as the only correct explanatory framework of the origin of the plurality of species on our planet). Hence, there are limitations on contingency, as our existence cannot bring with it the utter unintelligibility of nature. Otherwise, we would be in a position to wonder how much we might ever know about nature. Therefore, the very fact that we are able to work out a scientifically respectable sense of our own contingency proves that nature is at least in part intelligible, understandable and knowable by us. This is the basic structure of Schelling's overall philosophical project and his *Naturphilosophie* in particular.

As a matter of fact, it is misleading if one speaks at this point of the fact that evolution has spawned living beings endowed with minds. For "evolution" is a name for processes in which species emerge. The term does not designate an overall process, let alone a direction in which animals evolve. There are many independent trees of the evolution of species, and none follows any specific direction. We account for these processes by means of the theory of evolution. It is not the case that evolution is a "blind watchmaker," as Dawkins put it in his book of the same name.[20] Evolution is neither a watchmaker nor any other kind of maker; it does nothing at all, because it is neither a subject nor any other kind of person with blind intentions but our collective term for complex processes constitutive of the emergence of new species, which can be better explained with the aid of the theory of evolution than with any other available alternative.

Admittedly, one often reads that evolution does this or that or has led to this or that. That is absurd, since evolution leads to nothing at all. At best, genetic mutations caused by cosmic radiation, as well as other entirely natural processes that take place in the division of cells, lead to the transformation of phenotypes – that is, to the transformation of the external appearance of living beings of a particular species. If their environment has also been somehow transformed – all the way to great catastrophic upheavals that have affected the earth again and again – living beings with mutated genes will survive and reproduce under certain conditions, and so on. The basic ideas of Darwinism are well known.

The term "evolution" unfortunately suggests that the processes accounted for by the theory of evolution are connected as if there were still a kind of intention, even if a blind one, such as the survival of individuals and species. Evolution is unwittingly imagined as a process that is intentionally carried out, for instance as a struggle for survival. The crucial advance of evolutionary biology in comparison to older attempts at explaining the origin of species lies in the fact that evolutionary biology gets by without assuming any intentions. It has become clear from the progress of biology and massive leaps forward such as evidence for DNA and its decoding in the last century that one can dispense with blind watchmakers too. The theory of evolution has no need for such metaphors, which only accommodate the need to replace the old God full of intentions with at least an ersatz God: the blind watchmaker or evolution.

Schelling's *Naturphilosophie*, in contrast to Fichte's philosophy of the self, insists that living beings with minds, which identify as selves and in this way can attain knowledge about nature, do not fall from heaven. We are not angels bolted together with the bodies of apes or pure spirits imprisoned in animal bodies. But that only means that there are necessary biological conditions for the fact that we can identify ourselves as selves.

Within the framework of the self-investigation of the human mind, nature is thus discovered under the banner of the self and becomes a great theme of the nineteenth century, because it troubles the self, so to speak. *Naturphilosophie* and what succeeded it in the nineteenth century, including Marxism and psychoanalysis, objected to the idea of a complete autonomy of the self by pointing out that there are mental illnesses, and that the self is in general only able to develop a dimension of knowledge when it is not disturbed by its natural conditions or when it does not allow itself to be disrupted by them.

"Let Daddy take care of this": Freud *and* Stromberg

Against the backdrop of Fichte's philosophy and German Romanticism, Freud developed his influential concept of the self or the ego. He elaborates this with particular clarity in his text *The Ego and the Id* of 1923, in which he enriches his master distinction of the conscious and the unconscious with his equally famous conception of an ego, a superego and an id. In this context, Freud, unlike Fichte, understands the self or "the ego" no longer as a universal dimension of knowledge but, rather, as a facet of our psychical life. "We have formed the idea that in each individual there is a coherent organization of mental processes; and we call this his *ego*."[21] The self becomes a subject for psychology, a process whose groundwork was laid by Schopenhauer and Nietzsche, who heavily influenced Freud's way of thinking about the self.

Neurocentrists routinely point out in their favor that Freud was actually a kind of neuroscientist, since in fact he began early on to seek physiological causes of mental illnesses. Freud's *Project for a Scientific Psychology* of 1895, a text in which he developed a biologically grounded "neuron theory," as he himself called it, is often cited in support of this claim. Since we now know that a majority of the processes that run their course in the brain are not actually consciously experienced, even as they make our conscious life possible, some believe that a scientifically secure basis for psychoanalysis or something close enough has been discovered.

However, Freud actually discovered psychoanalysis because he understood that there are structures of our mental life that manifest in the ways in which we *describe* ourselves and our attitudes to others. In this vein, he founded psychotherapy – the talking cure – which consists in describing our attitudes to ourselves and others and questioning in what ways these attitudes are experienced as painful and how they can be transformed. An intervention into organic processes – for instance, by taking antidepressants – is thus necessary in some cases but by no means in all. There is a link between our self-descriptions and the quality of our conscious life. Whether this link is regulated by neuro-cocktails in *all* cases and whether biochemical regularities, which are subject to the release of neurotransmitters, are correlated in a law-like way with the regularities that emerge in the self-description of our conscious experience is *de facto* not known by anyone at this time. It is and will forever remain a purely speculative question as to what specific biochemical basis is supposed to correspond to Napoleon's ambition to conquer Europe – insofar as the question is even ever formulated.

Psychoanalysis has regularly been criticized for not being scientific enough. The success of any such critique depends on what one means by "science." In any case, psychoanalysis up to the present day is recognized as a legitimate form of therapy. Freud and, in his wake, the French psychoanalyst and philosopher Jacques Lacan (1901–1981), in particular, among other things critically evaluated the ultimately superstitious belief that there is an expert panel watching over humanity composed of scientists, who worship an absolutely objective goddess named "science."[22] Psychoanalysis is often associated with a critique of a false ideal of science that believes absolute objectivity can be achieved. That does not make it popular with everyone; it also lies behind the resistance summed up in the slogan that it is not scientific enough.

Since Freud and psychoanalysis are frequently cited by neurocentrism and sometimes honored as precursors, it is worthwhile looking a little more closely for a moment at what Freud understands by the self or ego and whether he wanted to identify it with the brain. What is "the self" or ego in Freud and which of his insights are relevant for our context?

Freud's seminal distinction consists in dividing the psychical into the conscious and the unconscious, which he called "the fundamental premise of psycho-analysis."[23] Accordingly, consciousness does not exhaust our mental life (the psychical). This distinction has remained intact to the present day, and there is only contention over how exactly one should understand it. According to Freud, it is crucial that the unconscious does not consist of purely organic processes but already belongs to the psychical. Of course, neurobiological processes ensure that protons, which affect my sensory receptors, can be registered as pieces of information. These processes are unconscious in the sense that I do not notice them as such but only experience their results: my conscious impressions. If I look at my hand, I do not simultaneously see the neurobiological processes that must have taken place in the background.

Yet these processes do not belong to the category of the unconscious in Freud's sense. For him, what is unconscious can be made accessible by giving up the resistance one has built up because one censors the particular ideas and wishes that one has. One need not immediately think here of repressed sexual fantasies or the (in)famous Oedipus complex. It suffices to consider entirely everyday experiences.

Let us consider the everyday experience of boarding an airport bus that travels from the terminal to the airplane. One boards and sees an open place to sit. While heading for the seat, one sees other people whom one has perhaps already observed at the airport. One takes an interest in some people (in whatever manner you like), though is not interested in others, "and the act of perception itself tells us nothing of the reason why a thing is or is not perceived."[24] Hence one constructs a proper theory that makes it possible to guide one's own behavior. It would be nice to see the apparently helpless older woman in the seat that one has selected. It is probably not a good idea to stand next to the man acting like a jerk, who spends the whole time talking on the phone to his business partner so that it is hard to avoid the impression that he wants to show everyone how important he is, and so forth. In all of these cases, different thoughts go through one's head that are not very pleasant and which one quickly puts aside, so to speak. According to Freud, such thoughts are subconscious messages that ensure that certain things attract our attention, that we are interested in certain people and have a disposition to evaluate them that has somehow become second nature.

Let us suppose that someone – let us call him Donald – is particularly irritated by tourists in shorts who swarm onto the plane. He could perhaps justify his irritation if questioned by complaining that people are being quite pushy, and he might even get worked up over the fact that someone in those kinds of shorts who is obviously going on vacation is now pushing their way past everyone else. While he complains to himself or to a fellow passenger, it suddenly occurs to him that in reality he himself would love to go on vacation and is instead flying on business to Palma de Mallorca. Furthermore, perhaps at some point he had the experience of someone not appreciating his legs and hence would never himself travel in shorts or even go out in public wearing shorts. Yet this flash of insight, so to speak, is at best a brief glimpse into the unconscious and is replaced by a bad attitude, apparently well founded, toward pushy travelers. Donald pushes back, as he is not in a position to face his unconscious fantasy and wish structure which actually tells him that he himself would like to be the tourist in shorts.

The basic idea of psychoanalysis is that everyday speech in which we justify ourselves, in which we articulate our attitudes to ourselves and to others, is always anchored in experiences, many of which we believe we have completely forgotten. However, they actually exert a decisive influence on us precisely because we have developed a resistance against them. The unconscious emerges through the development of resistance against ideas that we were once conscious of in our life. This is how we construct our personality or our "character," as Freud sometimes calls it with reservations.[25] "The ego" or the self in this context is Freud's term for the internal discourse of rational justification, the very level at which we believe that our attitudes toward others are justified and reasonable rather than merely personal, emotional and irrational. The ego serves the function of making us believe that we are fundamentally objectively justified in feeling the way we do about others and ourselves. It makes us look rational in our own eyes.

This can be illustrated with reference to a well-known phenomenon. Consider a workplace, for instance – an open-plan office, let us say. So that we are imagining roughly the same thing, think of *Stromberg*, the British or American versions of *The Office*, or the French *Le Bureau*, which are all variations of the British prototype originally created by Ricky Gervais. These TV series are concerned with the psychodynamics of the workplace.

The German open-plan office from *Stromberg* belongs to an insurance company named Capitol. At least since *Stromberg – the Movie* it is clear that "Capitol" is a name for German capitalism. The German social market economy appeals to the need for security, whereas the American model of economic exchange addresses us as potential consumers and business people interested in pure liberty. Capitalism in the German version is experienced as a contribution to security. This is, of course, a fantasy and not itself an economic fact. There just is no specific relationship between the production and exchange of goods and political emancipation or social progress and stability. Any such relation is negotiated between a network of subsystems of society that are in principle too complex in order for anyone to give an overall account of what is going on. This is one of the reasons why there is such a thing as ideology, a fantasy supplement that makes our lives as members of structures no one fully understands more bearable. Unfortunately, this can easily be exploited. A TV series such as *Stromberg* expresses unconscious ideas. Indeed, the unconscious is continually erupting in the series, which is part of the comedy – something that reaches its peak in the movie when the executive board meets with prostitutes for wild orgies under the pretext of a party for management. In the movie we see a brutal outburst of sexist and repressive authoritarian behavior among the management of Capitol insurance, something which unfortunately nowadays can even result in your being the president of a powerful country.

In any social situation, such as the one depicted in *The Office*, every individual projects a kind of psychical map onto the social space. Everyone in the network enters the personal interpretation space of the others in terms of specific evaluations. If one listens to their evaluations, every single person will describe the social network of the workplace in a different way. Besides the *legally regulated order* – which determines the positions in the company – there is always a *psychical order*, which partly overlaps with the legal order. This becomes all the more transparent as we gradually realize that there is no purely legal order that is utterly independent of our psychical orders and that the two are often connected (one should think here of the discussions of bullying, stress, sexual harassment, sexism, red tape, and so on – in short, one should think of business psychology).

The omnipresence of the psychical order is illustrated in *The Office* and *Stromberg* by the fact that short individual interviews with the various parties are conducted over and over again. The individuals who are interviewed speak in front of the camera that follows everyday life at the office, since a documentary is being produced about it. Those involved describe the social order in light of their evaluations, in the course of which it subtly becomes clear that their evaluations are far from rational. Participation in the game of giving and asking for reasons is not itself a rational business; it is always grounded in emotional experience and, thereby, in the unconscious of the members of a given social system.

The self or ego in the Freudian model boils down to a level of description for our social interaction. At this level, our descriptions appear to be justified and supported with good reason. This corresponds to Freud's understanding of the psychological function of science. He succinctly writes at the very beginning of his essay "Instincts and Their Vicissitudes" of 1915:

> We have often heard it maintained that sciences should be built up on clear and sharply defined basic concepts. In actual fact no science, not even the most exact, begins with such definitions. The true beginning of scientific activity consists rather in describing phenomena and then in proceeding to group, classify and correlate them. Even at the stage of description it is not possible to avoid applying certain abstract ideas to the material in hand, ideas derived from somewhere or other but certainly not from the new observations alone.[26]

Drives meet hard facts

In contemporary philosophy, there are different accounts of the relation between our rationality (from the Latin *ratio* = reason) and the structure of what Freud calls "the ego" and what we have been referring to as the self. Neo-pragmatism holds that to be a self is to be rational, which is in conflict with Freud's view that the ego is actually a part of the id – that is, that its primary function is to create the misleading impression (the illusion) that our drives are justified. The neo-pragmatist American philosopher Robert Brandom (b. 1950) speaks here of "the game of giving and asking for reasons," and he has made a case for conceiving of the self as the general name for our fellow players in this game.[27] To be a self means to be accessible at the level of description on which we support and justify our attitudes to ourselves and to others with reasons.

Unfortunately, despite his valid insight that rationalism cannot be the whole truth about the self, Freud himself was often inclined to treat the ego or self like a homunculus that in his view enters the scene because perceptions arise in us through mere sensory stimulation. "It is like a demonstration of the theorem that all knowledge has its origin in external perception."[28] To support this thesis he draws on "cerebral anatomy"[29] and considers the ego to be a kind of anatomically verifiable surface or interface in the neo-cortex. How confusing things thus become is shown by the following fundamentally indecipherable passage, in which Freud explicitly defines the ego as a homunculus:

> The ego is first and foremost a bodily ego; it is not merely a surface entity, but is itself the projection of a surface. If we wish to find an anatomical analogy for it we can best identify it with the "cortical homunculus" of the anatomists, which stands on its head in the cortex, sticks up its heels, faces backwards and, as we know, has its speech-area on the left-hand side.[30]

Here Freud brazenly reifies the ego. However, this can be avoided with the help of Brandom's suggestion that the self is to be understood as a social function, as the level of description of social interaction in the light of our justificatory speech. One thus already treads a fine path between bundle theory and substance theory, since the level of description belonging to the self is neither a bundle nor a bearer of mental states. If the self is not an entity but, rather, a capacity to participate in a certain practice, it ceases to make sense to try to locate it and identify it with some brain area (or any number of brain areas working together in whatever spectacular way).

However, Brandom is not bothered by the fact that the self is not merely a neutral player among others. He does not focus on the fact that every self describes the whole game from a standpoint that others do not immediately and self-evidently share. The reason for this is not only that each of us just has different theories with different experiential bases, which could then be aligned with one another in the game of giving and asking for reasons. Rather, one can learn precisely from Freud that the ego or self becomes individual because we have experiences that are evaluated by others and which we then acquire as habits.

In order to account for this, Freud introduces the superego and the id alongside the ego. The superego, which he also characterizes as the ego-ideal or the ideal ego, plays a constitutive role in our self-description as an ego, in our considering certain modes of conduct and attitudes to be acceptable or even imperative. The superego stipulates what we should accept in general as good reason, which allows the ego to transform an emotional attitude toward others into something that appears to be justified. To recognize that we find ourselves in certain recurring situations in a certain way due to certain experiences in the past (not only in childhood) is difficult for us because we thus to some extent surrender the conscious control for which the ego feels responsible. The ego as an advocate of good reason is simply not the only factor of mental life, and it does not merely exist alongside other factors. Feeling seems to be something that just somehow comes over us, which is why the task of self-knowledge is to make a practice of how not to become the victim of one's feelings, as it were. Such a practice would not be possible if we were already in full control of any feature of our mental lives, as we could just happily play the game of giving and asking for reasons without bothering with our emotions, habits, etc. But how could we ever be initiated into the game without having been taught to behave in certain ways prior to acquiring the (often ideological) belief that our practices are in play because they are justified?

In the case of the id, his name for the drives, Freud distinguishes between a positive drive (eros) and a death drive. The positive, often sexual drive strives for self-preservation, the death drive for self-destruction. Furthermore, Freud is of the opinion that both of these drives can be biologically verified. He even cites "simpler organisms" in support of his distinction of ego and id, "for it is the inevitable expression of the influence of the external world."[31] On this level, he attributes to the ego perceptions that enable our inner life to have contact with reality, while the id potentially resists the recognition of an independent reality by forming an inner world.

What Freud is proposing here can be to a large extent reconstructed without the absurd idea that ego, id and superego can be localized, as if they were literally a matter of three regions of the body. Unfortunately, Freud actually does accept this crude materialistic idea, which is why he calls his theory "topical" (from the ancient Greek *topos* = place).

We have beliefs and opinions about what is the case independently of our beliefs and opinions. To perceive something means to come into contact with the kinds of facts that we cannot change by means of our perception but can only take in. That already resonates in the popular notion among traditional German philosophers that the etymology of the word "perception" [*Wahrnehmung*] indeed suggests that one takes in [*nehmen*] something true [*wahr*] and thus conceives of something true, a fact. As a matter of fact, the German word for perception etymologically means to become aware of something rather than to believe that something is true. In languages that use a version of the Latin-derived *perceptio* for perception (as in English or French), the idea is expressed that we are collecting or gathering something in perception. For Freud, the ego is close to the **reality principle**, as he calls it – that is, the fact that we typically come into contact with given states of affairs in whose continued existence or coming about we do not participate.

Facts whose existence is not brought about by us in any manner can be characterized as **hard realities**. We perceive some hard realities simply because they act upon our sensory receptors. But this is not unconditionally true of all facts, of course: the fact that Napoleon crowned himself emperor, at any rate, exists independently of whether anyone living today was involved in making it happen. It is certainly not easy to specify just when something actually exists independently of us. Yet this should not concern us further here. Right now, the only thing that is crucial to note is that, at some level or other, the self encounters facts, some of which are hard realities whose existence must simply be accepted if one is at all interested in truth.

In contrast, the id stands for drives. These are able to exist independently of hard realities. Thanks to our drives, we are in a position actually to change some hard realities: for example, we used to be confronted by a mountain range that made it difficult to get to Italy from Switzerland (and vice versa). So we simply drilled the Gotthard Base Tunnel in order to travel more quickly from one country to another. And why do we want to do that? Because we want to do business with each other, go skiing and visit museums, meet up with friends who live elsewhere, and so forth. The reason for the existence of a tunnel is not that it is rational to have tunnels, but rather that tunnels help us realize our wishes. There is nothing essentially rational in turn about our wishes themselves.

Because we have drives we transform realities and create new ones. Without drives, we would be passive windows into reality that would not belong to this world. Animals are distinguished from many plants by their self-determined motion. We animals experience an impulse toward change of place as a drive. For this reason, Freud supposes that the id is a kind of energy center that is irritated by perceptions and reacts to them. For Freud, the ego is the eyes and ears of the id; he expressly considers it to be a part of the id, which raises difficulties for his distinctions. Ego, superego and id are much more closely connected than one might believe at first sight. The superego, according to Freud, is for its part the "representative of the internal world of the id,"[32] which communicates the id's wishes to the ego in censored form. "What has belonged to the lowest part of the mental life of each of us is changed, through the formation of the ideal, into what is highest in the human mind by our scale of values."[33] An odd construction.

In any case, it is clear that the very thing which Freud calls a "drive" can be understood as a striving for transformation, in distinction from "perception." Perception does not want to transform anything but, rather, simply accepts things, while the id drives us from one state to the next. It thus only actually obtains some specific form – that is, the form of concrete wishes – because it is articulated by the ego. The ego is a transformation engine which translates drives into more specific wishes by attaching the (ultimately illusory) notion to them that it is inherently rational to realize the wishes, to change reality so as to make what we wish for happen. This is part of why egoism is so hard to overcome and why humanity is so amazing at destroying itself by destroying its natural habitat, planet earth: we are prone to believe that what we want to have and want to do is the right thing to have and the right thing to do – a pure illusion, as thinkers as diverse as Buddha, Marx and Freud have rightly pointed out.

Let us choose another example which comes to mind for us inhabitants of wealthy globalized societies. We go into the supermarket and ask ourselves which kind of milk we want to buy. We allow the color and form of the packaging to stimulate our imagination (Mmm, that tastes just like milk at breakfast in Bavaria, and I will feel the way I did that time I was at Lake Starnberg). The very moment we pose ourselves the question as to which kind of milk we want to buy, calculations begin that put the energies of the id (Mmm, quite tasty!) in contact with the energies of the superego (Too expensive! Milk makes us fat!). In Freud's somewhat archaically tinged image of the human being, the pre-conscious and unconscious synchronization of the layers of consciousness is rather as follows: "Mmm, I am secretly recalling my mama's breast and my infantile love for my mother," whispers the id. "You are fat and should not be, otherwise you do not deserve mama's love," roars the superego. This, or something close to it, is probably how Freud would have seen it. One need not follow him in this regard.

Oedipus and the milk carton

The perception of various milk cartons always occurs in conjunction with evaluations that do not unconditionally have anything to do with actual facts. Our perceptions are embedded in systems of wishes and desires of all sorts and never arise in our life in some pure state that is free of wishes. All thinking always involves an element of wishful thinking. Even when, for instance, a scientist stands in the laboratory and is researching a protein, he or she must dissociate from his or her wishes in order to perceive or discern the bare facts. Yet in order to be able to dissociate from one's wishes, one must want to do precisely that. Indeed, one has already resolved to be a scientist and orders one's drives as expediently as possible in accordance with this decision. Consciously lived existence, about which we communicate in the form of reasons accepted in conversations with each other every day, is in that sense "a specially differentiated part of the id,"[34] as we do indeed experience quite a variety of things but never the manner in which the choice is made as to what we are or are not to concentrate on. Hence Freud can characterize the ego as a "poor creature,"[35] because he sees it as a surface on which perceptions are displayed on the one hand, and drives on the other, which are immediately filtered and censored by the superego. The ego for Freud is an interface inserted between drives and imperatives, and it deals with this by experiencing its drives as inherently rational and, therefore, justified (at least, generally or typically justified).

In the version of the distinction between perception and drive – between reality and wish – advanced by Freud, at the end of the day unfortunately everything gets so mixed up that, on closer inspection, the structure collapses. How, for instance, is the id supposed to be not merely an undifferentiated single drive, a feeling emotionally hot and bothered, so to speak, that we sense and that urges us on? How can there be many drives and not just a boiling emotional heat? It so happens that Freud understands the ego as part of the id and thus inserts an eye into the latter with which the blunt and stupid id now looks around at realities to which it can adhere, a mechanism Freud calls "cathexis." Lo and behold, the mother's breast is already there, onto which the id can latch – and the often caricatured psychoanalytic explanation of our sexual drive with reference to our deep desire to sleep with our mothers and their future surrogates or our fathers and their future surrogates runs its course in a hundred different ways in literature, film and television.

Yet what does the claim that the ego is a part of the id mean? To formulate the question in another way: If the id is unconscious and its messages or impulses reach the conscious ego only after having been filtered, how can the ego be a part of the id? It would have to be unconscious and instinctual. But then it could no longer be responsible for perceptions. The reality principle collapses into the pleasure principle, and from the science of psychoanalysis out comes Pippi Longstocking:

Three times three makes four,
widdle widdle wid,
and three makes nine,
I'm making the world,
widdle widdle wid,
how I like it.

Freud himself explains: "Psycho-analysis is an instrument to enable the ego to achieve a progressive conquest of the id."[36] Yet what is going on in this model? Is the analyst in his or her function as conversational partner who approaches another person a representative of the external world for this person – that is, the ego – or is the analyst the voice of conscience, the superego? Or is the analyst even the id? If the id is already the ego, which indeed is supposed to be a part of it, how is the ego's conquest of the id supposed to proceed at all?

It is evident that a few things are here conflated with each other. Like he did in replying to objections raised by representatives of the philosophy of his time, Freud would now presumably respond that he learned of the relations between ego, superego and id in clinical practice, that he has empirical, scientific ground to believe that his theory is true. Yet this claim, which retreats to supposed experiences that the specialist will have had, cannot be persuasive even according to Freud's own premises. If a contradictory model of the self or ego is presented, one cannot fast-talk one's way out of it by claiming that one has already seen this in psychotherapy or, as is more typical of late, in a brain scan. Surely there are no theoretically far-fetched contradictions to be seen anywhere, neither in the talking cure nor in a brain scanner. They are believed to be there only because one is looking for them.

And yet Freud is on the right track. His reflections must be modernized, however, which in this case means above all freeing them from the erroneous assumption that the self or the ego is a biological entity that is formed by the interaction between organism and natural environment (external world), and that, moreover, a long cultural history has led to the emergence of a superego. These assumptions by Freud led to legendary myth-making – to which we are admittedly indebted for genuine insights and many works of art. Without Freud there would be no surrealism, no films by Alejandro Jodorowsky or Woody Allen, and many other things would be missing. Without him, there would probably not have been a sexual revolution, even if, as a man of the nineteenth century, he still partly clung to its ideas, above all concerning feminine sexuality, but also concerning homosexuality and, well, sexuality as such.

We are indebted to psychoanalysis for decisive advances in the political emancipation of minorities or oppressed groups. The controversy over the fact that we repress sexual wishes, indeed that we all have sexual fantasies, which are not self-evidently to be classified as perversions or to be condemned as crimes, ultimately led to the fact that we no longer consider homosexuality to be a sickness (at least this is still true for many Western societies, as I am writing this) or believe that women are seductresses, akin the serpent in paradise (or even the converse, that they are projection screens for masculine desires and not really capable of desire themselves), who come between us and the voice of God. In general terms, Freud laid the groundwork for our recognition of sexuality as a central component of our very selves.

Different branches split off in the twentieth century from his original version, branches which for their part led to new emancipatory theoretical developments, such as **gender theory**, for example. These new theoretical developments fundamentally proceed from the fact that there are gender roles that cannot be completely explained by examining our organism and determining whether we are male or female. The most prominent advocate of gender theory today, the American philosopher Judith Butler, has referred to the fact that even the search for feminine or masculine elements in a human organism – by classifying hormones as "feminine" or "masculine," for instance – is often already determined by the fact that we bring certain ideas of gender roles to bear with us and project them onto bodies.[37] It is crucial that we do not ignore the insights from psychoanalysis or gender theory, despite the fact that they have been overgeneralized by their adherents and misused as an excuse to ignore new scientific evidence.

On closer inspection, Freud's psychoanalysis holds crude assumptions about gender roles in its pseudo-biological details which are, strictly speaking, rather absurd and mostly unfounded. For instance, Freud is never quite certain whether the superego represents the internalized father or the internalized parents. He does not consider the possibility that it could come from the mother, simply because he probably thought that religious and moral ideas were advocated and enforced only by men. Ultimately, his writings swarm with patriarchal assumptions supported by myth-making.

A typical procedure for the avoidance of self-knowledge is currently infected with Darwinitis. Instead of asking who or what the self really is and developing a coherent response to this question, a response that is at the same time conceptually and historically informed about what account of the self all this talk of the self brings along with it, an ultimately unknowable past is invoked. This past must go back far enough in time and be attested to only by a few archeological findings, such as skulls, perhaps also a spearhead, in any case by a cave painting. Then one is able to narrate popular histories of how we originated from this past in order to make it look as if one has thereby achieved a better self-understanding.

This is mythology. The **main political function of mythology** consists in forming an idea of the total social situation of one's own time by imagining a primordial time. The less one really knows about this past, the more inventive one can be. Freud himself, in his wonderfully written book *Moses and Monotheism*, tells a story according to which we have a conscience and believe that there are objective moral laws, and thus in general something like good and evil, only because a primal horde killed Moses in the desert. Having a bad conscience emerged as a reaction to this slaughter. But how would this have worked and how did they transmit their bad conscience to the next generation? Why did they feel so bad about this particular act of killing and how does Freud know any of this, as there is no written or other record of this extraordinary "fact"?

Freud famously thinks that the essential theme of individuation, the cultivation of a self, lies in the male wish to murder one's father and sleep with one's mother, the much discussed **Oedipus complex**, to which Carl Gustav Jung (1875–1961) added an Electra complex – that is, the equivalent for girls. Freud did not approve of Jung's addition, as he explained in his essay "Female Sexuality" of 1931. These themes are in fact found in many mythological texts from the past, primarily of course in Sophocles' tragedy *Oedipus the King*.

Today there is a widespread tendency to reduce good and evil to value judgments that came to prominence in the course of evolution because they were useful. Something which was conducive to survival counted as "good" and something which endangered the survival of the species *Homo sapiens* counted as "evil." In particular, there is discussion of why **altruism** emerged – that is, the fact that living beings sacrifice their own well-being or even their lives for other living beings, or take an interest in the well-being of others at all. The presupposition for this question is the assumption that from the outset all living beings are actually egoistic. This is how the opposition egoism–altruism emerges.

Against this backdrop, the evolutionary biologist Richard Dawkins, for instance, in his widely noted book *The Selfish Gene*, has attempted to explain why we consider our relatives to be morally closer to us than random strangers.[38] He thinks that what drives egoism is not the individual (that is, not you or I) but a certain gene which we represent. Since this gene is also present in our relatives, we protect them even if it brings about the sacrifice of our own interests. Thus it becomes understandable why we normally prefer a stranger to die rather than our own children (but how do things then stand with adopted children or friends? – one of the many problems immediately prompted by this line of thought).

And how does one know that any of this is actually the case? If we are asked in the context of our everyday socially arranged, more or less amicable relationships, many of us will quickly answer that we would protect our relatives before protecting random strangers. However, this is not simply a universal truth (moreover, it should be noted that our relatives do not all belong to the same gene pool . . .). Here is a simple counter-example from the present day. Until the end of August 2014, the town of Amirli, which was overwhelmingly populated by Shia Turkmen, was besieged by jihadist troops from ISIS, who threatened to massacre them. During the siege, an Iraqi helicopter occasionally flew into the town to ensure that food was provided and to fly the sick and wounded out. The local dentist was assigned the task of caring for all of the sick and wounded, while his own family was still stuck in Amirli. What is more, he told the German magazine *Der Spiegel* that he deliberately did not put his own family on the helicopter and have them flown out, since a panic would otherwise have ensued.[39] Things would have ended badly if the doctor had pulled strings to save his family. It is not difficult to find countless examples (but also countless counter-examples) in which someone acts altruistically, according to generally accepted standards, and subordinates his or her own relatives to the common good. Why is genetic egoism supposed to be the rule and altruism an exception that is hard to explain?

The point is that we just do not have any data that sheds light on whether and how some humanoid or human ancestor acted in prehistoric times, which principles they followed and why they did what they did. More or less arbitrary assumptions about ordinary behavior in one's own society (or what is considered to be ordinary behavior in one's own society) are simply projected onto the past and combined with facts from evolutionary biology. In this way, mythology appears to be scientific and one is not directly exposed to public criticism. Here we have a strategy for immunizing oneself that is easy to see through. This is only too willingly concealed behind a perfidious lip-service to science, which on the basis of universal human reason is supposedly opposed to appeals to authority. However, there is a significant gap between natural science and philosophical interpretations of natural science. You simply cannot read philosophical truths off from science without first and foremost resolving the conceptual philosophical issues. This does not rule out the fact that philosophers need to respect natural science and acquire as much knowledge as possible in its manifold fields. However, there is a widespread tendency in our culture (more so in the Anglophone than in the German-speaking world) to outsource philosophical issues from philosophy to natural science, which is a fundamental mistake.

It is simply not the case that overall we tend to be egoistic. But it is also not the case that we generally prefer to care for others and sacrifice ourselves. Precisely therein lies human freedom: we are able to dissociate ourselves from our own standpoint by understanding that others have standpoints, too. This insight is associated with the mind's account of itself as a self. In particular, the self is both something individual (just you or I) and something universal (each of us is a self). However, by now it should be evident that the self cannot be the brain or a gene, let alone a gene pool. Rather, it is the case that without brains of a certain type the dimension of the self would never have been able to develop historically. Brains are a *necessary condition* for the fact that there are practices in which selves are involved. Yet the discovery of the self takes place within the context of historical processes of self-knowledge.

To this point, I have reconstructed a few cornerstones of this history, which in the West stretches back to Greek philosophy. "The self" is a philosophical concept, and it fulfils a function in the account of ourselves. It belongs to our self-portrait. The point is to pay attention to this account and to ask what assumptions are in play and whether any kind of coherent picture of the self can be constructed from them.

The self was also introduced so that we might understand what it means to be able to act in a good or an evil manner. It does not help to want to get rid of the concepts of good and evil by replacing them with the conceptual pairings of useful and harmful, or altruism and egoism. This only obscures the intention to introduce another vocabulary to account for the self. Yet this other vocabulary then typically adopts elements of its antecedent, and one still speaks of the self – or of the ego, as Freud does, for instance – in order to suggest that it has been only a biological matter all along. The self thus became reified by considering the account of it to be a biological issue.

We can understand ourselves as selves, can experience ourselves as conscious and self-conscious, can know and communicate thoughts. None of this can be sufficiently explained by realizing that we need a specific kind of organism to be able to do this. If we believe that such an explanation is sufficient, we conflate the necessary biological or natural conditions for the fact that we are living beings endowed with a specific mind with elements of our account of ourselves that have arisen historically. This conflation is a basic form of ideology, and behind it lies concealed, in each instance in a new way, the attempt to get rid of freedom and ultimately to become a thing. Neurocentrism is an ideological fantasy of self-objectification.

5

Freedom

In recent years, the classical debate whether we are free, or, rather, whether we have free will, has assumed a new shape, as some neuroscientists have entered this discussion with supposedly new findings that might speak against free will. Some new discoveries in brain research seemed to suggest for a while that even decisions that we consciously make and which then determine our actions must have been unconsciously prepared in the brain.[1] It thus appears as though our decisions do not lie in our hands. The idea that our brain could be directing us was born.

The debate about free will is not new. It has been prevalent for a long time and took a new turn in the nineteenth and the early twentieth century, when the suspicion arose that the human will is defined or determined by the fact that, although we are living beings with minds, we nevertheless belong to the animal kingdom. At that time, it was Darwinism, nascent sociology, psychology and also brain research to which one looked for evidence that the human being did not really have free will.

In fact, we know that there are many factors that influence the decisions we make and the personality we develop. We are not in control of our preferences in the sense that we are able to choose all of them in the same way we are able to choose an appetizer in a restaurant or a brand of sausages in the supermarket. We come to the world with preferences that are in part genetically determined, and over the course of our life we cultivate further preferences in our association with other people and with authorities, without being consciously aware of the mechanisms for selection that in the end result in patterns of conduct.

Such truisms, which have fortunately long since been acknowledged, have certainly shaken the outdated (never uncritically predominant) image of the human being, according to which each of us is an autonomous self to the extent that there is a command

178

center for our life. On this view, we are situated in such a command center and decide with complete freedom, in a frictionless vacuum, who or what we are and what we want to do. This model has rightly been recognized as a variant of the homunculus fallacy. If we had free will only in this sense, if we were the helmsman of such a command center, we could not in fact have free will at all. The idea of a completely autonomous little helmsman within our skull or in the depths of our soul is simply incoherent. But we do not need neuroscience to tell us that, as the incoherence is a conceptual matter: it simply is not possible to be responsible for all your preferences in the sense of having to create them *ex nihilo*. If we had to create ourselves in this way, we would never come into existence in the first place. No one is absolutely autonomous; no one acts in a void. Hence, it cannot be a requirement of actual free will to be absolutely autonomous.

Furthermore, it is a fact that many decisions which we experience as consciously made are unconsciously prepared at the neural level. This seems to speak in favor of the claim that our brain directs us, in which case "we" would then just be a conscious user interface able to have experiences and the brain would be the real central processor. A part of the brain whose activity we do not experience would accordingly somehow direct the very activities of the brain that we consciously experience or in which consciousness arises.

That is roughly the basic structure which, along with many others, the German neurophysiologist Wolf Singer outlined in a much discussed article published in the newspaper *Frankfurter Allgemeine Zeitung* on January 8, 2004, entitled "No One Can Be Other Than They Are" – an idea that he further elaborates in his essay "Neural Connections Determine Us" as well as in subsequent books.[2]

Naturally, there is no reason to deny the fact that our organism functions as a biological entity in such a way that many operations of information-processing and decision-making must occur without our noticing them. In a similar vein, the Nobel prizewinner Daniel Kahneman (b. 1934), in his book *Thinking, Fast and Slow*, refers to how important it is for us as living beings with minds that we can think so quickly, that we make decisions without going through explicit and time-consuming reflections.

All of this has already been common knowledge for a long time in the philosophy of consciousness and is discussed there, for instance, under the heading of the **Dreyfus Model of Skill Acquisition**. As the name suggests, it was developed in particular by the philosopher Hubert Dreyfus (b. 1929), who teaches at

Berkeley and who has pointed out that actual *expertise* is distinguished from mere *competence* by the fact that an expert just sees
right away what action has to be taken in a given situation. To
be knowledgeable in an area consists in transforming consciously
available information into unconscious processes which structure
patterns of behavior.

There has been good research showing that the acquisition
of competence in chess does not happen in such a way that the
grandmaster can calculate better positions, as it were, and can
thus become ever more like a computer. In truth, the concept of
intuition plays a large role in the game of chess. Good players see
possibilities in a position and choose paths and moves intuitively
because they are short on time. Only then do they calculate the
paths they have chosen. Which paths and moves are arrived at
on the basis of calculations and which are excluded in advance
(because they are counter-intuitive) determines the playing ability
of a chess player, among other things. One certainly needs to be
able to calculate very well and to have a proper visual imagination, but without intuitive insight into the essential structure of
a given chess position chess masters would not be able to play as
well as they do (any more than we could drive from one exit on the
highway to the next without an intuitive overview of the situation,
which relies on unconscious information-processing and percepts
we do not take notice of).

We are all familiar with such phenomena: when one gets one's
first driver's license, one might think that good drivers would continually keep in mind all of the different skills and knowledge of the
rules that they have acquired. Yet, the more experience one has of
driving a car, the less one explicitly recalls the rules by which one
has learned to drive. The driver probably forgets the specific word-
ing of the rules, although they remain second nature. The same
holds true for those who know foreign languages. As soon as one
speaks a language fluently, one no longer needs explicitly to recall
the rules to be applied, which have probably been forgotten. Thus
it is generally true that we must make use of an **unconscious background of skills**, as Dreyfus's colleague Searle puts it. Accordingly,
even at the high level of playing chess or solving mathematical
problems, we are not necessarily conscious of the cognitive skills
we are engaged in, nor are we conscious of all the information-
processing required in order to carry out even mundane tasks, such
as crossing the street.

Yet why should the fact that the many processes we unconsciously call on to make decisions – processes which escape our

attention – somehow threaten our freedom or free will? Singer argues as follows: "If it is granted that conscious deliberation on arguments rests on neural processes, then it must be subject to neural determinism in the same way as the unconscious decisions where we concede this happens."[3] He assumes that there are "genetically determined . . . fundamental neural connections"[4] and that they determine all our conscious decisions (including his belief that his view is correct). Accordingly, he has not freely decided on his own theory of neural determinism. His brain dictated it to him. Had his theory been true, he would have been lucky to have a brain which communicated the theory to him.

At first glance, it might seem entirely plausible to some that their brain dictates their thoughts to them. On closer inspection, however, it turns out that any view along those lines is quite untenable. Let us have closer look, then! Let us start from the notion of **naïve determinism**, on which Singer's position is based. In a nutshell, naïve determinism is the claim that everything which happens in nature proceeds according to natural laws from which there can be no deviation and which at any moment determines exactly what will happen in the next moment. Just as everything that one throws out of the window falls onto the street – as a result of gravity, a law of nature – so everything in nature occurs inevitably in the way prescribed by the laws of nature. The statement of naïve determinism immediately invites all sorts of objections, since, for instance, some things that one throws out of the window fly upwards (a healthy bird, for instance, or balloons filled with helium). But the basic idea seems to be clear, in any case. The basic idea is that nothing goes against the laws of nature, from which the determinist concludes that everything which happens takes place in accordance with the laws of nature. Since our neural processes belong to nature, they too are simply reeled off according to fixed rules. And thus we would no longer be free, because we would be defined or determined by the fundamental neural connections of our brain. Free will would be an illusion whose advantages and disadvantages for evolution one could continue to discuss.

Many arguments in the history and philosophy of science speak against determinism in this sense, arguments that were recently elaborated in a particularly distinct way by the German philosopher and physicist Brigitte Falkenburg in her lucid book *Mythos Determinismus* (The Myth of Determinism). Let us take as an example the following simple line of thought: since the time of Galileo's formulation of the law of falling bodies, we know that, in a vacuum, a cannonball and a crystal ball fall with equal velocity.

Thus one can formulate a law of nature on this basis that expresses relationships which can be rendered mathematically precise. Yet, this law of nature says nothing about what actually happens when I throw a feather out of my window. What if a wind blows from below and propels the feather upwards? Furthermore, feathers and cannonballs do not actually fall out of my window with equal velocity, something which holds true only in a vacuum. It quickly becomes evident that laws of nature only hold true without exception when we carry out certain idealizations. Laws of nature do not describe what actually happens at some moment in nature or even what must happen; rather, they describe idealized conditions. Hence, one cannot predict on the basis of knowledge of natural laws alone what will happen in the next moment.

The laws of nature thus do not stipulate, so to speak, what must happen. They are not like rules of a game, which are fixed and which determine precisely what the next move will be. In contrast, this does hold true for movies, since the events that one can repeatedly view by fast-forwarding and rewinding always run according to the exact same pattern. In light of this, let us call naïve determinism the **movie theory of nature**. It claims that nature, in the eyes of an omniscient external observer (if such an observer were even possible), would be like a movie in which the exact same thing always happened every time it is replayed. To be sure, this is a widespread but quite untenable idea of how nature functions, as if it were a very complex machine that always proceeds from one state to the next according to the same principles. Of course, none of this follows from the present state of knowledge in physics. Determinism is metaphysical speculation, at best, and not a hypothesis that has been or even can be proven by physics. As Falkenburg notes: "... determinism can *always be saved* by *some kind* of speculative metaphysics. Indeed, this shows only that it is not an empirically testable scientific hypothesis but a sheer case of belief."[5] For this reason, the neuroscientist cannot simply appeal to the fact that our neural processes are determined, insofar as this is supposed to mean that they are somehow inserted into the gigantic machinery of nature that changes from one state to the next without our help, our wishes or our volition. Determinism is not a scientifically proven hypothesis but is actually a case of wild philosophical speculation.

In any case, it is certain that there are natural conditions for how we are able to act in general, and we cannot change all of these conditions. Whether we want to or not, we cannot travel anywhere near the speed of light and certainly not faster than that

– in any case, not by blasting off and accelerating into the universe in some kind of tin can. Hence recent science-fiction films such as *Interstellar* must introduce "wormholes" into space-time to keep alive the vain hope that one day we will live in outer space and on other planets in order to escape our earthly conditions and found colonies elsewhere.

It seems hard for many of us to recognize that as a biological species we are stuck on this planet – which is still a wonderful place to be – and that sooner or later human beings will not exist any longer. Sooner, if we do not live in a demonstrably more environmentally sustainable manner in the near future. Later, if we survive until our planet disappears for good along with all human intelligent life, never to be seen again, as our dying sun expands.

Unfortunately, the rejection of naïve determinism as bad metaphysics alone does not suffice to return our free will to us, as there is a more fundamental conceptual threat to our understanding of ourselves as the free agents we happen to be.

Can I will not to will what I will?

There is a serious problem with free will which goes beyond the metaphysical question of whether the movie theory of nature is true. The **hard problem of free will**, as I call it, is a paradox – that is, a series of claims all of which intuitively we must accept, but which together entail an untenable conclusion. The positive part of the paradox looks like this:

1 I can do what I want (this is **freedom of action**).
2 I can influence what I want by forming a will (an intention to do something).
3 To form such a will (an intention to do something) is an action.
4 Therefore, free will exists (this is **freedom of the will**).

This good news is unfortunately rescinded by the negative part of the paradox.

1 If the will is freely formed, I can also form another will.
2 I must thus not only be able to do what I want but must also be able to choose for myself what I want (to set an agenda for myself).
3 But I cannot choose for myself what I want ("I can do what I will . . . But I am not able to *will* it," as Schopenhauer put it).[6]

4 Consequently, the will is ultimately not freely formed and is thus unfree.
5 Therefore, free will does not exist.

Naturally, my freedom of action is limited since I cannot always do what I want. What is worse, if to do what one wants always presupposes the prior activity of forming a will, we would never be entirely free, because the fact that we have a will itself, of all things, would make us unfree. Schopenhauer is right to point out that I cannot choose my agenda from scratch. What is more, I cannot change my will from scratch either, since I would have to want this, too. The desire to change my will would then be what determines me to carry it out – something I cannot in turn choose on pain of a vicious infinite regress. Therefore, at some point, one must indeed assume that one simply just wants something for no reason whatsoever. However, one would apparently not be free then but, rather, determined by one's own will, which in principle cannot be chosen. If there were such a thing or agent as our will, she, he or it could actually not be free. It would lie in the nature of the foundation of the freedom of action that we are never really free.

In November 2010, I traveled to a philosophy conference through the state of Goa in India. At some point, a truck with an advertisement for a product named Zinzi drove in front of our taxi (no one has paid me yet for my covert product placement here). On the pink advertisement alongside the product's name was written only the memorable sentence "Find any reason." Until I wrote these lines, I figured that it must have something to do with a soft drink. I just found out that Zinzi is an Indian red wine.

The point of this is that, instead of giving us a reason to want precisely *this* drink, the apparent freedom to allow some kind of arbitrary reason to occur to us is demanded of us so as to justify the ultimately groundless wish to drink this beverage. In short, at some point in the system of our preferences we always run into groundless desires and patterns of preference, a fact the ad for Zinzi ironically exploits. One can often still do what one wants on this basis, but one can no longer want what one wants. Our reasons seem to be pretexts, convincing our will to "Find any reason!"

If neural processes run their course unconsciously and lie behind these patterns of preference (as Singer claims), we seem to have arrived at an improved argumentative version of his position of neural determinism. The groundless will, which we simply have in a given way, only has to be identified with a neural pattern. If you combine neuroscience with Schopenhauer's paradox, you might claim to have found empirical support for the paradox's conclusion that no one is ever really free, or that there is no free will.

In philosophy, there are a variety of attempts to solve the hard problem of free will. What needs to be made clear at the outset is that the problem has very little to do with the brain. Whether my will is identical to neural processes or is formed by unconscious neural processes – which is why I am not able to choose what I want but, rather, have to find it out – plays only a subordinate role in the hard problem. For thousands of years there have been other variants of the hard problem of free will which did not involve our brain.

For instance, for a long time **theological determinism** was central. It taught that, as an omniscient being, God already knew before creation everything that was going to happen. As a human being, then, one apparently cannot change this, since what was going to happen to one was already fixed before birth. Accordingly, as the classical argument runs, we have no free will (*liberum arbitrium*) but an unfree will (*servum arbitrium*). Incidentally, Martin Luther himself belongs to this tradition. In 1525, he composed an elaborate text *On the Bondage of the Will* (*De servo arbitrio*), in which he unmistakably notes that:

> It is most necessary and most salutary, then, for a Christian to know this also; that God foreknows nothing contingently, but foresees and purposes, and accomplishes every thing, by an unchangeable, eternal, and infallible will. But, by this thunderbolt, Freewill is struck to the earth and completely ground to powder . . . Hence it irresistibly follows, that all which we do, and all which happens, although it seems to happen mutably and contingently, does in reality happen necessarily and unalterably, insofar as respects the will of God.[7]

Luther calls this a "'paradox'" because it amounts to "publishing to the world that whatsoever is done by us is not done by Freewill, but by mere necessity."[8] There are countless attempts, some of which are ridiculous in their hairsplitting, at solving this theological problem. For now, it is crucial only to note that determinism does not necessarily have anything to do with the brain. God can also apparently threaten our freedom or not even allow it to emerge in the first place, as Luther believes.

In contrast to this, **physical determinism** (at least one prominent variety) claims that we are not free because, in truth, only the things and events that particle physics talks about exist, since the entirety of physical reality is composed of elementary particles (which, it should be noted, is a metaphysical claim, not something necessitated by physics). Depending on which laws one postulates to understand the behavior of elementary particles, everything happens according to necessity or at least according to laws of probability – perhaps with a dash of randomness or uncertainty in quantum reality. Yet randomness or uncertainty is nowhere near freedom, as we will soon see. Thus in this model, too, we are unfree, but not so much because the movie theory of nature is true but, rather, because we do not really exist according to this metaphysical interpretation of physics.

Neural determinism adds to the hard problem of free will the claim that unconscious neural processes, which run their course in the brain, merely follow basic established neural connections and thus make decisions for us – that is, in place of a consciously experiencing, supposedly autonomous subject – before any supposedly consciously made decision. The brain supposedly decides for us, and indeed it fundamentally does so in such a way that we have no more direct influence on it than we do on our blood sugar level or digestive processes.

All kinds of things accordingly seem to threaten our poor little freedom: God, the physical universe, and even our very own brain. Yet these are only a few examples of the hard problem of free will, which actually does not have much to do with such things. At bottom, the problem is much more troublesome than any machination of the brain, God, and the universe altogether could be. In the case of the hard problem, it is a question of whether the concept of free will is even coherent or whether it is not ultimately as absurd as the concept of the biggest natural number. Closer inspection of our concepts (or elementary mathematics) shows that there cannot be a biggest natural number. Perhaps closer inspection of the concept of free will will also show that this, too, cannot exist at all, since the concept itself is incoherent. In any case, this is the hard problem that really lies concealed behind theological, physical and neural determinism.

The hard problem of free will proceeds from the fact that our decisions are conditioned by something that for the most part we never survey. We are certainly never in a position to survey all necessary conditions for our acts, as we do not know all the almost infinitely many details that are involved in what we do and why we do it. Against this background, Spinoza already almost cynically pointed out that freedom is the consciousness of our actions without the consciousness of the determining grounds for our actions.[9] In other words: we consider ourselves to be free because we do not know what exactly is determining us. According to this view, free will is an illusion which arises on account of our ignorance of the determining factors of our actions.

The claim that we really only consider ourselves to be free out of ignorance of the necessary conditions for everything that happens is deeply unsatisfying. Our freedom would then consist only in the fact that we are too stupid to realize that, in reality, we are not free. We are quite justified in expecting more than such a cynical theory of freedom.

The self is not a one-armed bandit

Against the backdrop of the hard problem of free will, the very concept of the will was introduced to the history of philosophy. Admittedly, this concept was severely criticized, though it was also accepted by many. Contemporary philosophy mostly replaces it with talk of capabilities and capacities that we can or simply cannot put into practice. Freedom is thus sought in the fact that we have capacities and capabilities. Let us call this approach the **capacity theory of human freedom**. The capacity theory replaces talk of the will by talk of capacities in order to circumnavigate the hard problem of free will.

However, capacity theory, at bottom, is not really very helpful since, rather than solving the paradox of free will, it only defers it. The problem now runs as follows: suppose that I take measures to become a better swimmer. In order to reach this goal, I must decide both for and against certain actions. I must either wake up earlier to go swimming before work or schedule my daily routine in a completely different manner right away. I need to eat less Wiener schnitzel and more salad, and so on. To the extent that, in principle, no obstacles stand in my way, I could decide to become a better swimmer – something which could, however, fail to happen for various reasons. Thus situations arise in my life, after I have made decisions, in which I must choose: schnitzel or salad; sleeping in or getting up when I hear the alarm clock. Nothing prevents me from choosing salad. In this regard, I am free to do what I want.

But when I have chosen the salad, am I then still free not to have chosen the salad? Obviously not: I have indeed chosen the salad, as was already mentioned. I have made my decision. But how does this happen? One possibility is to claim that I have chosen between salad and schnitzel. But, in this case, I have not chosen between my choice of salad and my choice of schnitzel, but between salad and schnitzel. I choose not my choice but an action: to order salad or to order schnitzel. But is my choice then free at all?

If one wants to prevent the paradox at this point from resurfacing, one should absolutely not say that my choice is a further action that is free. For then the question would arise as to whether my action of choosing in turn was free or not. If it was free, there was another choice – the choice to carry out this action of choosing. This was in turn either free or unfree. Once again, we run into a vicious infinite regress: one must choose to choose to choose, and so on. At some point one must choose something without choosing that one chooses it. Sooner or later a decision needs to be made which cannot have a further ground.

But how does this decision come about? Capacity theory, as its name suggests, has it that the decision is the exercise of a capacity. Traditionally, this capacity was identified with the will. On closer inspection, capacity theory ultimately replaces the problems of the will by multiplying the problems with recourse to a bunch of capacities which are supposed to interact. Be that as it may, capacity theory needs to address the following regress: if I exercise my capacity of necessity in the sense that it is not up to me either to exercise it or not, I am unfree. However, if the reasons for the exercise of my capacity are supposed to be up to me, the regress begins. If Fred (the will) is unfree, he does not become freer by renaming himself Freddie (capacities). The hard problem of free will persists.

Naturally, the capacity theorist assumes that it is not the case that there is always a multitude of necessary conditions that compel my capacity to be exercised. The exercise of my capacity is supposed to be free, without my thus being permitted to have chosen ahead of time to exercise my capacity. In exercising my capacity, I need to be free and, hence, unconstrained by prior parameters which would undermine my capacity to act in one way or another.

This gives rise to a version of the **problem of chance**, however. One can illustrate this problem as follows. Imagine that our self functioned like a one-armed bandit in Las Vegas. Assume further (which of course is not quite right) that the reels were not preprogrammed to spin on the one-armed bandits. It would thus actually be a matter of chance whether the three reels, for instance, displayed "cherry, melon, 10" or "cherry, 10, 10." The problem of chance arises in that it is hard to avoid the claim that the decision as to whether we are exercising a capacity or not is like pulling on a one-armed bandit. In this case, our decisions would not be determined, they would not be preprogrammed. In each and every case, determinism would thus be false.

However, in its place the capacity theorist has so far merely put **indeterminism**, which claims that some events occur without either necessary or sufficient conditions compelling them to happen. The problem of chance consists in that our actions, according to capacity theory, are indeed free, but that the decision to exercise a capacity is ultimately left to chance.

A typical move of the capacity theorist at this point is to allow for the notion that we have various capacities that work together and thereby solve the problem of chance. I have the capacity to improve my swimming, to control my eating behavior, to change my sleeping habits. This interplay of various capacities is supposed to minimize chance, since they are all unified in me as an agent, a picture which makes the exercise of my capacities look less random and more specific to me. Yet, this maneuver just obscures the fact that, for every capacity, it is also true that either it is activated by necessary and jointly sufficient conditions or it is not. The problem of chance thus recurs. The more capacities, the more one-armed bandits.

A one-armed bandit is not free but a chance machine. Sure, the counter-argument against the capacity theory just sketched presupposes that there could actually be one-armed bandits that produce genuinely random outcomes – a strict naïve determinist would already doubt whether this is conceivable. But even if there were chance machines and our capacities were exercised like one-armed bandits, this would not make us one jot freer. If we are played like a throw of the dice, so to speak, this does not make us any freer than if we are "compelled" by necessary conditions or the neural connections in our brain to exercise our capacities, a thought that is reflected in a highly refined poetical manner in Stéphane Mallarmé's masterpiece *Un coup de dés jamais n'abolira le hazard* (A Throw of the Dice Will Never Abolish Chance). If the actual exercise of our capacities were activated by chance on every occasion, this would make us not free but dependent on chance. Whether one is dependent on fate, natural laws or chance plays only a subordinate role in the formulation of the hard problem of free will.

The American philosopher Peter van Inwagen (b. 1942) – incidentally, an avowed Christian thinker – introduced a famous and helpful distinction in his *Essay on Free Will* of 1983, one of the most influential texts in the literature on our theme.[10] On closer examination, I believe his distinction does not stand up to analysis, but it does point us in the right direction. He distinguishes two possible positions in the debate between free will and determinism, one of which he calls **compatibilism**. Compatibilism assumes that freedom and determinism are actually compatible, and so it is perfectly consistent, on the one hand, for there to be necessary and jointly sufficient conditions for everything that happens – conditions that can extend far into the past – and, on the other hand, for us to be free. Van Inwagen calls the other position **incompatibilism**. This position correspondingly claims that we can only be free if determinism is false, since freedom and determinism are incompatible.

In my view, incompatibilism fails to the extent that it cannot solve the problem of chance. At some point in their arguments, incompatibilists always assume that we have capacities – or a will – that are activated so as to trigger an action (or motivate it in some such manner that freedom, as they conceive of it, is not threatened). If the activation of our capacities at any point functions like a one-armed bandit, however, one has failed to salvage freedom, even if it is also true that one has reined in determinism. This is why compatibilism is the safer bet. As the German philosopher Thomas Buchheim (b. 1957) writes: "Ultimately all of our activity must be determined by *some* factors, otherwise it would be a product of chance and not a person's decision."[11]

Usually, incompatibilists reproach compatibilists for giving up freedom. There are very detailed points of disagreement here. One can, however, immediately reject the basic reproach: compatibilism maintains not that we are not free but that everything that happens to us is determined, and that determinism and freedom, seriously considered, are compatible.

In my view, the debate really hinges neither on freedom nor on free will but on the world picture or metaphysics that is operative in the background. Almost everything depends on the meaning of "determinism," as some forms of determinism are compatible with free will, whereas others are not. Evidently, if "determinism" referred to the view that non-conscious processes in the universe force us to do whatever we think we do out of our own choice, determinism would be incompatible with freedom. It is not hard to work out a meaning for the term "determinism" such that determinism clashes with freedom. Yet, this does not mean that determinism in the most plausible sense of the term (on which it has a chance to be true) conflicts with freedom.

The crucial first point of my own contribution to this debate is the claim that there is no all-encompassing reality through which a single causal chain runs from the beginning of all time. The claim that there is such a chain is a world picture against which I argued in more detail in *Why the World Does Not Exist*. Since *the* world that would connect everything together does not exist, there is no way to pose a problem for freedom on such a metaphysical basis. The universe is not an all-encompassing reality that reels off everything which happens on a single timeline, as though time were a chain on which everything that happens hung like pearls. The universe is also not a movie from which nothing and no one can escape. The movie theory of nature is simply false, which is not to deny that many elements in the universe can be understood deterministically. It is, however, not the case that absolutely everything that takes place falls within the domain of natural phenomena governed by strict deterministic laws which are incompatible with free will.

The hard problem of free will, however, does not even presume such a metaphysics of nature. It is not concerned with whether we are only pearls on a chain, which from the very beginning of time are continuously bound to the inexorable anonymous laws of nature. The fear that incompatibilists stoke is the fear that we could be the playthings of an anonymous causal chain. Yet one need not assume this at all in order to formulate a version of determinism. The idea of an anonymous causal chain is a red herring in the question of determinism. Since it presupposes a metaphysically false idea of the universe, every determinist should gladly disregard it because it does not contribute anything to what is at stake.

Let us return to the everyday level and simplify the thought at stake with recourse to an example. Imagine that I find myself at a buffet in a cafeteria during lunchtime and must choose whether I would prefer to have a baloney sandwich or pasta. My freedom of action consists in the fact that I can decide for myself whether to have the sandwich or pasta. Nothing prevents me from making this decision. On the contrary! Imagine now that I take the sandwich; this is no accident. Indeed, I can tell you exactly what led me to such a decision: yesterday I had pasta, the sandwich looks more appealing, I am not a vegetarian, and I would like to get a rise out of my vegetarian companion. Of course, neural processes are also taking place, without which I could not have any thoughts and which are possibly also guided by microorganisms that belong to my gut flora.[12] Moreover, these processes are restricted by laws of nature, since my thoughts rely on the existence of time, and no information can be conveyed at a velocity greater than the speed of light. In addition, the sandwich lies on a counter, which among other things is related to the fact that the earth's gravity is 1g. If it were greater, the sandwiches would be flat and I would not be able to lift anything. If it were less, the sandwiches would fly through the cafeteria.

Thus, there are a number of necessary conditions, including at the very least the ones just listed. All of this pertains to my choice of the sandwich. Otherwise I would have perhaps chosen the pasta or something else entirely. In this sense, all the necessary conditions, taken together, are sufficient. If they are all present, nothing is missing and I do indeed grab the sandwich. My freedom cannot lie in the fact that there is a kind of gap in between the conditions. If it did, we would again be at the mercy of a one-armed bandit. Freedom and determinism are thus not incompatible to the extent to which determinism means commitment to the absence of gaps in the set of necessary and jointly sufficient conditions for an event which actually takes place.

The point of this reflection is that not all conditions are causal or even anonymous and blind. It is not as if all conditions of my freedom of action are tangible causes that push me around, so to speak, urging me on and ultimately compelling me to opt for the sandwich. Furthermore, some conditions are just not causal at all.

A simple example: I must pay for the sandwich. It is for sale. But this does not cause me to buy the sandwich, even though it is a condition for my choice. Our economy indicates exchange of goods not governed by deterministic causes as it is built on the free negotiation of the exchange value of goods and services. Indeed, this is one of Marx's most basic insights: the reason why cigarettes cost what they do is not because they have a certain completely objective use value but, rather, because processes of negotiation have taken place that terminate in a given price. Thus, normally, things do not cost exactly what they are worth in themselves, which is why *exchange value* always differs from *use value*. This can be observed simply by noting that the price of a good can change in the course of time without the good itself changing. It is enough to keep things in storage and wait. Their value (their price) will change soon enough.

Our actions are thus free because they are not exhaustively caused by anonymous blind factors such as causal chains. We can nevertheless in principle completely understand our actions by listing all of the necessary and jointly sufficient conditions that lead to the fact that a given action results. That is no accident. Some of us are bandits but none of us is a one-armed bandit (in the sense of what is to be found in casinos, since there may well be bandits who have had an arm amputated).

Why cause and reason are not the same thing and what that has to do with tomato sauce

Leibniz – one of the great thinkers of early modernity who has already been mentioned a number of times – formulated a famous principle: the **principle of sufficient reason**. This principle, which states that nothing happens without a sufficient reason, lies concealed behind the hard problem of free will. Leibniz's basic idea is very simple: if something happens (for instance, the kick-off of a soccer match), there is a series of conditions for why it does so. One can identify these conditions in a list:

- Twenty-two (sufficiently healthy) players are on the field.
- The referee has a whistle.
- The referee absolutely wants the match to begin on time (since last time he got in trouble with FIFA for blowing the whistle too late).
- The playing field consists of an appropriate turf (and not of concrete or ice, for instance).
- The spectators are behaving themselves (they are not throwing cups of beer onto the playing field).
- The earth's gravity is 1g.
- There are agreed-upon rules of soccer.
  . . .

Each item on this list is a necessary condition for the fact that a soccer match can begin with the starting whistle. If one of these conditions were not met, the soccer match would not start. Not one of the conditions is sufficient on its own. If the spectators are behaving themselves, but there are no players on the field, the referee cannot blow the whistle to start the match. And the fact that the earth's gravity is 1g alone has precious little to do with the soccer match.

Leibniz's principle states that an event occurs if and only if its list of conditions is complete. There are no gaps in the tapestry of conditions. Indeed, the match would not begin if the referee did not have a whistle, and so forth. The necessary conditions are only sufficient for the fact that a soccer match can start on the referee's whistle when they are present altogether in the right way.

However, some readers will already want to object here: what happens if the referee suddenly loses the desire to begin the match, calls the whole thing off and heads home? In that case, a different event occurs, namely the referee's trip home. In such a case, however, there is once again a list of conditions for this event, which includes the fact that the referee suddenly no longer had the desire to officiate the match, but likewise includes the fact that neural processes occurred that are connected to his lack of desire. For instance, perhaps he is extremely depressed because for the last few months he has binged on cocaine. In this scenario he would actually be guided by his brain's neurochemistry, which is something that can occur (far be it from me to cast doubt on this!). The fact that the referee no longer wants to officiate matches does not fall from heaven, and even if this were the case – if he thus went home by chance instead of remaining – it would just add a new condition that explains why the football game lacked a starting whistle.

The point of this line of thought is that, whenever an event takes place, necessary conditions (the reasons, causes, conceptual and legal preconditions, and so on) are present for its taking place. Taken altogether they are sufficient for the fact that the event takes place. In my view, **the principle of sufficient reason** accordingly states: *for every event that takes place there is a collection of necessary conditions that are jointly sufficient for the event to take place.*

At first sight, one might think that the principle of sufficient reason limits our freedom or even renders it void. It does indeed state that we do not do anything just so or without any reason. It also rules out the possibility of there being a list of necessary conditions for the occurrence of an event that then activate, as it were, a will that is free of what comes from outside in order for the event actually to take place. The fact that one decides for this or for that does not fall from heaven but, rather, stems from all of the necessary conditions being present, which can include the fact that we would like something specific to happen. One cannot free oneself from the corset of necessary conditions, as it were. If that were to happen, one would not be free but, once again, at best be a one-armed bandit who depends on chance.

The impression that the principle of sufficient reason means that we are not free is deceptive. In order to see why this is so, a first step is to distinguish between hard anonymous causes and reasons. A **hard anonymous cause** is a cause that will have an effect, whether one wants it to or not. For instance, if someone were to strangle me for ten minutes I would be dead, whatever my wishes might be. If I am stabbed in the leg with a knife, it will hurt me, whether I want it to or not. If gravity follows Newton's law, one will be able to observe from the earth at a particular time precisely the same stars and constellations, whether one wants to or not. On many conceptions, laws of nature are supposed to express the actual connections between hard anonymous causes and their effects. Laws of nature are, so to speak, particularly hard, necessary and unyielding.

In contrast to this notion of hard anonymous causes, there is the concept of a reason. It is indeed true that there are many reasons that would never compel me to do something. Let us imagine that Olaf – a longstanding chain smoker – were to have the best possible reason finally to quit smoking. The reason might be that he would live longer, cough less, smell better, have better teeth, etc. It does not follow from his insight into this reason or this set of reasons that he will necessarily quit smoking. He will quit smoking if he wants to, but otherwise he will just go on smoking regardless of any list of reasons we might give him. Of course, we can try to compel him to quit smoking if we threaten him with prison if he carries on smoking. Yet, even then, there is always still a chance that, should he consider a life without cigarettes not to be worthwhile, Olaf will prefer not to be free to give up smoking. Reasons generally do not compel; they merely suggest that following the path of action they recommend might be a good idea. Reasons are proposals and not some kind of spiritual cause. Reasons can become motives for actions, which is not in any obvious way the circumstance with hard anonymous causes. In any case, adhering to the laws of nature is not a typical motif. Unless we are God, we do not usually intend to follow the laws of nature because it would make no sense to attempt not to follow them. To respect a reason for doing something, to incorporate it into one's life, means to accept that we could also not have incorporated it. Accepting a reason as a guiding motif for a course of action categorically differs from being compelled to do something.

This distinction of hard causes and reasons can lead to the paradox of free will. To that end, one must accept that nature is merely the reeling off of hard anonymous causes that lead to effects, which will in turn be hard causes for something else, and so on. In addition one must accept that nature is all there is. Then, there is no place for us as free agents in such a mechanism, since everything that happens at all happens whether one wants it to or not. Any kind of reasonable will that allows itself to be led by reasons seems to be opposed to this kind of mechanism.

Our freedom indeed has no place in the hard anonymous chain of cause and effect of an inexorable nature that is not concerned with us. And, conversely, nature has no place in what many contemporary philosophers call the "space of reasons," precisely because reasons are not supposed to be a case of hard causes. One is supposed to follow them by understanding them and not by being compelled by them, otherwise they would coincide with hard causes. In this sense, the philosopher John McDowell (b. 1942), in his very influential book *Mind and World*, distinguishes a "space of causes" from a "space of reasons."[13]

But is that really enough? How do we know whether we are ever guided by reasons? If we comply with a reason, such as a wise bit of advice, or do not comply with it, how does that happen? Does it simply lie in our neurochemistry? If that were the case, we would always be guided by our brain and its mechanism of hard anonymous causes after all. So it seems, at any rate. Hence, many believe that it is not sufficient to lay out a concept of reasons if one cannot show in addition that we are ever really free to follow them without being secretly compelled to follow them.

However, this impression is deceptive. Everything hinges on recognizing that both reasons and hard anonymous causes can guide our behavior at the same time. We do not have to choose between a depiction of the human being, on the one hand, as fully autonomous and, on the other, as being fundamentally part of non-human nature. Assume that on the basis of my neurobiological make-up, tomato sauce tastes better to me than Alfredo sauce. In that case, the relevant neural connections could be cited as hard causes for the fact that tomato sauce tastes better to me than Alfredo sauce. But perhaps today I have a good reason to opt for the Alfredo sauce, since it contains more protein and fat, which I would like to incorporate into my diet. In such a case, this reason would take precedence despite the fact that my overall preference for tomato sauce might turn out to be biologically hardwired.

Let us imagine that I pick the tomato sauce as usual. We can now draw up a list that includes the necessary conditions for this specific, actually occurring event. Hard causes will not be the only things on this list, as it will include some reasons. Here is an excerpt from the list of necessary conditions.

- My neurochemistry predisposes me to tomato sauce (this is expressed by the fact that it tastes better to me).
- My gut microbiota (my gut flora) are inclined to tomato sauce.
- I know that I get tomato sauce when I order spaghetti al pomodoro.
- Tomatoes are available today.
- Tomatoes have a certain price.
- I can afford the spaghetti al pomodoro.
  . . .

Some of the entries on the list are not hard anonymous causes. That tomatoes have a certain price surely has to do with the fact that they grow on our planet. But their price (their exchange value) is not itself a natural fact. Prices do not grow like tomatoes; they result from negotiations in complex economic systems. I could not order tomato sauce in a restaurant if there were no economic system that consisted in a set of negotiations driving the exchange value of goods. But such a set does not obey the laws of nature, as negotiations do not follow physical laws. This is one of the many reasons why economics is not at all like a natural science. Too bad, it is still in the grip of the ideological illusion that it can be expressed in a mathematical symbolism supposed to resemble the expression of laws of nature. And thereby hangs a tale ...

In any event, the principle of sufficient reason does not state that everything which happens does so as a result of hard anonymous causes. Since it is simply not the case that in all circumstances all necessary conditions that underlie an event are hard anonymous causes, what happens on our planet cannot be explained entirely by taking only the latter into account. It is simply an error to reduce all events to natural events. This mistake makes it look as if freedom could not find a place in nature. This impression of an incompatibility of freedom and nature derives from a misguided conception of nature and our overall place in it.

For instance, if one explains why a car thief is punished, one will employ all sorts of concepts that are considered necessary conditions for the event of punishment, even though these concepts do not all pick out hard causes. Naturally, this means that it is not the case that there is a single, very long causal chain which determines, directs or governs everything that exists. In other words, neither the Big Bang nor the Big Bang taken together with all laws of nature and the initial conditions of the universe is a cause for today's exchange rate of the US dollar or the election of Donald Trump as US president. Rather, there exist an enormous, completely incalculable number of necessary conditions, and given events happen because of them. *We are free because many of the necessary conditions for our actions are not hard causes. And we are not one-armed bandits because there is no room for chance thanks to the principle of sufficient reason. Everything has a sufficient reason (the collection of necessary conditions that jointly suffice for an occurrence), and nothing happens without reason and/or cause.*

I have claimed above that determinism and freedom are

compatible. But have I not ultimately denied that determinism is true? Not necessarily! If determinism were the thesis that there are only hard causes for events and no other kinds of conditions, it would in fact be false. However, one does injustice to determinism by associating it with such an outdated and at any rate false metaphysics.

Metaphysics, in general, is concerned with absolutely everything, with absolute totality, the world, the universe, reality as a whole, the cosmos, or whatever else you want to call it. But, as I have argued at length in *Why the World Does Not Exist*, absolute totality does not exist anyway. Hence, there is no overall metaphysical reason to assume that there is a single enormous causal chain by which everything that ever happens is linked. For this reason, determinism should not offer itself as a metaphysical thesis and attempt to inflate itself into a world picture which weakens its case. Also, qua metaphysical world picture, determinism would be fundamentally unscientific, as one could neither prove nor falsify it by actually observing the universe – or, for that matter, the brain. It would have already been decided in advance that there is a single enormous causal chain, which is neither a presupposition of physics and neuroscience nor anything that follows from empirical, scientific discoveries that have been made up to this point. Causal determinism is simply a myth from the past. At best, it is a philosophical, metaphysical claim.

Traditionally, the principle of sufficient reason is considered to be the epitome of a metaphysical thesis. Does it not state that everything that happens is determined by a sufficient reason? Do I not therefore simply replace one metaphysics with another? Some even think that the principle of sufficient reason tells us not only something about events but literally something about absolutely everything that exists. The principle would then in fact be metaphysical in the problematic sense I reject. For this reason, on my construal, the principle of sufficient reason is restricted; it talks not about absolutely everything but only about events. In my preferred version, it says that no event can occur without the necessary conditions for its occurrence being jointly sufficient.

An important twist that should be noted in this line of thought is the fact that I do not assume that all conditions can ever be reduced to a common category. Not all conditions are (hard causes or) reasons. The list of conditions is open. There are countless types of conditions that we cannot survey in a single theory, a metaphysics. Hence, all we need to safeguard our free will is a categorical distinction that allows us to understand that we have no credible evidence which forces us to identify all conditions of human action with hard anonymous causes.

My resolution of the hard problem of free will is thus a specific form of compatibilism. It claims that determinism in the form of the principle of sufficient reason is true and that nevertheless at the same time we are free, because some conditions of those events which we conceive of as emerging through freedom are properly referred to as free. We are free, because many of the necessary conditions of human action are precisely such that we cannot understand them without ascribing free will to agents. And we have no credible, non-metaphysical evidence which undermines this image of the human being as a free agent.

Friendly smites meanie and defeats metaphysical pessimism

An exemplary case can further illustrate the resolution of the hard problem of free will. Romeo sends Juliet a rose to make her happy. We would normally say that Romeo was free to do this – unless we were to learn that he did it under the influence of a drug that limits his freedom or something similar. However, we have no reason to suspect that Romeo was drugged or otherwise manipulated into sending the rose. Here are a few conditions for our classifying this event as an expression of freedom. Let us call this list the **friendly list:**

- Romeo likes Juliet.
- Romeo has the little bit of money needed to buy the rose.
- Romeo knows where to find Juliet before the rose withers.
- Romeo is able to move.
- Romeo wants to send Juliet a rose to make her happy.
- Romeo is someone who is made happy when others are happy, but most of all when Juliet is happy.
    . . .

No element on this list has a compulsory or coercive character that would limit Romeo's freedom. To be sure, the actual list is quite long. A skeptic about freedom would have to deal with the problem of having to argue that no entry on the list requires Romeo's freedom. Accordingly, he would have to replace the friendly list by one that deprives him of freedom. Let us call the alternative list the **meanie list,** because it undermines the expression of freedom with a mean-spirited maneuver.

- Romeo likes Juliet – only because of a genetic disposition.
- Romeo has the little bit of money needed to buy the rose – it is on hand just by chance (it fell off of a roof), while he just happened to be stumbling around the florist's.
- Romeo knows where to find Juliet before the rose withers. His knowledge is purely instinctive: he heads to Juliet's place because his nervous system sniffs out her scent trail, without his even noting this himself.
- Romeo can move – he is blown around by gusts of wind. He is moved about like a piece of paper in the wind.
- Romeo wants to send Juliet a rose to make her happy – but only because a certain hormone is released due to a brain lesion.
- Romeo is someone who is made happy when others are happy, but most of all when Juliet is happy – because he has just gotten over a long clinical depression that did not allow him to feel happy about anything other than someone else being happy, which made him into a compulsive do-gooder.

  . . .

We are all familiar with the fact that we are sometimes uncertain of the motivations of our action, both with respect to ourselves and in our encounters with others. Hence, we look for **action explanations** – that is, explanations which allow us to understand why someone (including ourselves) does something or did something. In this context, we can always suppose either benevolence or ulterior motives. The former lies behind the friendly list: one attributes freedom to someone, which is a charitable interpretation of an event that has every appearance of being a happy one (such as Romeo sending Juliet roses). Meanie lists substitute the appearance of benevolence either with ulterior motives (base motivations) or with explanations that allow us to disburden someone of the imposition of freedom. For example, if I am stumbling around and bump into someone on the street, no one will accuse me of having a base motive. In this respect, I simply was not free.

At this point of the argument, we need to realize that there is no sufficiently justified general suspicion that permits us to replace *all* motives for human action and *every* appearance of benevolence or freedom with an all-encompassing meanie list. If we had reason to believe that, in general, human action is never free, that would lead to a form of **metaphysical pessimism**, a philosophy prominently advocated by the grim Arthur Schopenhauer. He thought that there was no room for freedom in the structure of this world and preferred to understand every apparently benevolent action as the bare will to survive or the equally bare, purely biological will to reproduce. As he notes in his "The Metaphysics of Sexual Love," chapter 44 of the second volume of *The World as Will and Representation* (one should call this volume: The Second Part of the Tragedy): "For all amorousness is rooted in the sexual impulse alone, is in fact absolutely only a more closely determined, specialized, and indeed, in the strictest sense, individualized sexual impulse, however ethereally it may deport itself."[14] Schopenhauer goes to great lengths to explain the increasing rate of divorce in modern times in this way, too, for he believes that divorce is merely a consequence of the lie concealed in the miserable world's eternal cycle of rebirth, meaningless in itself. He does not explain divorce as a social phenomenon or as a series of free decisions. For him, it is simply the necessary consequence of falling in love, and love itself is nothing but a side-effect of the imperative to procreate. Schopenhauer's social agenda, which is fairly obvious, incidentally, is a justification of the Indian caste system along with its practice of arranged marriage.[15]

Accordingly, on this view, Romeo sends Juliet roses only because his motive is to sleep with her. Whatever he might think of tender motives, they play no actual role for Schopenhauer, who was still willing to credit some men (but no women) for sometimes breaking through the fatal cycle of rebirth if they make it to the special status of genius or saint. However, as his awful essay *On Women* makes unmistakably clear, he allotted to women only the role of "nurses and governesses of our earliest childhood"[16] or that of sexual temptress. Women, so we read, are "by nature ... meant to obey."[17] What happens if one renounces the cycle of the Indian caste system is clear to Schopenhauer: then, as in France, there is a revolution!

> In Hindustan no woman is ever independent, but each is under the guardianship of a father, husband, brother, or son ... That widows burn themselves on the corpses of their husbands is of course shocking [a brief flash of insight in Schopenhauer]; but [and thus the flash of insight is immediately extinguished] that they squander on their lovers the fortune which has been acquired by the husband through the incessant hard work of a lifetime, and in the belief that he was working for his children, is also shocking ... Was not the ever-growing influence of women in France from the time of Louis XIII responsible for the gradual corruption of the court and government which produced the first revolution, the consequences of this being all the subsequent upheavals?[18]

Schopenhauer, scorner of freedom, misogynist, and also not very sympathetic in other regards, is at the same time the master of the meanie list, as this passage proves in a paradigmatic way. At a historical remove from him, we recognize that these texts are purely ideological, that they lay claim to a discovery of a nature (for instance, "of women") in order to justify social structures that exist because of freedom and which can accordingly be transformed (abolished!).

Schopenhauer's purely ideological ensnarement should be more or less obvious to most readers of this book. At this point in history, one can only hope that the contemporary scientific and philosophical literature weighed down with Darwinitis and neuromania will in the future be perceived as ideological. Since one should not wait until then and hope for better times, one must intervene today.

There is no reason for an all-encompassing metaphysical pessimism that replaces all of the friendly items on the lists that express our action explanations with mean-spirited ones. Such an imposition is unacceptable, as well as being a form of paranoia supported by pseudoscience that is to be mistrusted in principle, both on its own account and for other reasons, too.

The resolution of the paradox of free will sketched here consists in the claim that the principle of sufficient reason is true and that both physical and neural determinism might be true (we simply do not know if they are). However, these two kinds of determinism only threaten our freedom if all events, including all human actions, belong entirely only to the realm of physics-cum-biology. Among other things, this presupposes the unwarranted assumption that we can always understand and explain our actions better if we phrase our accounts of what we are doing in the language of the natural sciences. This amounts to the thesis of naturalism, which under the scalpel of philosophical analysis turns out to be largely unfounded and certainly overly metaphysical (and unscientific).[19] Naturalism is ultimately simply not true, because many events take place only if agents are involved in them, and agents can only be involved in events if they actually exist. Yet, agents cannot be ontologically reduced to epiphenomena of purely natural events. We can do what we want to do. Our actions are mostly free – or, rather, we have no good reason to doubt this. Naturalism in general and neurocentrism in particular are forms of ideologically driven metaphysical paranoia. They are neither scientific findings nor warranted suspicions that human action never has the motivation the agents ascribe to themselves.

However, I do not mean to convey the idea that there is a will which is just as free as our actions are. The claim that such a will exists as a second agent located somewhere in ourselves (either in the brain as a neurobiological homunculus or in some more spiritual layer of ourselves as souls) is a source of much confusion. For this reason, Nietzsche, in his critique of Schopenhauer, considered a properly radical solution by pointing out that *the* will does not exist, that there is never an interplay of capacities and capabilities which one could characterize as *the* will. "I laugh at your free will and at your unfree will, too. What you call your will is an illusion to me, there is no will."[20] In contrast, Nietzsche argues that "will" is "a false reification."[21] Thus he responds to Schopenhauer, who was initially a great model, an "educator," for him.[22]

This is all the more significant given that Schopenhauer took the concept of the will to extremes. And, indeed, he did this especially in the framework of the debate over human freedom. Schopenhauer produced the most influential version of the notion that we can indeed do what we want to do (freedom of action) but cannot choose what we want as an act of our own volition, a paradox definitive of debates about free will up to the present day. In this context, Schopenhauer claimed that the will determines us, that we are directed or "willed" by the will itself, so to speak, without ever being able to change this heteronomy. The will is our fate as humans because we have a character as respective persons only by our being committed to want this or that. Schopenhauer, like many popular neuroscientists, sees us as victims of ourselves qua brains.

Yet Schopenhauer falls into the very trap into which he had earlier tried to run his opponents. In particular, he accepts that there is a capacity, the will, whose activation is not up to us but without which we would not have any freedom of action. How are we supposed to be able to do what we want to do without wanting anything in the first place? This is a valid question and rightly posed. But it does not follow that there is such a thing as *the* will. Why should we not simply say that we want, wish for, like, prefer, or choose all kinds of things, without it being the case that this is because "the will," "the wish," "the liking," "the preference" or "the choice" is operative in us, like an alien being lodged behind our consciousness, directing us from there? Errors of this sort are known as **reifications**. Schopenhauer, like Freud and the neurocentric enemies of their own free will, reifies his own vocabulary in which we couch our self-portrait as minded animals. This is a form of avoidable self-alienation.

Let us briefly return to the self. One might think that we bear a self-thing inside ourselves or are a self-thing that dwells behind our eyes (the good old homunculus). One might even seemingly "provide reasons" for this, for instance, by means of the following fallacy (which Kant calls a "paralogism," as we have seen).

1 We are able to observe things (cats, worms, trees, and so forth).
2 If we observe things, we have thoughts.
3 If we have thoughts, then someone must exist who has these thoughts.
4 Since we are only too happy to say "I" [*ich*], let us call the bearer of thoughts "the self" [*das Ich*].
5 We are able to observe the bearer of thoughts.
Conclusion: Therefore, the self (the bearer of thoughts) is a thing.

The mistake here is the identification of a formal object of our thought (the self) with a thing in the world (a brain, say, or a soul for that matter). It is simply not the case that everything we can think about with true or false thoughts is an object or thing in the natural world. There are some things we can observe and track with thoughts that are not part of the natural world, and the self is precisely one of those "things." Neurocentrism ideologically assumes that we are a natural thing among natural things and that it is only such things that exist. But it is false that only natural things exist, since values, hopes and numbers exist, *inter alia*, which do not self-evidently qualify as natural things.

The basic error lies in the idea that there is a world out there that, as a metaphor commonly used by contemporary philosophers suggests, has furniture which is completely independent from us, namely the "furniture of reality." The object furnishings of reality are then supposedly tangible things that are pushed around through space and time according to inviolable laws of nature. As corporeal things, we would then only be one thing among all other things. In that case, the existence of consciousness, numbers, values, open possibilities, and so forth, would of course be an enigma. However, consciousness, free will, and so on, are not objectively enigmatic things in the natural world. This seems plausible only if one is in the grip of the misguided metaphysical fantasy of a completely reified universe of which everything and everyone is a part.

If we reify everything, we get caught in contradictions. We then all too quickly have to introduce a self-thing and identify it with a brain-thing in which a will-thing is lodged (or several will-things which are located in different areas of the brain). The next thing we know, we are now supposed to believe that nothing can be free because all things are related to each other according to laws of nature that govern what happens to each and every thing. Yet this building-block metaphysics that conjures up an image of the world in which things bump into each other and sometimes get stuck to each other, and so on, does not of course fit very well with our self-image as freely acting persons among other such persons (nor does it fit with actual physics, by the way). I call this kind of metaphysics **legocentrism** (in honor of the well-known toy). Persons are simply not natural things (they are neither like Playmobil nor like Lego).

Human dignity is inviolable

This line of thought has important ethical consequences. Article 1 of the Basic Law for the Federal Republic of Germany famously states: "Human dignity shall be inviolable. To respect and pro-tect it shall be the duty of all state authority." Of course, one can interpret and explain this article in different ways. In any event, it is important to respect the valuable insight that human dignity and human rights are conceptually linked.

What should not be overlooked here is that human dignity is literally inviolable, since it is not a natural thing. One cannot grab hold of human dignity or even perceive it with one's senses as natu-ral things are perceived. It does not belong to us because we are human-things whose brain-things have been installed to grow and flourish within our skulls.

Here Kant's famous **distinction between economic value (price) and dignity** can be of further help:

> ... everything has either a price or a dignity. What has a price is such that something else can also be put in its place as its equivalent; by contrast, that which is elevated above all price, and admits of no equivalent, has a dignity. That which refers to universal human incli-nations and needs has a *market price* ... but that which constitutes the condition under which alone something can be an end in itself does not have merely a relative worth, i.e., a price, but rather an inner worth, i.e., dignity.[23]

In this passage, Kant points out that our condition as human agents is an end in itself. Here one has to make the reader aware of a common wordplay in German philosophy. The German word for "condition" is *Bedingung*, which contains the word *Ding* (= thing). A *Be-Dingung* turns something into a thing without necessarily being itself a thing. A condition makes a thing into what it is with-out all conditions necessarily having to be hard causes. According to Kant, human dignity belongs to us because we live in the "realm of ends."[24] It is part of our constitution as agents to be conditioned by human dignity. The realm of ends is a system of concepts that we use to make human actions understandable to ourselves. This includes concepts such as friendship, deception, gift, president, copyright, exploitation, free will, alienation, ideology, revolution, reform and history. These concepts are distinct from the ones that we use to make natural processes understandable, processes which automatically run their course without any help from us.

In Kant's time, the dividing line between natural automatic processes and free actions was admittedly in dispute, which received literary treatment in Romanticism. It is sufficient to think of famous automata such as Olimpia from E. T. A. Hoffmann's *The Sandman*. In another well-known passage, from the *Critique of Practical Reason*, Kant opposes "mechanism of nature" and "freedom" to each other, in the course of which he formulates the suspicion that we could after all be automata. Kant emphasizes the central thought that things which are not subject to the "*mechanism* of nature" need not "be actual material *machines*."[25] In distinction to many contemporary advocates of determinism, Kant explicitly takes issue with the hard problem of free will as formulated by Leibniz and made popular by Schopenhauer.

> One is here taking account only of the necessity of the connection of events in a time series as it develops according to natural law, whether the subject in whom this elapsing occurs is called *automaton materiale*, inasmuch as the machinery is driven by matter, or, with Leibniz, [*automaton*] *spirituale*, inasmuch as it is driven by presentations; and if the freedom of our will were none other than the latter [kind] (say, psychological and comparative freedom, not simultaneously transcendental, i.e., absolute, freedom), then it would basically be no better than the freedom of a turnspit, which, once it has been wound up, also performs its motions on its own.[26]

On the basis of an admittedly somewhat unorthodox reading of Kant, one can claim that, as inhabitants of the realm of ends, we are really free insofar as we can only understand each other if we allow for genuine teleological explanations of action. Let us recall Larry and his brown bread: Larry goes into the supermarket to buy brown bread that is not moldy. Thus, he is not moving around merely in the realm of hard causes. It is not the case that Larry has been blown into the supermarket by hurricane-force winds and has landed in front of shelves of bread. Larry goes to the supermarket of his own accord. His action is an element of a whole system of actions that constitutes Larry's biography.

Actions are distinguished from natural events by the fact that a natural event need not be an element of a teleological system where someone does something in order to achieve an end. For this reason, natural events (such as having to answer the "call of nature") are involuntary. Having to answer the "call of nature" indeed has a function in the organism, but it is not an end toward which someone has decided to aim.

A large part of human civilization consists of the fact that we eliminate natural events from occurring around human bodies or at least make them look more beautiful: we trim our fingernails and cut our hair, we clothe ourselves, have private bathrooms that can be locked, make use of technology with which we improve our natural potential (calculators, trains, and so on). This also includes the fact that we do not live with wild animals but would like to know that they are somewhere else entirely. They are supposed to remain in wilderness areas undisturbed by human beings, or in zoos, and not bother us.

Be that as it may, the idea of a dignified human life is the idea of a life that is able to move in the "realm of ends." If we are sick or terminally ill, natural events take over our lives. However, this is not the normal state of affairs, as neurocentrism would have us believe. We are governed by hard causes and neural connections in our body only when we are sick. Whoever supports environmental conservation and the protection of animals does not do this only because there is an electrical storming of neurons within the skull that drives one against one's will to engage in such actions, or that implants the will, whether one wants it or not, to be used in this way for the community.

Human dignity is inviolable because we are *not only* organisms and animals of a specific kind but are those particular animals who live in the realm of ends. Please note that I do not mean that other animal species are excluded from this realm. Indeed, domestic animals already live with us in our realm of ends, even if they do not understand it nearly as well as we do. Admittedly, no single person comes even close to knowing everything about the realm of ends in general, because innumerably many people and institutions contribute to it. Hence it sometimes seems to us to be more like a natural force than a manifestation of freedom.

We create soft conditions, so to speak, through which we partially free ourselves from the concatenation of hard anonymous causes. Other animal species do not have a kind of reflexively, philosophically grounded legal system like ours, which resulted from millennia-long reflections on the structure of a just political system, among other things. Such reflections were paradigmatically elaborated at an advanced theoretical level by the ancient

Greeks (primarily Plato and Aristotle, but also tragedians such as Aeschylus and historians such as Thucydides and Herodotus). Jurisprudence and political science have been established on this ancient foundation. They are expressions of free will, because they are constitutive elements in the self-portrait of human agents. Such elements are subject to historical change, a change not governed by laws of nature.

We are not more valuable than other animal species because of these reflexive achievements. As Kant writes, dignity is not a relative value and thus not something that elevates us above the rest of the animal realm. From the fact that human dignity exists, which is perhaps also what establishes our human rights, it does not follow that we may treat other animal species badly just because they are unfamiliar with our realm of ends. Otherwise, our dignity would be reduced to a relative value, one that allows us to look good in relation to other living beings. However, according to Kant, dignity is an inner value that I see substantiated in the fact that our actions are free because not all necessary conditions of our actions are hard causes.

On the same level as God or nature?

I have already cited Cavell's insightful dictum that "Nothing is more human than the wish to deny one's humanity."[27] Sartre famously advocated a similar thesis, namely, the thesis that a large part of human behavior aims to absolve us of our own freedom. As he puts it, "man fundamentally is the desire to be God."[28] I call this **dehumanization from above**: human beings become inhuman through self-divination.

Sartre's basic philosophical idea is not hard to understand. He distinguishes between in-itself and for-itself. Something that is in itself is completely identical to itself without any conceptual mediation turning it into the thing it is. Think of a rock. It has an absolute being. To be sure, it can be destroyed, but it cannot change itself by changing its beliefs about itself – because it has no beliefs. Rocks are an example of the in-itself. Some primitive organisms, too, should undoubtedly be included in the category of the in-itself (we do not know at this time at what "level" in the animal realm the for-itself begins). In contrast to such beings, "human reality," as Sartre calls it, entails that we belong to the for-itself. This is Sartre's version of the already well-known idea that our image of ourselves (even if it is a false image) expresses something essential about us, something in light of which we can change. We are always to some extent what we consider ourselves to be. Even if we are wrong about who or what we are, this error constitutes who we are. If I consider myself to be a good dancer (without being one), I am a person who considers himself to be a good dancer. This says something about me (for example, that I am too vain to admit that I am a bad dancer or that I would love to be a good dancer).

For Sartre, human beings devise the idea of God because God stands for a perfect combination of in-itself and for-itself. God has no false beliefs about himself; he cannot be self-deluded, vain, envious, etc., while he is at the same time also not like a stupid, lifeless rock. Rather, he is imagined to be an exceptionally perfect person (in any case, this is how philosophers imagine their god, who is for that reason called the "God of the philosophers"). In Sartre's view, we are free because there is a gap between our in-itself (our body, our parents, and so forth) and our for-itself. This gap can never be closed, even if we like to develop a variety of strategies to cover it up. In particular, a classical strategy for covering up the gap at the very center of our being is **essentialism**, which in this context is the claim that a human being or a social group is determined by their essence to engage in specific patterns of conduct that are only apparently free. Racist and sexist ideas are essentialist in that sense, as are nationalist ideas that claim Bavarians or Greeks have an essence that manifests itself in their actions: for instance, Bavarians like to drink beer and vote CSU, while Greeks are corrupt, lazy, congenial, radically left-wing or radically right-wing, and so forth. Stereotypical notions such as these are currently part of the portfolio of German ideology, not to mention the ideological regression of the US. Ideology is as widespread as humans, of course. It is not restricted to a specific nation-state or time in history.

Unfortunately, there are countless stereotypes of the essentialist kind, and from the perspective of neo-existentialism they serve only to deny our own freedom by denying it to others. If others are automata, we cannot be blamed for not making any use of our own freedom to treat them like free living beings. Ideology has harmful consequences for others, as it relieves those who cling to their ideology from the moral imperative to change their behavior and their very selves by giving up cherished, but ultimately ungrounded and even evil assumptions about others.

That said, one can combine the existentialist motifs of Cavell and Sartre and identify two dangers: a dehumanization from above and one from below. Dehumanization from above is a threat if we choose God as our ideal self – that is, if we want to become like God (something religion itself in all of its varieties typically prohibits). **Dehumanization from below** is a threat if, infected with Darwinitis, we believe that all human behavior can be completely explained by evolutionary biology.

In present-day society, dehumanization from above is not associated with religion as much as it is with the fantasies of omnipotence of post-humanism and trans-humanism, as well as the idea of a digital revolution, engulfing everything, lying in the hands of the gods of Silicon Valley. There are currents of thought that proceed by claiming that, due to our technology, we human beings have already been cyborgs for a while now. The laptop on which I am composing these lines, according to the advocates of the thesis of the "extended mind," supposedly belongs to me just as much as my liver does. At the extreme, think of scenarios like those from the film *Transcendence*, which many take to be desirable as they come with the hope that we can be uploaded to an online platform after death, where we will enjoy an eternal life on the exciting internet.

Dehumanization from above stems from "progressive cerebration" – that is, the cephalization of our culture, pithily described by the German poet and medical doctor Gottfried Benn. Recent neuromania is another chapter in the progressive cerebration. Benn opposes a thesis advanced by the Austrian neurologist Constantin von Economo (1876–1931), who was well known for, among other things, having discovered the brain inflammation *encephalitis lethargica*, which we have already discussed (p. 70). Von Economo hypothesized that the history of mind is understandable via the evolution of the brain. In accordance with this, he claimed that there was a kind of progress of the growing brain that drives cultural progress in its train.

Benn rejects Economo's idea, which he considers along with nihilism to be a symptom of decline of an unsteady modernity, primarily in the first half of the last century. Benn – who sadly opted politically for National Socialism, which he wrongly thought was going to be a political system supportive of the arts – in 1932 asked in his essay "After Nihilism":

> Do we still have the strength, asks the author, to oppose the scientific-deterministic world view with a self that is grounded in creative freedom? Do we still have a strength drawn from the power of traditional Western thought, not from economic chiliasms and political mythologems, to break through the materialistic-mechanical form-world and to design the images of deeper worlds out of an ideality that posits itself as such, and in a measure that sets its own limits?[29]

In place of materialism and nihilism, Benn posits "constructive intelligence ... as an emphatic and conscious principle of far-reaching liberation from materialisms of every stripe."[30] Within the framework of progressive cerebration, Benn recognizes in the combination of "Newton Imperator, Darwin Rex"[31] an unbridled "intellectualistic exponential increase of becoming"[32] – in short: a dehumanization from above.

This dehumanization from above is also operative in **functionalism**, which claims that consciousness or mind is a formal functional structure that can be implemented or realized in various materials – in the age of Silicon Valley, silicon is repeatedly cited as an alternative to our brain tissue. One might think that functionalism is a new thesis that came into play with the arrival of computers. But here Benn is remarkably clear-sighted. In his "Speech to the Academy," he describes the basic structure of neurocentrism, which has not changed to the present day, as follows:

> A new stage of cerebration seems to be around the corner, a more frigid, colder one: to conceive our own existence, history, the universe in only two categories: the concept and the hallucination. From Goethe's time, the *disintegration of reality* has transgressed every measure, so that even the wader, if he notices it, must plunge into the water: the earth is ruined by pure dynamics and by pure relation. *Functionalism*, you know, means the time of unbridled movement, inexistent being.[33]

Just like Goethe and Nietzsche before him, Benn recommends that we reflect on the historical background of modern intellectualization. In Goethe's epic *Faust: The Second Part of the Tragedy*, a homunculus succeeds in escaping from the phial in which he had been living by smashing it on "the bright throne."[34] As the philosopher Thales – who appears on the scene in the "Classical Walpurgis Night" – remarks, the homunculus is "beguiled by Proteus"[35] into giving himself over to "Eros ... who gave all things beginning"[36] and causes the glass in which he is trapped to shatter. Nietzsche will later call this "the Dionysian,"[37] which in any case is not of much help, since even the Silicon Valley bandits, to relieve themselves of functionalism, participate in "Burning Man," a festival of intoxicated ecstasy in the Black Rock Desert of Nevada. There, appropriately enough, a very large wooden effigy is set on fire and burned. Post-humanism receives its sacrifice. "Burning Man" is a post-humanist celebration of Silicon Valley's dehumanization from above.

With the homunculus's act of shattering, Goethe alludes to Schelling's *Naturphilosophie*. Schelling radically broke with the

idea that the human mind as an intellectual self, as pure consciousness, confronts a nature that is inanimate and without self
or consciousness. Schelling and Goethe both thought that Fichte
advocated precisely this position – and Fichte, as we have already
learned, was a thorn in the side of Goethe, who was politically
very influential. As professor in Jena, let us recall, Fichte became
involved in the atheism dispute, since he ultimately advocated a
form of purely rational religion that viewed God not as a person or
an authority beyond human reason but, rather, as the moral order
immanent to the world: "That living and active moral order is itself
God; we require no other God and can grasp no other. There is
no ground in reason from which one can proceed and, by means
of an inference from that which is grounded to its ground, assume
some separate being as the cause of that which is grounded."[38] In
complete contrast, Goethe and Schelling (represented by Proteus in
Faust: The Second Part of the Tragedy) object that we should not
imagine nature as a mechanical contraption. If we belong to nature
at all, we must assume that our mind, including our emotional
world, is no stranger to a nature devoid of meaning and morality. For this reason, these two authors mobilize the human being's
pre-logical, irrational prehistory against progressive cerebration.
In other words, they rightly insist on the fact that there is no intentional consciousness without phenomenal consciousness, that as
thinking beings we also feel. The idea that our life is governed by
an egotistical calculus for survival is corrected with reference to
our capacity for erotic enthusiasm. Dehumanization from above is
thus foiled.

As an argument against neurocentrism, Benn accurately points
out that "the biological basis of the personality is not the cere-
brum, as was assumed in an earlier scientific era, but the whole
organism."[39] Yet, at the other end of the spectrum, there is all too
easily the threat of a dehumanization from below, which today
assumes the form of Darwinitis. I am thinking in particular of the
attempt to ground human goodness – that is, our moral capacity –
in non-human nature by studying primate communities in order to
find altruistic social relations there.

Authors such as the ethologist Frans de Waal (b. 1948) are surely
right when they point out that a dualism "which pits morality
against nature and humanity against other animals" is untenable.[40]
The idea that brutality exists in the rest of the animal realm, while
the human being alone has somehow tamed itself – or has been
tamed by God – is not empirically supportable. For this reason,
primatology is of course also philosophically relevant. However,

it never proves that morality is merely a side-effect of evolution. At best, it shows that other primates also participate in the moral realm of ends, that they also have a mind in a full sense of the term, and maybe even a history. We do not know any of this yet, as we have not deciphered the languages of other animals. In any event, it seems clear that they have no written records and institutions based on traditions – but, again, this does not elevate us above the rest of the animal kingdom in any special sense.

PS: There are no savages

In modern political philosophy there has been a prolonged debate over the question of whether "savages" (in other words, the inhabitants of North and South America who were newly discovered by Europeans at the end of the fifteenth century) lived in a natural condition free of states, and indeed of morality. In modern anthropology, it became clear that humanity could not be classified into the supposedly "savage" on the one hand and the "civilized" on the other – one of the reasons being that, from antiquity, this classification has been used in order to justify slavery, which was finally recognized as a moral evil in the nineteenth century. Instead of such classifications, the French sociologist Bruno Latour (b. 1947), in his book *We Have Never Been Modern*, aptly postulates a "symmetrical anthropology."[41]

Symmetrical anthropology no longer divides humanity into a premodern (the formerly "savage") group and a modern (the formerly "civilized") group. Rather, it proceeds from the fact that we appear just as different in the eyes of every genuine or supposed other as they do in ours. Here a symmetry prevails in which we are no longer conceptually privileged in understanding the human mind because we are more technologically advanced.

After a long course of events that consumed many human lives, it finally became clear that universalism really has no philosophical alternative, even if recent political events can be read as a rebellion against the truth of universalism. **Universalism** is the thesis that all human beings are fundamentally equal, that there are no different species (or, even worse, races) of human beings who are somehow situated at different stages of development and hence have fundamentally different values that are incompatible with the advanced values of modernity.

The realization of the truth of universalism means that a typical justification of political power should no longer function. This justification – which has been extensively used both politically and ideologically – proceeds from the claim that human beings are naturally anarchistic and tend to raid, plunder and instrumentalize each other for egotistical ends.

This ideological representation of the "state of nature," as Thomas Hobbes quite influentially described it in his gloomy, visionary *Leviathan*, is familiar today primarily in the Hollywood genre of apocalyptic movies. As soon as public order is threated by an alien invasion, by zombies, by a natural catastrophe of unimaginable magnitude or simply by the end of the world, such movies usually depict raids on supermarkets and a state of generalized civil war. The first thing human beings do in that genre, now that the police are no longer watching, is take advantage of their newly won freedom to seize hold of every conceivable good by force. Such scenarios imply that public order protects us from ourselves, so to speak. If public order were to disappear, man would again be "an arrant wolf to man," as Hobbes puts it in his famous formulation.[42]

In any case, it should no longer be officially acceptable today to justify the state's monopoly on violence by referring to the brutal savages who supposedly lie concealed inside all of us, because this has long been perceived as an ideological construct by advanced sociology and anthropology. Fortunately, our idea of constitutional democracies is still in many places aligned with universalism – that is, it is not justified by claiming that we view constitutional democracy as our contingent system of government, which the state merely uses to justify its retention of power over us evil, brutal citizens. This model would not be compatible with our claims to political freedom. If we all thought that the state and only the state imposes on us codes of conduct such as morality, so that we do not continually threaten each other with murder and mayhem, we would be right not to feel very free. It would be hard to escape the impression that we are a "nation of devils"[43] tamed by the equally brutal government.

In contrast, in his famous text *Toward Perpetual Peace*, Kant recognizes that we are not such devils, even though the justification of a public order would have to function even if we were devils. The assumption that we are evil by nature is only a fiction that we employ to make it understandable to ourselves why institutions are reasonable both for good and for evil human beings.

> The problem of establishing a state, no matter how hard it may sound, is *soluble* even for a nation of devils (if only they have understanding) and goes like this: "Given a multitude of rational beings

all of whom need universal laws for their preservation but each of whom is inclined covertly to exempt himself from them, so to order this multitude and establish their constitution that, although in their private dispositions they strive against one another, these yet so check one another that in their public conduct the result is the same as if they had no such evil dispositions."[44]

The point is that the state (in other words, its chosen representatives) can proceed neither from the supposed fact that we are a nation of angels nor from the supposed fact that we are a nation of devils. Rather, the state is a matter of guaranteeing political freedom for everyone, whether they are good or evil, or, to put it better, whether they act in a good way or in an evil way. Fortunately, many of us have been more or less able to free ourselves from the idea that there is a human nature which can be determined phenotypically – for instance, as race – or in historical-nationalistic terms (the Germans, the Norwegians, the Chinese) – by linking essences instead to the state of economic development, for instance. We need to recognize fully that our essence as human beings is a function of the historical structure of our mind as *Geist* – i.e., of our capacity to create images of what it is to be a human being and act in accordance with these images. In this context, it is important to emphasize, with Kant, that the creation of self-images is constrained by moral norms: how we conceive of ourselves as human beings in part determines the moral value of our actions. This is one of the many reasons why ideologies can be dangerous, as they impose distorted representations of the human mind on us and are thereby able to manipulate us into acting against our own interests and those of everybody else.

Certainly, there is a lot to be done to spread the insight into universalism. For example, I fear that, if one were to launch a survey of how a typical German looks, many people would probably believe they have an answer. The point, however, is that "a German" has no appearance, since being German is a normative status. A German is someone who has German citizenship. One need not have a particular kind of appearance for that. Admittedly, citizenship is associated with values, since, in the case of Germany, as it is right now, it is anchored in the framework of a free democratic constitutional order. Since this includes human rights, equality of opportunity, indeed a universal idea of freedom and equality before the law, it follows from all of this that, politically speaking, we have a great chance to rid ourselves of the idea that human beings can be broken up into different subspecies.

However, it remains true that we are nowhere near a universal realization of the universal structure of morality. If human rights are supposed to distinguish us from other animal species, the fact that we can arbitrarily misuse animal species for our own purposes once more brings us back to the idea of the "savage." In this case, one imagines that "wild animals" are a danger to civilization so that one can claim a universal human monopoly of violence against the rest of the animal realm, a thought process underlying the current ecological disasters we are witnessing. The current ecological crisis, among other things, is a function of the dehumanization from above: humans believe they are beyond nature and that God may even tell them to exploit the planet at will (think of the dangerous association of Christian fundamentalism and Republican climate change denial in the US).

Kant offered a well-known **dehumanization argument** that refers to the fact that "violent and cruel treatment of animals is . . . intimately opposed to a human being's duty to himself," since it thus "dulls" the "shared feeling of their suffering" even toward other human beings.[45] Hence, with Kant, we could derive animal rights from the very foundation of human rights: "Even gratitude for the long service of an old horse or dog (just as if they were members of the household) belongs *indirectly* to a human being's duty *with regard to* these animals; considered as a *direct* duty, however, it is always only a duty of the human being *to* himself."[46] We should thus remain human beings and only become better at understanding what moral and political opportunities this entails. To this end, one must criticize the ideologists who, as I have sketched in this book, are associated with a double dehumanization. An important step in overcoming one's ideological ensnarement is to draw the lesson from modernity that there are no savages, indeed that even other animal species are not savages. We have fundamentally distinguished ourselves from them so that we could go around with a glorified self-image. We are different from other animals – that is all. Our dignity does not derive from this difference. It is not given to or implanted in us as nature but, rather, assigned in advance as a task that we are still far from completing. The human being has not yet established a moral and political order in which all human beings are recognized for what they are: minded animals with a history which all share the capacity to lead a life in light of their conceptions of what it is to be a human being.

Man is not a face drawn in the sand

In this book, I have sketched the outlines of a philosophy of mind
– or, rather, of *Geist* – for the twenty-first century. In so doing,
my intention was to elaborate the concept of spiritual freedom
and to advocate it against reductionist and eliminativist programs
that would like to persuade us that we have neither minds in
any demanding sense nor freedom. The neurocentric opponent
represents a widespread form of ideology, whose main intention
from epoch to epoch I see in the various attempts of the human
being to get rid of itself. This self-alienation of the human mind
assumes many forms today, which to some extent revolve around
the thoughts of trans-humanism and post-humanism. That is, they
revolve around the idea that the era of the human being has come
to an end because, heading into the future as cyborgs, we have
outgrown our biological nature.

A problem that contributes to the ideology of our time can be
linked to the fact that the humanities, which in German are called
Geisteswissenschaften – i.e., sciences of *Geist* – after World War
II began radically to dismiss *Geist*. The famous title of a series of
lectures that was held at the University of Freiburg encapsulates
this: *Die Austreibung des Geistes aus den Geisteswissenschaften*
[The Expulsion of *Geist* from the Humanities].[47] The organizer
of this lecture series, the literary theorist Friedrich Kittler, who
died in 2011, explained this expulsion in the following manner.
According to him, the concepts of a "mind" and of a "human
being" were first constructed in early modernity and consolidated
by different domains of knowledge. The former spiritual realm
[*Geisterwelt*] of superstition was in this way replaced by a single
spirit, a *Geist*, or a human mind. Yet this notion for him is now
itself to be overcome as a superstition, because it involves an
untenable construct that in any case is about to disappear in favor
of new technological orders as well as of an overall new order of
things.

Modernity in German is also called the time of the new
[*Neuzeit*], because it is the epoch based on the belief that one
could start something radically new which changes everything so
fundamentally that we will finally arrive at the end time or a state
of post-history. The time of the new longs to be the end time, as
numerous apocalyptic films, novels and television series make
clear. Like good old Christians, many people wish for a decisive
final event to occur, a revolution after which nothing will be as it
was before, but everything will be better and settled definitively,

once and for all. In particular, one might wish that demands for freedom will eventually come to an end.

In a nutshell: modernity fosters imaginary forms of relief. Yet, one must stand up in opposition to this in the name of freedom. True progress consists not in the illusory ideal of overcoming the mind and the human being but in improving the moral and juridical order in light of our insights into who we are as free human agents, without identifying us with things in the natural world (such as a brain, an assortment of genes or a race).

Thus, there is no utopia still to come, no time after historical times that would in principle be better placed for freedom to be advanced than the one in which we already find ourselves. There is no better place, neither in the future, nor in the past, nor on Mars. Neither postmodernity nor post-humanism will better fulfill the demands for freedom than our current era. We have the improvement of humanity in our hands, as individuals and as institutions. No one can take this away; it can only be oppressed.

The expulsion of *Geist* and the human being from the humanities has an ominous historical background, since it springs not least from Martin Heidegger's *Letter on Humanism*. Heidegger explicitly composed this work to distance himself from existentialism, which he scorned because it was a modern urban, progressive and liberal philosophy. In contrast, as the publication of his so-called *Black Notebooks* has once more called to mind, he preferred to align himself with National Socialism and an idea of the essence of the German people that was utopian to the point of madness.[48] Heidegger exchanged the concept of *Geist*, which refers to the fact that our freedom consists in working in historically and socially relevant ways on our self-portrait in the light of conceptual and ethical demands, for a concept of essence that is supposed to bind us surreptitiously to our soil. Thus, in a seminar from 1933–4 on *Nature, History and the State*, he speaks of the supposed fact that "the nature of our German space would definitely be revealed differently" to a "Slavic people . . . from the way it is revealed to us; to Semitic nomads, it will perhaps never be revealed at all."[49]

Another source for the supposed overcoming of humanism is the Heidegger-inspired *The Order of Things* by the influential French sociologist, historian and philosopher Michel Foucault (1926–1984). This book describes how the concept of the human being emerged in the modern life sciences and human sciences and how it has changed over time. From this Foucault draws the absurd conclusion that the human being has existed for only a few hundred years, because he considers the human being to be only a point of intersection in different scientific discourses, and thus a construct, which is a terrible philosophical confusion: "Taking a relatively short chronological sample within a restricted geographical area – European culture since the sixteenth century – one can be certain that man is a recent invention within it."[50] Foucault concludes from this that the epoch of the human being could also be brought to a total end – indeed, just like Heidegger and other eschatologists, he even hopes for "some event of which we can at the moment do no more than sense the possibility."[51] The book closes with the prospect, indeed with the wager, "that man would be erased, like a face drawn in sand at the edge of the sea."[52] I venture to bet against this!

Of course, the human being will disappear someday, simply because – this is a detail of my bet – we will never reach the Star Trek universe via androids and warp-drives and colonize planets that are far enough away from our sun when the latter dies one day, and we have already long since been pulled into the abyss.

Humanity as a whole is not to be preserved for eternity. We will be extinct sooner or later. Humanity is finite, as is each individual, too. We find ourselves in dimensions of unimaginable vastness and will never sufficiently understand the universe in order to be able to provide an exact assessment of our place in it. And yet, in modernity we have much progress to report. We live in an age of knowledge. However, this will lead to further progress only if we stop fooling ourselves into believing that we are on the verge of realizing that we are neither minds nor human beings which are still free to make progress.

Hence an important task for us in our century is to take a new look at our situation as minded animals. We must overcome materialism, which would have us believe that all that exists is what is found in the universe (in the sense of the reality of hard anonymous causes, of matter and energy), and which for that reason desperately seeks a conception of the mind that is able to reduce *Geist* to consciousness and then reduce consciousness to an electrical storming of neurons. We are citizens of many worlds, we move in the realm of ends. This provides us a series of conditions for freedom.

There is no reason in principle to engage in escapism. But there are many reasons to further social and political progress, because untold numbers of human beings live at present under conditions which make it difficult simply to tell them to live with human dignity. Man is still an arrant wolf to man. This is our real problem, and we cannot get rid of it by all becoming vegetarians in affluent

societies, by attending meditation classes, or by identifying mind
and brain. Euro-Hinduism is only another evasion, a looking away
from the real problems. The human being's greatest enemy is still
the human being, and this spoils for many the only prospect which
we human beings have: this life that we are living right now.

There is no reason to pin our hopes on a utopian future. We
exist here and now, and that is all. The poet Rainer Maria Rilke
celebrated this in his *Duino Elegies* with his concept of our being-
here (which we should oppose to Heidegger's being-there, always
in the future).

> Life is glorious here. You girls knew it, even you
> who seem to have gone without it – you who sank under
> in the cities' vilest streets festering like open sewers.
> For there was one hour for each of you, maybe
> less than an hour, some span between two whiles
> that can hardly be measured, when you possessed Being.
> All. Your veins swelled with existence.
> But we forget so easily what our laughing neighbor
> neither confirms nor envies. We want to make it
> visible, even though the most visible joy reveals
> itself to us only when we've transformed it, within.[53]

Actually, life can be glorious here, but not always and not for
everyone. We human beings are to blame if we do not work in
common to improve the conditions for freedom, prosperity, health
and justice on this planet for everyone. We have no other planet,
and we should not seriously count on another life after death in
which we can make everything better. For this reason, it is a central
task of philosophy to work on an avatar of the human mind that
can be led into the field, in the sense of an ideology critique, against
the empty promises of a post-human age. I would like to conclude
this book with the words of Schelling, who wrote them in a letter
to his friend Hegel on February 4, 1795: "The alpha and omega of
all philosophy is freedom."[54]

Notes

Introduction

1 Francis Crick and Christof Koch, "Towards a Neurobiological Theory of Consciousness," *Seminars in the Neurosciences* 2 (1990), pp. 263–75.

2 Concepts in bold print play a central role and for that reason, if possible, are introduced in the form of a definition or gloss.

3 See Markus Gabriel, *Why the World Does Not Exist* (Cambridge: Polity, 2015).

4 George H. W. Bush, "Presidential Proclamation 6158," *Project on the Decade of the Brain*, July 17, 1990, www.loc.gov/loc/brain/proclaim.html. See also Felix Hasler, *Neuromythologie: Eine Streitschrift gegen die Deutungsmacht der Hirnforschung* (Bielefeld: Transcript, 2013).

5 Brigitte Stahl-Busse, "Dekade des menschlichen Gehirns," *idw – Informationsdienst Wissenschaft*, November 5, 1999, https://idw-online.de/pages/de/news15426.

6 Ibid.

7 Gabriel, *Why the World Does Not Exist*, pp. 38–44.

8 Rainer Maria Rilke, *The Selected Poetry of Rainer Maria Rilke*, ed. and trans. Stephen Mitchell (New York: Vintage, 1989), p. 25.

9 Martin Hubert, "Teil 1: Des Menschen freier Wille," Philosophie im Hirnscan, April 4, 2014, www.deutschlandfunk.de/philosophie-im-hirnscan-manuskript-teil-1-des-menschen.740.de.html?dram:article_id=283145 [trans. MG].

10 Volkart Wildermuth, "Die Welt, wie sie scheint," Philosophie im Hirnscan, May 29, 2014, www.deutschlandfunk.de/philosophie-im-hirnscan-manuskript-die-welt-wie.740.de.html?dram:arrticle_id=287724 [trans. MG].

11 Ibid.

12 See at length the contribution in Markus Gabriel, "Wir haben Zugang zu den Dingen an sich," *Gehirn und Geist* 3 (2014), pp. 42ff.

13 Christian Weber, "Der Mensch bleibt unlesbar," *Süddeutsche Zeitung*, October 18–19, 2014 [trans. MG].

14 Thomas Schmidt, "Die Wirklichkeit ist anders!," *Die Zeit*, April 3, 2014, www.zeit.de/2014/15/neuer-realismus [trans MG]. See also the other contributions in the series on new realism in the issues of *Die Zeit* from April 16 to July 16, 2014. There is an overview of the state of the debate in Gabriel (ed.) *Der neue Realismus* (Berlin: Suhrkamp, 2014).

15 Hasler, *Neuromythologie: Eine Streitschrift gegen die Deutungsmacht der Hirnforschung*, pp. 159ff.

16 Christoph Kucklick, *Die granulare Gesellschaft: Wie das Digitale unsere Wirklichkeit auflöst* (Berlin: Ullstein, 2014), p. 11.

17 Stanley Cavell, *The Claim of Reason: Wittgenstein, Skepticism, Morality, and Tragedy* (Oxford: Oxford University Press, 1999), p. 109.

18 Immanuel Kant, *Critique of Pure Reason*, trans. Paul Guyer and Allen W. Wood (Cambridge: Cambridge University Press, 1998), p. 695 [A840/B868].

19 European Commission, 2013; website no longer active.

20 *Das Unbehagen in der Kultur* is the original German title of Freud's *Civilization and its Discontents*. The German literally means "Discontent in Civilization" [Trans.].

21 Raymond Tallis, *Aping Mankind: Neuromania, Darwinitis and the Misrepresentation of Humanity* (Abingdon and New York: Routledge, 2011).

22 Plato, *The Republic*, trans. Paul Shorey (Cambridge, MA: Loeb, 1930), 338c.

23 Christian E. Elger et al., "Das Manifest: Elf führende Wissenschaftler über Gegenwart und Zukunft der Hirnforschung," *Gehirn und Geist* 6 (2004), pp. 31–7; www.spektrum. de/thema/das-manifest/852357.

24 D. F. Swaab, *We Are Our Brains: A Neurobiography of the Brain, from the Womb to Alzheimer's*, trans. Jane Hedley-Prôle (New York: Spiegel & Grau, 2014).

25 Ibid., p. 3.

26 Sam Harris, *Free Will* (New York: Free Press, 2012).

Chapter 1 What is at Stake in the Philosophy of Mind?

1 In English in the original.
2 Bertrand Russell, *The Analysis of Mind* (London: Routledge, 1995).
3 Wolfram Hogrebe, *Riskante Lebensnähe: Die szenische Existenz des Menschen* (Berlin: Akademie, 2009), p. 17.
4 *Truth and Method* (London: Continuum, 2004), p. 470.
5 *The Philosophy of History* (Kitchener: Batoche, 2001), p. 90; translation modified.
6 Karl Marx and Friedrich Engels, *The Marx–Engels Reader*, ed. Robert Tucker (New York: W. W. Norton, 1978), p. 85; translation modified.
7 Jean-Paul Sartre, *Essays in Existentialism*, ed. Wade Baskin (Secaucus: Citadel Press, 1965), p. 34.
8 Gilbert Ryle, *The Concept of Mind* (London: Routledge, 2009), pp. 5ff.
9 Richard Dawkins, *The God Delusion* (Boston: Houghton Mifflin, 2008), p. 180.
10 Ibid., pp. 180–1.
11 Peter Bieri, *Handwerk der Freiheit* (Munich: Carl Hanser, 2001), p. 32.

Chapter 2 Consciousness

1 Thomas Nagel, *Mind and Cosmos: Why the Materialist Neo-Darwinian Conception of Nature is Almost Certainly False* (Oxford: Oxford University Press, 2012). See my review of this, "*Da schlug die Natur die Augen auf*," in the *Frankfurter Allgemeine Zeitung* of October 7, 2013.
2 Michael Patrick Lynch: *The Internet of Us: Knowing More and Understanding Less in the Age of Big Data* (New York and London: Liveright, 2016).
3 Immanuel Kant, *Dreams of a Spirit-Seer*, trans. Emanuel F. Goerwitz (London: Swan Sonnenschein, 1900), p. 49.
4 Ibid.
5 Ibid., p. 51; translation modified.
6 Geert Keil, *Willensfreiheit* (Berlin: De Gruyter, 2012), p. 208. Keil understands the homunculus fallacy somewhat differently than I do. He writes that a homunculus is "a human-like entity that is posited in recent philosophy of mind, which is

either explicitly or implicitly called upon to explain the human mind's way of functioning" (ibid.).

7 Thomas Nagel, "What is it Like to be a Bat?," *Philosophical Review* 83 (1974), pp. 435–50.

8 Aristotle, *On the Soul; Parva Naturalia; On Breath* (Cambridge, MA: Harvard University Press, 1957), p. 73 (413a).

9 Ludwig Wittgenstein, *Philosophical Investigations*, trans. G. E. M. Anscombe (Oxford: Blackwell, 1958), 94e.

10 Immanuel Kant, *Groundwork for the Metaphysics of Morals*, ed. and trans. Allen Wood (New Haven, CT: Yale University Press, 2002), p. 67 (Ak 4:450–451).

11 Hermann von Helmholtz, "Über das Sehen," in *Abhandlungen zur Philosophie und Geometrie* (Cuxhaven: Traude Junghans, 1987), p. 21.

12 Eric R. Kandel, James H. Schwarz and Thomas M. Jessell, *Principles of Neural Science* (4th edn, New York: McGraw-Hill, 2000), p. 412.

13 See, for example, the following statement by Krauss: "the ultimate arbiter of truth is experiment, not the comfort one derives from one's a priori beliefs, nor the beauty or elegance one ascribes to one's theoretical models." Krauss, *A Universe from Nothing: Why There is Something rather Than Nothing* (New York: Free Press, 2012), p. xvi.

14 Richard Dawkins, *The God Delusion* (Boston: Houghton Mifflin, 2008), p. 177.

15 Ibid., p. 13.

16 Lynne Rudder Baker, "Cognitive Suicide," in Robert H. Grimm et al. (eds), *Contents of Thought* (Tucson: University of Arizona Press, 1988), pp. 1–18; http://people.umass.edu/lrb/files/bak88cogS.pdf.

17 Paul Churchland, "Eliminative Materialism and the Propositional Attitudes," *Journal of Philosophy* 78/2 (1981), p. 88.

18 In her book of the same name: Patricia Churchland, *Neurophilosophy* (Cambridge, MA: MIT Press, 1989).

19 See, for instance, the interview with both in Susan Blackmore, *Conversations on Consciousness: What the Best Minds Think about the Brain, Free Will, and What it Means to be Human* (Oxford: Oxford University Press, 2006), pp. 50–67.

20 *Caroli Linnaei Systema naturae: A Photographic Facsimile of the First Volume of the Tenth Edition, 1758.* London: British Museum, 1939.

21 Plato, *Euthyphro. Apology. Crito. Phaedo. Phaedrus* (Cambridge, MA: Harvard University Press, 1982), p. 81 (20e).

22 Donald Davidson, "Rational Animals," *Dialectica* 36 (1982), pp. 317–27.
23 Geert Keil, *Willensfreiheit* (Berlin: De Gruyter 2012), p. 159.
24 Jacques Derrida, *The Animal That Therefore I Am* (New York: Fordham University Press, 2008), p. 3.
25 Blackmore, *Conversations on Consciousness*, p. 27.
26 René Descartes, *Meditations on First Philosophy* (Cambridge: Cambridge University Press, 1986), p. 21.
27 Christoph Kucklick, *Die granulare Gesellschaft: Wie das Digitale unsere Wirklichkeit auflöst* (Berlin: Ullstein, 2014), p. 67.
28 Ibid., p. 90.
29 Kant, *Critique of Pure Reason*, trans. Paul Guyer and Allen W. Wood (Cambridge: Cambridge University Press, 1998), pp. 193–4 [A51/B75].
30 Ibid., p. 235 [A112].
31 Daniel Dennett, *Consciousness Explained* (New York: Back Bay Books, 1991), p. 218.
32 Frank Cameron Jackson, "Epiphenomenal Qualia," *Philosophical Quarterly* 32/127 (1982), pp. 127–36. See also "What Mary Didn't Know," *Journal of Philosophy* 83/5 (1986), pp. 291–5.
33 Kandel et al., *Principles of Neural Science*, pp. 586–7.
34 Blackmore, *Conversations on Consciousness*, p. 206.
35 Jackson, "Epiphenomenal Qualia," p. 134.
36 Brian Greene, *The Hidden Reality: Parallel Universes and the Deep Laws of the Cosmos* (New York: Vintage, 2011).
37 Keil, *Willensfreiheit*, p. 41.
38 Wolfram Hogrebe, *Riskante Lebensnähe: Die szenische Existenz des Menschen* (Berlin: Akademie, 2009), p. 40.

Chapter 3 Self-Consciousness

1 Tyler Burge, *Origins of Objectivity* (Oxford: Clarendon Press, 2010), p. 157.
2 René Descartes, *Meditations on First Philosophy* (Cambridge: Cambridge University Press, 1986), p. 18.
3 This model of self-consciousness as an inner mind's eye with which we observe our mental processes has been refuted numerous times in twentieth-century philosophy, by thinkers as diverse as Martin Heidegger, Ludwig Wittgenstein, Gilbert Ryle, Jacques Derrida, the so-called Heidelberg School

and Ernst Tugendhat (b. 1930). An excellent and clear overview of this discussion can be found in Tugendhat's classic *Self-Consciousness and Self-Determination*, trans. Paul Stern (Cambridge, MA: MIT Press, 1986).

4 Eric Kandel, *The Age of Insight: The Quest to Understand the Unconscious in Art, Mind, and Brain, from Vienna 1900 to the Present* (New York: Random House, 2012).

5 Gottfried Wilhelm Leibniz, *Philosophical Essays*, ed. and trans. Roger Ariew and Daniel Garber (Indianapolis: Hackett, 1989), p. 215.

6 Ibid.

7 Erwin Schrödinger, *What is Life?* (Cambridge: Cambridge University Press, 1967), p. 129.

8 Ibid.

9 Ibid., p. 93.

10 Brigitte Falkenburg, *Mythos Determinismus: Wieviel erklärt uns die Hirnforschung?* (Berlin: Springer, 2012), pp. 354ff.

11 David Chalmers, "What is it Like to be a Thermostat?" in *The Conscious Mind* (Oxford: Oxford University Press, 1996).

12 Wolfram Hogrebe, *Riskante Lebensnähe: Die szenische Existenz des Menschen* (Berlin: Akademie, 2009), p. 17.

13 Wolfgang Prinz, *Open Minds: The Social Making of Agency and Intentionality* (Cambridge, MA: MIT Press, 2012).

14 Hilary Putnam, *Reason, Truth and History* (Cambridge: Cambridge University Press, 1981), pp. 1–21.

15 Unfortunately, Putnam's argument, on close examination, does not suffice to strictly prove that we are not brains in a vat. For more details, see Gabriel, *Antike und Moderne Skepsis* (Hamburg: Junius, 2008), pp. 93–109.

16 Sigmund Freud, *Totem and Taboo*, trans. James Strachey (London: Routledge, 1950), pp. 87–115; Putnam, *Reason, Truth and History*, p. 3.

17 Sigmund Freud, *Introductory Lectures on Psycho-Analysis (Part III)* (London: Hogarth Press, 1953), p. 285.

18 Sigmund Freud, *On the History of the Psycho-Analytic Movement: Papers on Metapsychology and Other Works* (London: Hogarth Press, 1957), p. 53.

19 In reference to this, see the useful overview of the major arguments from Fichte all the way to higher-order theory in Manfred Frank's *Präreflexives Selbstbewusstsein: Vier Vorlesungen* (Stuttgart: Reclam, 2015).

20 Heinrich von Kleist, "On the Marionette Theater," trans.

Thomas G. Neumiller, *Drama Review* 16/3 (1972); trans. modified.

21 Kant, *Critique of Pure Reason*, trans. Paul Guyer and Allen W. Wood (Cambridge: Cambridge University Press, 1998), p. 414 [A346/B404].

22 Georg Christoph Lichtenberg, *Philosophical Writings*, ed. and trans. Steven Tester (Albany: SUNY Press, 2012), p. 5; translation modified.

23 Prinz, *Open Minds*, p. 63.

24 Ibid., p. xvi.

25 Johann Gottlieb Fichte, *Foundations of Natural Right According to the Principles of the Wissenschaftslehre*, ed. Frederick Neuhouser, trans. Michael Baur (Cambridge: Cambridge University Press, 2000), p. 37 (§3).

Chapter 4 Who or What is This Thing We Call the Self?

1 Thomas Metzinger, *The Ego-Tunnel: The Science of the Mind and the Myth of the Self* (New York: Basic Books, 2009).

2 Susan Blackmore, *Conversations on Consciousness: What the Best Minds Think about the Brain, Free Will, and What it Means to be Human* (Oxford: Oxford University Press, 2006), p. 153.

3 Ibid.

4 Thomas Metzinger, *Being No One: The Self-Model Theory of Subjectivity* (Cambridge, MA: MIT Press, 2003).

5 Blackmore, *Conversations on Consciousness*, p. 203.

6 Ibid., pp. 198–9.

7 Karl Vogt, "Physiologische Briefe: 12. Brief," in Dieter Wittich (ed.), *Vogt, Moleschott, Büchner: Schriften zum kleinbürgerlichen Materialismus in Deutschland* (Berlin: Akademie, 1971).

8 Georg Wilhelm Friedrich Hegel, *Phenomenology of Spirit*, trans. A. V. Miller (Oxford: Oxford University Press, 1977), p. 210 (§346).

9 Ludwig Büchner, *Force and Matter: Empirico-Philosophical Studies, Intelligibly Rendered* (London: Trübner, 1864), p. 117.

10 Ibid., p. 112.

11 Raymond Bernard Blakney, *Meister Eckhart: A Modern Translation* (New York: Harper & Row, 1941), Sermon 52, pp. 231–2; translation modified.

12 Ibid., Sermon 48, pp. 220–1.

13 Thomas Nagel, *The View from Nowhere* (Oxford: Oxford University Press, 1989); Gabriel, *Why the World Does Not Exist* (Cambridge: Polity, 2015), p. 7.

14 Hegel, *Phenomenology of Spirit*, p. 110 (§177).

15 Johann Gottlieb Fichte, *The Science of Knowledge*, ed. and trans. Peter Heath and John Lachs (Cambridge: Cambridge University Press, 1982), p. 162n.

16 Ibid., p. 96.

17 Ibid., p. 110.

18 John Searle, *Intentionality: An Essay in the Philosophy of Mind* (Cambridge: Cambridge University Press, 1983), pp. 141–59.

19 Nagel, *Mind and Cosmos: Why the Materialist Neo-Darwinian Conception of Nature is Almost Certainly False* (Oxford: Oxford University Press, 2012).

20 Richard Dawkins, *The Blind Watchmaker: Why the Evidence of Evolution Reveals a Universe without Design* (New York: W. W. Norton, 1996).

21 Sigmund Freud, *The Ego and the Id and Other Works* (London: Hogarth Press, 1961), p. 17 (the Standard Edition of the Complete Psychological Works of Sigmund Freud, Vol. 19, 1923–1925).

22 The German word for science, *Wissenschaft*, is feminine and hence becomes a "goddess," *Göttin*, when fetishized in this manner [Trans.].

23 Freud, *The Ego and the Id and Other Works*, p. 13.

24 Ibid., pp. 15–16.

25 Ibid., p. 28. See also Freud's "Character and Anal Eroticism," in *Jensen's "Gradiva" and Other Works* (London: Hogarth Press, 1959), pp. 167–75 (the Standard Edition of the Complete Psychological Works of Sigmund Freud, Vol. 9, 1906–1908).

26 Freud, "Instincts and Their Vicissitudes," in *On the History of the Psycho-Analytic Movement: Papers on Metapsychology and Other Works* (London: Hogarth Press, 1957), p. 116 (the Standard Edition of the Complete Psychological Works of Sigmund Freud, Vol. 14, 1914–1916).

27 Robert Brandom, *Articulating Reasons: An Introduction to Inferentialism* (Cambridge, MA: Harvard University Press, 2000), p. 11.

28 Freud, *The Ego and the Id and Other Works*, p. 23.

29 Ibid., p. 25.

30 Ibid., p. 26.

31 Ibid., p. 38.

32 Ibid., p. 36.

33 Ibid.
34 Ibid., p. 38.
35 Ibid., p. 56.
36 Ibid.
37 See, for instance, Judith Butler, *Gender Trouble: Feminism and the Subversion of Identity* (New York: Routledge, 1990).
38 Richard Dawkins, *The Selfish Gene* (Oxford: Oxford University Press, 1976).
39 Christoph Reuter and Jacob Russell, "Die Vergessenen von Amirli," *Der Spiegel*, August 25, 2014; www.spiegel.de/spiegel/print/d-128859935.html.

Chapter 5 Freedom

1 See with reference to this claim the book *Mind Time: The Temporal Factor in Consciousness* (Cambridge, MA: Harvard University Press, 2004) by the neuroscientist Benjamin Libet, who has become famous for his experiments. The best critique of the entire experimental setup and of the philosophical theses associated with it can be found in Alfred R. Mele's *Free: Why Science Hasn't Disproved Free Will* (Oxford: Oxford University Press, 2014).
2 Wolf Singer, "Verschaltungen legen uns fest: wir sollten aufhören, von Freiheit zu sprechen," in Christian Geyer (ed.), *Hirnforschung und Willensfreiheit: Zur Deutung der neuesten Ergebnisse* (Frankfurt am Main: Suhrkamp, 2004), pp. 30–65.
3 Wolf Singer, "Keiner kann anders, als er ist," *Frankfurter Allgemeine Zeitung*, January 8, 2004 (www.faz.net/aktuell/feuilleton / hirnforschung - keiner - kann - anders - als - er - ist - 1147780-p4.html).
4 Ibid.
5 Brigitte Falkenburg, *Mythos Determinismus: Wieviel erklärt uns die Hirnforschung?* (Berlin and Heidelberg: Springer, 2012), p. 255.
6 Arthur Schopenhauer, *The Two Fundamental Problems of Ethics*, trans. David E. Cartwright and Edward E. Erdmann (Oxford: Oxford University Press, 2010), p. 69.
7 Martin Luther, *On the Bondage of the Will*, trans. Edward Thomas Vaughan (London: Hamilton, 1823), pp. 32–3.
8 Ibid., pp. 58–9; translation modified.
9 "Therefore, the idea of their freedom is simply the ignorance of

230   Notes to pp. 189–203

the cause of their actions." Baruch Spinoza, *Complete Works* (Indianapolis: Hackett, 2002), p. 264.

10 Peter van Inwagen, *An Essay on Free Will* (New York: Oxford University Press, 1983).

11 Thomas Buchheim, "Wer kann, der kann auch anders," in Christian Geyer (ed.), *Hirnforschung und Willensfreiheit: Zur Deutung der neuesten Experimente* (Frankfurt am Main: Suhrkamp, 2004), pp. 158–65 (here, p. 162). See also his *Unser Verlangen nach Freiheit: Kein Traum, sondern Drama mit Zukunft* (Hamburg: Meiner, 2006).

12 I would like to thank the biologist Michael Hoch for an interesting conversation about the notion that one could also actually formulate interesting objections to free will on the basis of our discoveries of microbiota, which play a crucial role in our understanding of eating habits. Thus potential determination by nature actually begins in the stomach.

13 John McDowell, *Mind and World* (Cambridge, MA: Harvard University Press, 1994).

14 Arthur Schopenhauer, *The World as Will and Representation*, Vol. 2, trans. E. F. J. Payne (New York: Dover, 1966), p. 533.

15 Ibid., p. 557:

> Marriages from love are contracted in the interest of the species, not of individuals. It is true that the persons concerned imagine they are advancing their own happiness; but their actual aim is one that is foreign to themselves, since it lies in the production of an individual that is possible only through them. Brought together by this aim, they ought then to get on with each other as well as possible. However, the two persons, brought together by that instinctive delusion that is the essence of passionate love, will in other respects be very often of quite different natures. This comes to light when the delusion vanishes, as it necessarily must. Accordingly, marriages contracted from love prove as a rule unhappy . . .

16 Arthur Schopenhauer, *Parerga and Paralipomena: Short Philosophical Essays*, Vol. 2, trans. E. F. J. Payne (Oxford: Clarendon Press, 1974), p. 614.

17 Ibid., p. 626.

18 Ibid.

19 To learn more about this critical analysis in detail, I recommend Geert Keil's informative *Kritik des Naturalismus* (Berlin und New York: De Gruyter, 1993).

20 Friedrich Nietzsche, *Nachgelassene Fragmente 1882–1884*, Vol. 10 of *Sämtliche Werke: Kritische Studienausgabe in 15 Bänden* (Munich: Deutscher Taschenbuch, 2009), p. 420.

21 Nietzsche, *Nachgelassene Fragmente 1885–1887*, Vol. 12, p. 26.
22 Nietzsche, "Schopenhauer as Educator," in *Untimely Meditations* (Cambridge: Cambridge University Press, 1997), pp. 125–94.
23 Immanuel Kant, *Groundwork for the Metaphysics of Morals*, ed. and trans. Allen W. Wood (New Haven, CT: Yale University Press, 2002), p. 53.
24 Ibid.
25 Immanuel Kant, *Critique of Practical Reason*, trans. Werner S. Pluhar (Indianapolis: Hackett, 2002), p. 123.
26 Ibid.
27 Stanley Cavell, *The Claim of Reason: Wittgenstein, Skepticism, Morality, and Tragedy* (Oxford: Oxford University Press, 1999), p. 109.
28 Jean-Paul Sartre, *Being and Nothingness*, trans. Hazel E. Barnes (New York: Citadel Press, 1969), p. 566.
29 Gottfried Benn, "After Nihilism," in *The Weimar Republic Sourcebook* (Berkeley: University of California Press, 1994), p. 380.
30 Ibid.
31 Gottfried Benn, *Gesammelte Werke* (Wiesbaden: Limes, 1968), p. 197.
32 Ibid.
33 Ibid., p. 433.
34 Johann Wolfgang von Goethe, *Faust: Parts 1 and 2*, trans. Louis MacNeice (New York: Continuum, 1994), p. 220 (Verse 8472).
35 Ibid. (Verse 8469); translation modified.
36 Ibid. (Verse 8479).
37 For an extensive treatment of this term, see Nietzsche's *The Birth of Tragedy* (Cambridge: Cambridge University Press, 1999).
38 Johann Gottlieb Fichte, "On the Ground of Our Belief in a Divine World-Governance," in *J. G. Fichte and the Atheism Dispute (1798–1800)*, trans. Curtis Bowman (Farnham: Ashgate, 2010), pp. 17–29 (here p. 26).
39 Benn, *Gesammelte Werke*, p. 97.
40 Frans de Waal, *Primates and Philosophers: How Morality Evolved* (Princeton, NJ: Princeton University Press, 2006), p. 8.
41 Bruno Latour, *We Have Never Been Modern* (Cambridge, MA: Harvard University Press, 1993).

42 Thomas Hobbes, *De cive, or, The Citizen* (New York: Appleton-Century-Crofts, 1949), p. 1.
43 Immanuel Kant, "Toward Perpetual Peace," in *Practical Philosophy*, ed. and trans. Mary J. Gregor (Cambridge: Cambridge University Press, 1996), p. 335.
44 Ibid.
45 Immanuel Kant, *Metaphysics of Morals*, trans. Mary J. Gregor (Cambridge: Cambridge University Press, 1996), pp. 192–3.
46 Ibid.
47 We lose something of the force of the German here by rendering the title of this lecture series in a manner consistent with the rest of the book, so the reader is here advised to consider the title more literally – "Driving the Mind out of the Sciences of Mind" [Trans.].
48 See my reviews of the three volumes that have appeared to this point: "Wesentliche Bejahung des Nationalsozialismus," *Die Welt*, April 7, 2014; "Der Nazi aus dem Hinterhalt," *Die Welt*, March 8, 2014; and "Wo 'Geschick' waltet, darf keine Schuld sein," *Die Welt*, March 21, 2015.
49 Martin Heidegger, *Nature, History, State, 1933–1934*, trans. and ed. Gregory Fried and Richard Polt (London: Bloomsbury, 2013), p. 56. See also the references in Emmanuel Faye's *Heidegger: The Introduction of Nazism into Philosophy in Light of the Unpublished Seminars of 1933–1935*, trans. Michael B. Smith (New Haven, CT: Yale University Press, 2009), ch. 5.
50 Michel Foucault, *The Order of Things: An Archeology of the Human Sciences* (London: Routledge, 1989), pp. 421–2.
51 Ibid., p. 422.
52 Ibid.
53 Rainer Maria Rilke, *Duino Elegies and The Sonnets to Orpheus*, trans. A. Poulin, Jr. (Boston: Houghton Mifflin, 1975), pp. 49–51.
54 Friedrich Wilhelm Joseph Schelling, *Briefe von und an Hegel*, Vol. 1, ed. Johannes Hofmeister (Hamburg: Meiner, 1952), p. 22.

Index